VIRGINS, VAMPS, AND FLAPPERS

The American Silent Movie Heroine

Sumiko Higashi

EDEN PRESS

Monographs in
Women's Studies

Series Editor:
Sherri Clarkson

VIRGINS, VAMPS, AND FLAPPERS.

The American Silent Movie Heroine

Sumiko Higashi

© Eden Press Women's Publications, Inc. 1978

Published by:
Eden Press Women's Publications, Inc.
1538 Sherbrooke Street West, #201
Montreal, Quebec, Canada
H3G 1L5

and

Eden Press Women's Publications, Inc.
Box 51
St. Albans, Vermont 05478
U.S.A.

ISBN 0-88831-028-5

Library of Congress Catalog Card Number 78-74106

Printed in Brattleboro, Vermont, U.S.A.

For Toi

As does the individual, each generation reveals in the choice of its loves the undercurrents which give it form. This is true to such an extent that one of the most instructive avenues for assessing human evolution would be to attempt a history of the feminine types which have successively been preferred.

Jose Ortega y Gasset
On Love

ACKNOWLEDGMENTS

I would like to thank the staff of the Motion Picture Section, Library of Congress; the Film Study Center at the Museum of Modern Art in New York; and George Eastman House in Rochester, New York for their assistance. Also, I am grateful to James Card, former curator at Eastman House, for his graciousness and some delightful conversations. Special thanks go to Bill Coffman and Bill Field for recreating the days of silent movies and the Wurlitzer at the Old Music Hall in El Segundo, California. My friend, Diana Hernando, provided much needed camaraderie while I was working on this project, and Toivo Maki gave me invaluable moral support. Finally, I am indebted to Alexander Saxton, not only for his encouragement and perceptive criticism, but also for projecting a rare humane quality into an institutional environment.

CONTENTS

LIST OF ILLUSTRATIONS

i

PREFACE

Virgins, vamps, and flappers were female screen types who projected
and reflected the image of woman in vogue before and during the Jazz
Age. This study is based on the premise that a society's feminine ideal
is related in complex ways to its moral climate and values. Changes in
the popular image of woman are consequently a manifestation of larger
social, economic, and cultural developments. In a technological society,
the movies as part of the media play an important function in
perpetuating or modifying for a large audience certain feminine types
and heterosexual role models. The mirror relationship between film
and society is difficult to gauge but significant nonetheless. As
Siegfried Kracauer wrote in the introduction to his study, *From Caligari
to Hitler,* films are a reflection of "psychological dispositions--those
deep layers of collective mentality which extend more or less below the
dimension of consciousness."

A study of the screen image of woman during the silent period is
pertinent for at least two reasons. This was an era when an estimated
ninety to one hundred million people went to the movies every week. By
the late twenties, the motion picture industry, representing a total
investment of $,1,500,000,000, ranked fourth in the United States and
produced 90 percent of the world's film output. The teens and
especially the twenties were also years when an acknowledged revolution in manners and morals produced the flapper as a "new woman"
and greater permissiveness in sexual relations. The question of
whether the movies raced ahead or lagged behind actual social and
moral change results in inconclusive answers. F. Scott Fitzgerald,
spokesman of the Jazz Age, wrote in retrospect that motion pictures
inhibited by censorship displayed a lag and had no effect upon the
moral climate. A film historian such as Lewis Jacobs appears to have

iii

taken provocative film titles and advertisements at titillating face value and records that the dissolution of marriage and family life proceeded apace on celluloid and in reality.

Fitzgerald and Jacobs assert extreme positions, but the very nature of film as mass media would actually result in a moral conservatism. The movies were after all a product of technological innovation and became a source of mass entertainment in an urban and industrial society. After motion picture stock was floated on Wall Street in 1919, the process of filmmaking became subject to streamlining in production, distribution, and exhibiting to yield maximum profit. Although films were not commodities such as automobiles, the attempt to ensure a degree of predictability in the industry meant an organization with a conservative front office that would discourage artistic experimentation. As a result, the industry settled upon formulated plots, such as the triangular love story with hero, heroine, and villain, which gave the viewers recurrent déjà vu.

The movies also had a conservative effect with respect to the image of woman because the industry discovered that in a mass consumption society, sex was stimulating both as motion picture content and form of exploitation. The films of the DeMille-Swanson era, for example, depict sex appeal in the environs of the rich as a commodity to be acquired like expensive furnishings. The role of these films in stimulating consumers was noted even then and in this sense, Hollywood promoted in a postwar society what Malcolm Cowley referred to as the "consumption ethic." Although mass consumption undermined such traditional values as the Protestant work ethic, in the long run it also reenforced the system of capitalism. And to the extent that it was based upon the sexual sell, its effect on the image of woman was negative.

Finally, the motion picture acts as a conservative force because in providing an escape from reality, it functions as a medium for vicarious living. The movies as a form of popular entertainment necessarily express mass desires and fantasies which interact with realistic situations on screen and in the lives of filmgoers. One consequence is that the superimposition of make-believe upon reality serves to complicate the latter. In a contemporary film, *Minnie and Moscowitz,* Minnie drinks with a female companion on a Saturday night and complains

iv

about the way in which the movies "set you up." The movies disarm the viewer in confronting life's realities.

As a study of the silent screen heroine, this monograph is divided into two parts. The first four chapters deal with the archetypes of woman as virgin and vampire so popular during the Victorian era. The beginning chapter on Lillian Gish analyzes the sentimental heroine as both victim and redeemer, while the succeeding one presents Mary Pickford as a contrasting Victorian paradigm in the guise of a manipulative little girl in a fatherless world. Chapter III discusses the bifurcation of woman in terms of the vampire image and the attenuation of the powers of the "vamp." The supernatural Vampire proved a figure too threatening to the male ego and was therefore made susceptible to love. Chapter IV traces the persistence of the image of the sentimental heroine throughout the twenties, even after the decline of the Gish-Pickford era. An analysis of the career of vamps during the decade is also revealing in that bad women subject to redemption through love came to resemble their virginal counterparts. The second half of this study is devoted to images of then contemporary women such as the working girl, socialite, and flapper and assesses the changes in the popular concept of woman during the Jazz Age. A final chapter studies the few uncharacteristic heroines who pursued an independent course in relating to men and their families while redefining their roles as women. For the most part, the silent screen heroine did not provide the "new woman" of the twenties with alternative models of non-traditional life styles.

As an analysis of the screen image of the American woman, this work is based on the viewing of more than one hundred sixty-five silent features, both box-office films and lesser known poverty row or independent productions. Although none of the films viewed contradict the basic argument regarding the image of woman set forth in these chapters, not all have been analyzed in order to give the thesis structure and proportion. A filmography is appended for the more specialized reader.

Since this is a study which uses film as evidence about social and cultural developments in early twentieth century America, works in film scholarship were not helpful to the extent that emphasis was upon the cinematic. Although film theorists and critics have a point in faulting so-called sociological studies for utilizing content analyses and neglecting film as film, there is a basic problem in terms of a conflict regarding methodologies and underlying assumptions. Briefly, sociological approaches are empirically based whereas film studies, especially those in the category of structuralism and semiology, emphasize close readings of a filmic text according to theoretical models (such as the spectator as subject based upon concepts of the unconscious articulated by Freud and Jacques Lacan) which are applicable irrespective of sociohistoric context. The utilization of Freud also poses certain difficulties for some feminist film theorists, be they interested in adaptation or repudiation, with respect to the analysis of women in film.

As for non-scholarly works, a great deal written about motion pictures and the people involved in their production reflects the movie world in that fact and fantasy merge. Even detailed descriptions of films can prove misleading. As journalistic or personal observations, these writings are valuable but it would be difficult if not impossible to substantiate many statements. The films themselves are sometimes difficult to discuss in sharp detail because visual impressions fade. The use of stills has been extremely helpful in recapturing those impressions and photographs are therefore included within these pages. The stills and discussions are meant to complement each other to recreate the films for the reader.

Sumiko Higashi
Assistant Professor, Department of History
Women's Studies Director
SUNY Brockport

Chapter I

LILLIAN GISH: APOTHEOSIS OF THE VICTORIAN HEROINE

On the dedication page of her autobiography, *The Movies, Mr. Griffith and Me,* Lillian Gish honors the memory of her sister Dorothy, her mentor, D.W. Griffith, and her parents, about whom she writes: "To my mother who gave me love," "To my father who gave me insecurity." Mary McConnell Gish, a courageous and determined woman, brought up her two daughters by herself. James Leigh Gish influenced the lives of his wife and daughters mostly by his absence. Significantly, the relationship between mother and daughter has proved the most essential family tie in the lives of certain successful women like Gish.

James Leigh Gish met and courted Mary Robinson McConnell during a trip to Urbana from neighboring Springfield, Ohio, where he clerked for a wholesale grocery business. After their marriage, the young couple set up housekeeping in Springfield. Gish quit his job and opened a small confectionary shop. Lillian Gish was born a little over a year later in 1896. The family moved to Dayton, where Lillian's sister Dorothy was born, and then to Baltimore, where Gish again set up a candy store. Two years later, he sold his share of the business to his partner and moved on to New York, but without his family. Unable to manage on what she earned in the candy shop and occasional sums sent by her husband, Mary Gish moved to New York and installed her daughters in a flat. She paid expenses by taking in boarders and working as a demonstrator in a Brooklyn department store. James Gish was apparently without a job and made irregular appearances in their lives. Financially desperate, his wife was persuaded by a friend to go on

1

stage with her daughters despite the obloquy directed against theatrical performers. Lillian was five years old at the time. She grew up on the road and her life became a succession of train rides, cheap hotels, and one night stands. Always, mother and daughters budgeted and saved for the off season. But there came a time when road companies ceased to be the main attraction in the small towns and cities on their circuit. The nickelodeon had made its appearance.

The story of how the Gish sisters began their movie career is an oft-repeated episode in film history, though versions differ. [1]   Lillian and Dorothy had gone to the "flickers" one afternoon and were surprised to see an old friend, Gladys Smith, demean herself by appearing in a photoplay called *Lena and the Geese*. Curiosity led them to the Biograph Studio on Fourteenth Street in New York where they were reunited with Gladys, now Mary Pickford, and introduced to D.W. Griffith. The director terrified the sisters by chasing them around the studio with a gun and satisfied with their reaction, engaged them at the standard five dollars a day.

When he became a director for Biograph, Griffith, who admitted that "blondes seem to have a fatal effect on me," had a particular type of leading lady in mind. [2]   (Curiously, Linda Arvidson, the actress he married, was a brunette.) Griffith hired Mary Pickford, soon to be known for her masses of blond curls, after Biograph and Essanay had previously rejected her for movie roles. According to his biographer, Robert M. Henderson, it was Gish who really entranced Griffith. The director later recalled their first meeting in paternal tones and described Lillian's blond beauty as "exquisite" and "ethereal." [3] Blanche Sweet, one of his leading ladies, also recalled the encounter and observed that Griffith was so attracted to Gish he had to force himself to maintain his professional composure. Henderson conjectures that Gish herself developed an infatuation for Griffith though she has always alluded to him publicly as her friend and mentor. [4] Unable to pursue his attraction for Gish, Griffith idealized her in his greatest commercial successes. Lillian Gish became the apotheosis of the Victorian heroine.

The films of D.W. Griffith strongly appealed to an audience whose values were for the most part rooted in prewar America. Griffith himself never transcended these values nor achieved a unique vision within

2

their framework. The moral dimension of his work is best revealed by the characterization of the heroine since the hero was an accessory to the plot. The focus upon woman's essential goodness and purity reflected Griffith's Southern background and sentimental Victorian temperament, but it was a concept of woman very much in vogue during the nineteenth century. Accordingly, the Griffith-Gish heroine was the incarnation of innocence. She was an adolescent girl on the verge of womanhood. The youthful, girlish figure was tall but lithe and slender. Gish's face had indeed an "exquisite, ethereal beauty," and it expressed the artlessness and modest reserve of a virgin. Whether photographed in a frontal shot or in profile, that extraordinary face with its wide eyes and rosebud mouth was captivating. Altogether, there has never been another image on the screen which captured the "essence of girlhood," as Griffith put it. [5]

Parker Tyler has analyzed the sexual psychology of the Griffith-Gish heroine whom he dubs "the canary." Another critic complained that Griffith's direction of young girls consisted of "the dental floss variety (the finger perpetually in the mouth), the hand developer type (incessant twisting of handkerchiefs), the St. Vitus Dance genre (severe jumping up and down...), and occasionally the gymnastic school (violent straightening and unstraightening of the elbow to show enthusiasm)." [6] As a matter of fact, this description is unfair to the acting abilities of such Griffith heroines as Mae Marsh and Gish. According to Tyler, the psychology underlying such excited girlish gestures is explained by the synthesis of fear and desire, which is the Gish style of femininity. The more actively the female flutters, the more her fragility excites. [7]

The tension in the Griffith-Gish films was created by threats to the chastity of the innocent young girl thrust out into the cruel world. In the best of all possible Victorian worlds, such a girl would have been sheltered from the rigors of life outside the drawing room, and the obligation to protect her transmitted from father to husband at the wedding altar. The world as seen through a rose-colored lens hardly lent itself to exciting cinematic treatment, however, and certainly not to Griffith's last minute rescue sequences. So the Griffith heroine had to forego the protection which was her birthright and her wedding march involved a detour. She was exposed to the full horrors of the male world in which the ultimate threat was rape.

All would be lost for the Griffith-Gish heroine if she were left unaided, a prey to the lustful instincts of evil men. If her virginal qualities aroused intense sexual desire among the beasts of the male population, she exerted a moral force by appealing to that which was noble in others. The very fact of her inexperience, both sexual and in the ways of the world, aroused a reverential and protective feeling in the hero. Not that Griffith heroes were lacking in their romantic inclinations for Gish. With the exception of *Broken Blossoms* and its threat of miscegenation, there was an impending marriage at the end but its consummation takes place out of time and story. The hero, in the meanwhile, has achieved his manhood by proving both his devotion and courage. The lovers, separated during the course of their trials and tribulations, would reunite as moral equals. Virtue is virginity, but the ultimate reward of virtue is marriage.

The historic film which established Griffith's reputation, *The Birth of a Nation,* is a story about Civil War and Reconstruction from a Southern "bourbon" point of view. The film begins with the introduction of a Southern family, the Camerons, who live in the town of Piedmont, and a Northern family, the Stonemans. Phil Stoneman and his younger brother are visiting the Camerons on the eve of war. Phil discovers a love interest in the elder Cameron daughter, Margaret, while Ben Cameron finds "the ideal of his dreams" in a miniature portrait of Phil's sister, Elsie. The two friends are parted by civil war and fight on opposite sides. The war's devastation is depicted from a Southern point of view and the Union's victory portends evil days for the white South. Unknown to the Camerons, the rise to power of Austin Stoneman (a fictionalized and much-maligned Thaddeus Stevens) will affect their future and that of the reconstructed South. After the assassination of Lincoln, a mulatto maid who is also Stoneman's mistress, designates him "the greatest power in America." In the ensuing "era of cruel chicanery and political upheaval," Stoneman effects his plan to place the South under the black rule of his mulatto lieutenant, Silas Lynch (a curious name), and sets up headquarters in Piedmont. But the legacy of war, as well as Reconstruction and racial politics, exacerbate relations between the Camerons and the Stonemans. Elsie (Gish) is torn between loyalty to her father and her romantic feelings for Ben (Henry B. Walthall), whom she has nursed in a Northern military hospital at the close of war.

The elections result in a predominantly black state legislature which quickly enacts a bill providing for intermarriage. White visitors in the gallery depart while blacks break out in joyful celebration. In Piedmont, a black renegade named Gus covetously eyes the younger Cameron daughter, Flora (Mae Marsh), accosts her in the woods, and insists that she marry him. Terrified, Flora runs away and in desperation throws herself off a cliff. Ben reaches her moments before she dies. The title reads, "For her who had learned the stern lesson of honor, we should not grieve." Better dead than dishonored. A threat of miscegenation also awaits Elsie, who is horrified by Lynch's marriage proposal, resists his crude advances, and is imprisoned as a result. In the ensuing cross-cutting sequence, rightly famous in motion picture history, Elsie's struggle with Lynch is juxtaposed against the siege of the defiant Camerons, surrounded by Stoneman's black troops, and the ride of the Ku Klux Klan to their rescue.

The most fascinating aspect of *The Birth of a Nation* for purposes of this study is the rape complex. The myth of the purity of Southern woman-hood persisted into the Reconstruction period. Thomas Dixon, Jr. author of *The Clansman,* stated in an interview with a Boston editor that "one purpose of his play [the screen version of his novel] was to create a feeling of abhorrence in white people, especially white woman, against colored men. [8] Significantly, Elsie Stoneman, the feminine ideal of the film, is a Northerner. The enemy is no longer the damn Yankee. The enemy is the unfettered black man. Blacks are feared and despised because their political supremacy is a tool to enforce miscegenation, heretofore the ultimate taboo. Silas Lynch and his follower Gus become intoxicated with power and lust after white women. The South has become a nightmare in which seething blacks are about to run riot and commit sexual atrocities.

Griffith's projection of sexual innocence upon white women and sexual excess upon black men revealed a preoccupation with sexual extremes and the violent exercise of power. Woman became the helpless victim. The black man was the aggressor. The white man, who formed the apex of this perverted triangle, acted as rescuer. The assertion of the white man's power thus resulted in both the castrated black and the ideal Southern woman--blond, delicate, and asexual. The expense was repression of white male sexuality within the antiseptic confines of marriage. The ideal woman hardly necessitated an enthusiastic bed partner. Ben Cameron will wed Elsie Stoneman and the alliance between North and South so repressive to blacks after the Compromise of 1877, will be celebrated. But in what style will that marriage be consummated? The answer to that indelicate question lay outside the scope of the picture. And the evasion was one of the roots of the problem of sexual denial, for the rape complex betrayed an excessive preoccupation with woman's virtue. Although characterized as virginal and frigid, powerful fantasies in which she was cast as the victim of a black stud constituted both an affirmation and a disavowal of her sexuality. In the final analysis, knowledge about the real nature of female sexuality was to be avoided for the sake of the myth of Southern womanhood.

The release of *The Birth of a Nation* was no ordinary film premiere but provoked protests, lawsuits, and race riots. In Boston, that "abolitionist" city, the state legislature passed a special censorship bill to enable a newly constituted board to block the film's exhibition. The board voted in favor of the film. The State House was stormed, blacks marched on the Tremont Theater, and there were threats of dynamite. Both the N.A.A.C.P. and Booker T. Washington clubs attempted to have the film banned. Bills were introduced in Congress to prevent its screening in the nation's capitol. The Boston branch of the N.A.A.C.P. distributed a pamphlet titled *Fighting a Vicious Film: A Record of Protest against The Birth of a Nation,* which quoted such well-known critics of the film as Charles W. Eliot, president of Harvard, and Jane Addams. Also quoted in the pamphlet was a letter to Congressman Thatcher of Massachusetts from President Wilson's secretary, J.P. Tumulty, who denied that the President expressed approval after a private White House screening. [9] Interestingly, Griffith cited Wilson's *A History of the American People* as one of the sources used for the film. [10]

The Birth of a Nation was made in 1914, a year which some historians designate as the high point of progressivism. As a white, middle class, Protestant reform movement, progressivism had never held much promise for the inclusion of immigrants, certainly not blacks, into the mainstream of American life. Racial bigotry persisted into the postwar period when the Klan, revived in 1915, the year in which *The Birth of a Nation* was released, experienced a brief but powerful resurgence. With the outbreak of the war, however, nativist distrust was channeled

6

into anti-German sentiment. During World War I, Griffith and the Gishes went on location in Europe to film *Hearts of the World*. The movie was made in the English countryside and perilously close to the fighting in France. Griffith photographed actual war scenes and later incorporated these into the picture. *Hearts of the World* was an anti-German propaganda piece. Gish suggested that the ads for the film carry the slogan, "Do You Want to Go to France?" Karl Brown, a Griffith cameraman, recalls that the film had a powerful impact on a Los Angeles audience who witnessed its premiere. *Hearts of the World* was released in the spring of 1918 and enjoyed a successful run until the Armistice. Griffith continued to edit after its release to satisfy his requirements but also to adapt it to the postwar situation. The various studios shelved at a loss a spate of war pictures produced with the intention of profiting from the anti-German hysteria which Hollywood had helped to create.

The beginning title of the picture describes *Hearts of the World* as the triumph of a love story. The setting is a peaceful French village, soon to be destroyed by war. A young boy (Robert Harron) aspiring to be a writer finds his inspiration in the love of a girl (Lillian Gish) so innocent that she sews her wedding dress with "white threads and even whiter dreams." Their idyllic romance is abruptly interrupted when mobilization orders arrive and the Boy marches off to war. The Germans invade the countryside, terrorize the population, and force the Girl to do hard labor in the fields. Apart from physical abuse, the Girl is subjected to the lecherous impulses of the Hun. While attempting to steal some food for orphaned children, she encounters a German who is seated on a chair and imprisons her against the wall within the triangle of his legs. Only the arrival of his superior officer saves her. Back in the street, the Girl is shocked to see the Boy who has been trapped behind enemy lines on a volunteer mission. The couple seek refuge in her room, but a German discovers them and soldiers arrive at a stairway in the rear and also penetrate inside the building. In typical Griffith fashion, the siege of the beleaguered couple is juxtaposed against the war as French soldiers advance steadily towards the village. The lovers prepare to face death as man and wife and recite their marriage vows. Just as the Germans are about to batter down the door, the Girl pleads with her lover, "Do not leave me to worse than death," but French troops come to the rescue.

The same preoccupation with the rape complex which figured in *The Birth of a Nation* recurs in *Hearts of the World*. Gish plays a more expansive role as the young girl who matures into a woman during the horrors of war. Robert Harron registers a passive quality as an actor but he points a gun at his sweetheart lest she fall into the clutches of the Hun. The order in Griffith's sexually antiseptic world is especially precarious, for on balance the forces of destruction always threaten to overwhelm. The last minute rescue operates as a deus ex machina since the result of an actual confrontation between innocence and lust is never so rosy. In the last analysis, Griffith's inability to explore this dilemma on any realistic or complex level limited his vision as a filmmaker.

In the fall of 1919, Griffith joined Mary Pickford, Douglas Fairbanks, and Charles Chaplin as part of the "Big Four" to form United Artists. The corporation was designed as a distributor for the stars' individual productions and enabled them to take a cut of producer as well as distributor profits. Griffith's first release for United Artists was *Broken Blossoms,* based on a story by Thomas Burke called "The Chink and the Child." The director had made the film while he was still under contract to film magnate, Adolph Zukor. The story goes that Zukor's reaction to it was blunt. "You bring me a picture like this and want money for it? You may as well put your hand in my pocket and steal it. Everybody in it dies. It isn't commercial." [11] Griffith raised $250,000 to obtain the rights to the film and released it through United Artists. Zukor was wrong. *Broken Blossoms* became an enormous critical and box-office success. And by 1934, the picture had netted a profit of $700,000. [12]

The story line of *Broken Blossoms* is simple and centers about three characters: Lucy, a poor, mistreated, waiflike girl who grows up in the disreputable Limehouse section of London (Gish); her father, Battling Burrows, a besotted boxing champion (Donald Crisp); and the Yellow Man, a sensitive and gentle Chinese who has emigrated to spread the pacifist philosophy of Buddhism (Richard Barthelmess). The film focuses upon the tragic fate of Lucy, a motherless child, who lives in terror of her father since he does not confine his pugilism to the ring. Alternatives to her miserable existence with her father are just as wretched, however. A forlorn creature in tattered dress, Lucy sits huddled together on the wharf and in a flashback recalls the advice of

8

a poverty-stricken mother, "Whatever you do, dearie, don't get married." Life as a streetwalker is depicted as equally depressing. What lies ahead for Lucy is bound to be cruel. She is a child who is especially sensitive to the beauty of flowers though she lives in Limehouse squalor. As indicated by the film's title, however, Lucy herself will never bloom into womanhood.

After a particularly brutal beating, Lucy runs away and collapses inside the Yellow Man's shop. The Chinese man shelters her in an upstairs room, arrays her in costly silks, and displays the only tenderness she has ever known. The "alabaster cockney girl" becomes his "White Blossom." This dreamlike idyl is short-lived. Burrows discovers the whereabouts of his daughter and drags her home in a murderous rage. Clutching the little doll which the Yellow Man gave her, Lucy protests her innocence, "T'ain't nothin' wrong! T'ain't nothin' wrong!" The final scene in the Burrows home is the celebrated sequence in which Lucy, having locked herself in the closet, reels around and around--her screams a crescendo of terror--as her father breaks in the door with an axe. Severely beaten, she lies dying and with a last gesture lifts the corners of her mouth in a forlorn smile.

The Yellow Man arrives too late but carries the broken body of his White Blossom back to the haven where she had been happy for such a brief moment and stabs himself.

Lucy represents the extreme logical characterization of the stereotyped Victorian heroine. She is a twelve year old child but no Lolita. Unlike other Griffith-Gish heroines, she gives no evidence of an awakening sexuality. According to Gish, *"Broken Blossoms...was a thing before sex. The difficulty I faced with that character was that it was a child... and we couldn't have any suggestion of a girl. We had to show only the sympathy that the Chinaman felt for this abused child and the goodness of feeling that the girl expressed in return."* [13] Since Lucy is still a child, the external threat is posed not by the lust of a man who would rape her, but the brutality of her own father. And the sexual overtones involved in a scene where a man beats his twelve year old daughter and literally falls upon her in bed provide not a little fascination. As for the Yellow Man, he perceives Lucy as more than a lovely child, to be sure, but his intentions must remain strictly honorable within the context of the story. Given the ultimate taboo of miscegenation and the quality of innocence in Lucy, the child-not-yet-a-woman, there could be no last minute rescue. The only setting in which marriage promises the legendary happy ending, moreover, is one in which the economics are not so bleak. As the Victorian heroine cast in the sordid environment of Limehouse, rather than in middle class comfort, Lucy becomes completely the victim. She has to be killed off. What else could Griffith do with her?

In 1919, Griffith paid $175,000 for the rights to an old stage melodrama, *Way Down East,* and an additional $10,000 for a scenario. Lillian Gish states in her autobiography that everyone thought Griffith had lost his touch, and she herself almost burst out laughing when she read the play. But the film eventually grossed $9,000,000.[14] Gish was aware that the success of the picture would depend on the credibility of the heroine, and she achieved a real tour de force as an actress in making Anna Moore so believable. *Way Down East* became a sensational hit due to the fine performances of both Gish and her co-star, Richard Barthelmess, and to Griffith's most spectacular last minute rescue sequence. *The New York Times* critic dismissed the film as "hokum," but Griffith's biographer rejoins that one man's fakery in the movie business is another man's showmanship.[15]

Way Down East opens with a Griffith sermon masquerading as a title: although man has been polygamous for centuries, the ideal of one man for one woman is gaining acceptance. Since the monogamous ideal has yet to be realized, woman is made to suffer. The woman in this case is Anna Moore, a shy, inexperienced country girl who goes to the city to appeal to wealthy relatives for support. A rich, suave man-about-town named Lennox Sanderson (Lowell Sherman) eventually lures her to his apartment but when he makes advances, she becomes tearful and frightened. Changing tactics, he proposes marriage and finds the young girl less alarmed but still abashed in his embrace. Only a villain would take advantage of Anna, but Sanderson rises to the occasion. He arranges a mock marriage which, he insists, must be kept a secret and then spirits his bride away to a suite at the Rose Tree Inn. Anna dresses in the evening gown which Sanderson has bought for her, but she is painfully shy and haltingly calls him, "my--my husband." The large bed in the background of the suite serves as a glaring reminder of the seduction which is about to occur.

Some time elapses before Anna reveals to Sanderson that there is a "tender new reason" why their secret cannot be kept any longer, but he horrifies her with the blunt revelation that they are not married at all. Shortly thereafter the heroine suffers the death of her mother, also that of her newborn child, and social disgrace and ostracism as well. She is forced to leave town. With her few possessions packed in a paper box, the figure of Anna trudging down a country road brings a lump to the throat. She arrives at the Bartlett farm and is taken in as a hired girl but becomes a much loved member of the household. David, the squire's son, begins to fall in love with her. Then, Lennox Sanderson reappears in Anna's life as the neighbor who owns the adjoining estate. Sanderson is annoyed by Anna's presence on the farm and predicts dire consequences should her past be disclosed. When she alludes to *his* past, he blandly remarks, "Oh it's different for a MAN. He's supposed to sow his wild oats." Consequently, when David declares his love, Anna reacts with joy and then despair as she exclaims, "I can never be ANY MAN'S WIFE--."

The plot reaches its climax when an old town gossip discloses Anna's past to the Bartletts. Squire Bartlett, a stern Calvinist who believes that a fallen woman remains fallen, takes an uncharitable stand and orders Anna out into a raging snowstorm. David quarrels with his father and rushes outside into the darkness. The famous sequence which follows was filmed during a blizzard in sub-zero temperatures.[16] Anna is driven by the wind and snow towards the river's edge. Exhausted, she collapses on a sheet of ice which breaks away from the shore and starts to move downstream towards the fall. She lies immobile, her bedraggled hair and a hand trailing in the icy water, her dark dress a tiny spot on an immense field of moving ice. Back on shore, David finds her cloak and frantic with the knowledge that she lies somewhere adrift, leaps from one block of ice to another, stumbles, almost falls into the water, and reaches her as they are about to be pitched over into the fall. In actuality, these scenes filmed at White River Junction, Vermont were skillfully edited in the studio with shots of Niagara Falls. The audience could not tell the difference and so spectacular was the rescue, in several theatres they broke out in loud cheers. When I first saw the film in a poorly attended theater, the phenomenon repeated itself and the audience clapped and cheered. The Griffith magic still works.

Way Down East is a film in which there were variations on the usual Griffith theme. Although the film ended with a last minute rescue and a wedding--this time a real one--the seduction of the heroine has already taken place and she has given birth to an illegitimate child. As Anna's lovers, Sanderson represented the hypocritical double standard and David, the monogamous ideal. The contrast between the wholesome country boy and the callous scoundrel from the city was stressed throughout the film. The city was the scene where rural values had gone to pot. Richard Barthelmess, whom Gish billed "the most beautiful face of any man who ever went before a camera," was ideally suited to play opposite her.[17] As David, he was handsome and virile yet clean-cut. The all-American boy could be quite as appealing a lover as the dark Latin type, but without seeming promiscuous.

The sexual model of *Way Down East* stood curiously in contrast to the freedom resulting from the urban, Jazz Age revolution in manners and morals. Griffith condemned the double standard and upheld a restraint associated with the Victorian concept of womanhood. Gish informs us that he himself was quite circumspect and never saw a woman in his office without a third party present. Also, he lectured his young actresses about the dangers of promiscuity and venereal disease. Ironically, Griffith may have been subverting the very code he idealized in his films by demonstrating its implausibility. The fact is that some women were then beginning to adopt a freer attitude towards sex--an attitude which had previously been a male prerogative. The greater sexual permissiveness of the twenties may not have paved the way to sexual nirvana any more than did the repression of the genteel era, but at least the flapper stepped off the pedestal and became a creature of flesh and blood.

After the completion of *Way Down East,* Griffith's brother Albert persuaded him to release Gish and encourage her to sign with Frohman Amusement Corporation to save the expense of her salary. Griffith's biographer states that Gish was both shocked and hurt by this dismissal but put the best construction on it. The Frohman corporation went bankrupt and feeling somewhat guilty, Griffith brought Gish back into his company. The nature of their relationship had altered however. Gish no longer stood quite in awe of the master and realized that she had her own career to pursue, apart from him if need be.[18] The final Griffith-Gish vehicle, *Orphans of the Storm,* was also Griffith's last big moneymaker and critical success. The film was a melange of the popular melodrama, *Two Orphans,* and Dickens' *A Tale of Two Cities.* It was premiered in Boston on December 28, 1921 and in New York on January 3, 1922. The country had just passed through the Red Scare and the film was a mirror of its times.

According to Gish, *Orphans of the Storm* was partly based on the works of such conservative French historians as Hippolyte Taine and François Guizot. The Red Scare undoubtedly influenced Griffith's conception of the French Revolution as that historic revolt is equated with Bolshevism and anarchy. The exhibition of the film in France was reportedly an occasion for riots. Although the film contrasts the extravagant waste of decadent nobles with the abysmal poverty of the people, the specter of an unrestrained mob is worse than the tyranny of kings. The hero of the French Revolution is Danton, designated by some chronological lapse in metaphor as the Abraham Lincoln of his day. Danton's oratory is the spark which rouses a discontented people to arms. The revolution which occurs is no timid affair. The soldiers and populace square off and fire cannon into each other's ranks. The people go mad with power, revel, and snake dance in the street. Unfortunately, the loose women who symbolize the moral degeneracy attributed to revolution and anarchy resemble Jazz Age flappers rather than revolutionary Parisiennes.

The principal characters in this melodrama are the two orphans, Henriette (Lillian Gish) and Louise (Dorothy Gish), who depart for Paris on the eve of the Revolution to find a cure for the latter's blindness. Enroute, their coach becomes entangled at an intersection with the carriage of the lecherous Marquis de Prailles, who is fascinated by Henriette's "virginal beauty." The unsuspecting young girl confides her story to the nobleman, whereupon he orders his henchman to abduct her. A handsome aristocrat, the Chevalier de Vaudrey, rescues Henriette from the lascivious de Prailles, secures her lodging, and begins to woo her. Unfortunately, the outbreak of the revolution endangers his life and Henriette's as well. At a sensational trial, the unsympathetic judgment of figures such as Robespierre condemns the lovers to the guillotine and they are carted away to the scaffold. Enter Danton. His thundering plea for moderation and justice wins over the crowd and he secures a pardon for the condemned lovers. In a typical Griffith cross-cutting sequence, Danton gallops off to the rescue and arrives at the guillotine just in the nick of time.

The Birth of a Nation, Hearts of the World, and *Orphans of the Storm* were all set in historical periods of turmoil and great upheaval. According to Griffith's conception of history, periods of chaos and disruption upset not only political stability, but the moral order of society as well. And standards of morality related to sexual behavior, for the libidinous instincts of those who achieved political power were far guarded. In fact, the very exercise of power encouraged sexual license as demonstrated by blacks during the Reconstruction, German soldiers at the French front, and the aristocrats prior to the French Revolution as well as their plebeian successors. Within these circumstances, the Griffith-Gish heroine was imperilled in the worst of all possible worlds. By contrast, films such as *Broken Blossoms* and *Way Down East* were not set in historical periods and focused upon human relationships which did not compete with the panorama of history. Absence of a political upheaval which unleashed primitive instincts meant that the heroine was not directly threatened by rape. The nature of her predicament, however, was still victimization by man. The maturation of the Griffith-Gish heroine into a woman capable of taking charge of her own destiny lay outside the scope of these pictures. Gish's image of imperilled young womanhood--chaste, virtuous, and defenceless--was too captivating to invite change. The Victorian concept of femininity was cherished because it disturbed neither male prerogative nor female claims to protection. Nevertheless, a revolution in manners and morals had already begun by the time that the Griffith-Gish era in motion picture history came to an end.

Although *Orphans of the Storm* enjoyed a financial success, Griffith's brother Albert again pointed out that Gish's salary was a drain despite the fact that she was only earning one thousand dollars a week while Paramount had reputedly offered Dorothy a million. After having cast Gish out into the cruel world in his film melodramas, Griffith ironically found himself compelled to do so in real life. Gish merely states with her usual reticence in her autobiography, ''Thus, in the most friendly way, an artistic and business association of many years was broken off as casually as it had begun.''[19] Robert M. Henderson suggests that the feelings involved were not so casual. Griffith had lately transferred his attentions from Gish to Carol Dempster and spent a considerable amount of time and expense trying to make her a star. When his efforts failed, Dempster decamped without a word of warning and married a shipping heir.[20] During the twenties, Griffith's career fell into decline while Gish continued to receive critical acclaim for her roles. The Griffith-Gish combination had been a magic Hollywood formula and was never again duplicated.

POST-GRIFFITH GISH

In contrast to the screen heroines she played, Lillian Gish was perfectly competent to assume control of her own destiny. Griffith had remarked that she knew as much about making pictures as he did and even gave her a directing assignment in 1919. Gish did not feel that a woman had the strength to direct because it required "a man's vigor and imagination."[21] Yet, *Remodeling Her Husband,* a comedy she directed, turned out to be Dorothy's biggest money-maker for Paramount and according to Gish, the profits helped to make possible the studio which Griffith set up at Mamaroneck. When she left Griffith in 1922 and began a separate career as a film actress, Gish was capable of leaving her own mark on the film industry.

After leaving Griffith, Gish made two films in Italy with Inspiration Pictures, a small independent company. She earned a salary of $1,250 a week plus 15 percent of the profits after a certain intake. The first of the pictures, *The White Sister,* was very much Gish's own film. She had read the novel about a young girl who enters a cloister and became convinced that it had possibilities as a movie. Although religious pictures were not then considered commercial, Gish proceeded with her plans. She and her director, Henry King, discovered a British stage actor named Ronald Colman to play the male lead and rehearsed him on board ship. *The White Sister* was filmed in Rome and Naples. The plot centers on the fate of an aristocratic young girl, Angela Chiaromonte, and her lover, Captain Giovanni Severi, who is leaving on an expedition to Africa. A close-up of a newspaper headline, "Engineers Massacred in Africa," reveals his fate to the audience. The film cuts to Angela, blissfully unaware of disaster, as she sits by the window and reads a treasured love letter. When she learns of Giovanni's death Angela falls gravely ill, recovers in a hospital run by the White Sisters of Santa Giovanna D'Aza, and makes the fateful decision to become a bride of Christ.

1. Lillian Gish

2.   Lillian Gish and Robert Harron in *Hearts of the World*

Angela cannot know that Giovanni has escaped from an Arab prison and is that very moment returning to her. When the lovers meet by accident in a hospital corridor, Angela rushes upstairs to pray for strength to accept her destiny. Giovanni is not so passive. Confronting a priest who argues that "marriage to the holy Church is just as binding as marriage to a man," he angrily decries "the tyranny of the Church--enslaving women who should be wives and mothers!" In desperation, Giovanni lures Angela away from the hospital and threatens to hold her captive as his mistress, but she is adamant. The young man is finally moved by her sincerity and releases her. As Angela clutches her rosary to recite a prayer, he falls to the ground, kisses the hem of her robe, and vows never to see her again. The novel ended happily, but Gish felt that the heroine could not repudiate her vows a half-hour after she had taken them. The film ends on a cataclysmic scale with the sudden eruption of Mount Vesuvius and a gigantic flood. Giovanni drowns.

Gish's biographer, Albert Bigelow Paine, was critical about the ending of the film. "A volcanic eruption, an earthquake and a flood, for no better reason...than to kill a poor soldier who had already spent five years shut up in a rabbit-hutch. Nothing he had done warranted his being drowned like a rat in a flooded ditch." [22] In fact, the ending, though a bit overdone, was appropriate. Angela Chiaromonte as the white-robed sister was consecrated to God and became inaccessible to her lover. With the removal of the only man who could lay claim to her feelings as a woman, she became an ethereal being, but the erotic overtones of the ceremony in which she takes the veil revealed the affinity between heavenly and earthly love. Angela was married, but she has become the bride of Christ.

The White Sister was premiered at the Forty-fourth Street Theater in New York on September 5, 1923. The distributors were skeptical about releasing a religious film but after its enthusiastic reception by critics and moviegoers alike, Nicholas Schenck arranged to distribute the film through Metro Pictures. In fact, exhibitors regarded Metro's acquisition of The White Sister as a coup, especially after its successful run in New York. [23] The negative cost $270,000 but the picture eventually grossed $4,000,000. [24] Gish cut the final version of the film from twelve to nine reels before returning to Italy to make her next picture, Romola, also directed by Henry King and co-starring her sister Dorothy, William Powell, and Ronald Colman. The film, based on a work by George Eliot, was set in fifteenth century Florence.

Romola is the aristocratic and intellectual daughter of an elderly scholar; she marries a clever adventurer named Tito (William Powell) in hopes that he will complete the prodigious work of scholarship to which her father has devoted his life. As a young bride, she is ignorant both of her husband's unsavory background and his relationship with a peasant girl named Tessa (Dorothy Gish) who eventually bears him a son. Not satisfied with having won the hand of Romola nor his elevation to the position of gonfalonier, Tito schemes to seize the Medici throne and engineers his own downfall by alienating the people. Entreating Romola to care for her child, the faithful Tessa follows him to his self-destruction. A madonna-like figure, Romola attempts to intercede for the life of still another target of mob fury, the monk Savanarola, played with a touch of Protestant evangelism, but she fails. After these tumultuous events pass, an earlier suitor described as "the ever faithful Carlo" (Ronald Colman) arrives at the palace and reconciles with Romola. As the film ends, he declares that women like her, standing at the foot of the cross, will ever teach men to be good. In fact, the angelic figure of Romola triumphs neither in redeeming the treacherous Tito nor in saving Savanarola from the mob. Carlo has already been predestined for grace. As she stands increasingly in contrast to a world of base and turbulent passions, the saintly Romola is all but elevated from it.

Romola was premiered at the George M. Cohan Theater in New York on December 1, 1924 and five days later at Sid Grauman's new movie palace, the Chinese Theater in Los Angeles. The Gish sisters attended both the East and West coast premieres. Although *Romola* enjoyed both critical and popular success, Gish felt that the drama moved too slowly and never matched the marvelous tapestry of its fifteenth century background. The success of the two Inspiration pictures made in Italy did prove, however, that Lillian Gish without D.W. Griffith was an actress and filmmaker in her own right. The rest of her silent film career was tied to the fortunes of a rising new studio, Metro-Goldwyn-Mayer.

In 1925, Lillian Gish signed a contract with M-G-M, a studio which rose to challenge the hegemony of Paramount at the close of the silent era. The exclusive contract stipulated a production schedule of six films in two years for a salary of $800,000. Gish moved back to Hollywood and settled in a bungalow at the Beverly Hills Hotel. She found that big business had changed the movies. When she and her sister Dorothy first arrived on the West coast in 1913, Hollywood had not yet put Los Angeles on the map. The industry was unstructured and directors like Griffith could work independently and make a film like *The Birth of a Nation* without a script. The huge Culver City complex which welcomed Lillian Gish with banners flying was the product of increasing concentration and streamlining within the industry. The year before, the Goldwyn corporations, Marcus Loew's Metro, and Louis B. Mayer's producing companies had merged to form the studio. The corporation was controlled by Loew's Incorporated which, together with Paramount and First National, cornered the vital exhibiting branch of the industry by monopolizing theater chains across the country.

When Gish arrived at the studio, she found that no preparations had been made for her first film. As a matter of fact, she herself was to exert a considerable degree of control over the better known pictures she made at M-G-M. The first production, a movie version of *La Boheme*, co-starred John Gilbert, one of the silent screen's great lovers. Gish selected King Vidor to direct, requested that her favorite photographer, Hendrich Sartov, be her cameraman, and became involved in technical details concerning film stock, lighting, rehearsals, sets, and costumes.

In his autobiography, Vidor relates how Gish succeeded in imposing her conception of the love story in *La Boheme* upon him and Gilbert.[25] She felt that the intensity of the love scenes, as well as the tragic ending, would be enhanced if the lovers never embraced and kissed but were always separated by space. The glow of the unattainable began to exert its fascination upon both director and leading man. According to Gish's secretary, Phyllis Moir, Gilbert fell in love with Gish, penned love letters, and sent a proposal of marriage. The front office was worried about Gilbert's image as a lover, however, and ordered a retake of the love scenes. Gish complied but used to sigh before rehearsals, "Oh, dear, I've got to go through another day of kissing John Gilbert." [26]

After *La Boheme*, Gish decided to make a film version of *The Scarlet Letter*. Louis B. Mayer was concerned about the opposition of churches and women's clubs to a dramatization of the novel, but Gish's personal appeal won their approval. As a result, she had considerable control

20

over the film's production.[27] Frances Marion, a successful screen writer who had previously worked in collaboration with Mary Pickford, adapted the film and wrote both scenario and titles. Gish requested that Victor Seastrom direct the film and agreed upon Lars Hanson as the leading man. She felt that the Swedes had a spirit in common with New England puritanism.

The screen version of *The Scarlet Letter* was a melodrama which portrayed the fate of Arthur Dimmesdale and Hester Prynne as lovers in a repressive New England society.[28] Lillian Gish in the role of Hester revealed qualities more vibrant than any Griffith heroine, but her appearance was rather girlish for the part.[29] The novel begins with the public branding of Hester as an adultress but in the movie, the seduction takes place as the result of a growing attraction between the two lovers. The appearance of Chillingworth as the wronged and vengeful husband thus occurs late in the film, and his threat to pursue the couple in any attempt to secure happiness elsewhere convinces Dimmesdale that the only escape is revelation. In the final scene, he mounts the scaffold to proclaim his guilt alongside Hester and collapses in her arms. With a last gesture, he removes the scarlet letter from her dress and it falls on his chest next to the letter which he had branded upon himself. The ending of the film is thus more literal than that of the novel, which leaves the disclosure of what was on the minister's breast a matter of conjecture for the villagers.

Critics differed about the quality of the film as an adaptation of the novel but for the most part, reviews were favorable.[30] In effect, *The Scarlet Letter* was intellectually deficient because it focused on the narrative as melodrama rather than attempting a cinematic representation of a moral dilemma. Absent was the sense of a tragic and ineluctable fate binding together Hester, the child as a living counterpart of the scarlet letter, the Reverand Dimmesdale, and Chillingworth. And since the sinister role of Chillingworth was minimized, the complex psychological and philosophical aspects of the problem of guilt were not explored. The film, moreover, contained scenes of comic relief which showed women laundering their undergarments away from masculine eyes and an engaged couple conducting their restrained courtship through a speaking tube. Such interpolations underscored the contrast between novel and film.

While filming *The Scarlet Letter,* Gish received word that her mother had suffered a stroke in London. She completed the picture in a few days and then traveled cross country to board a liner in New York. When she returned, she found that the studio had already begun the production of her next picture, *Annie Laurie,* a costume drama about feuding Scottish clans. She was not involved in preparations for the film and concluded that "the heroine lacked the emotional depth and stature of Mimi and Hester."[31] After the debacle of *Annie Laurie,* Gish assumed charge of her next feature, *The Wind,* based on a novel by Dorothy Scarborough, and worked again with director Victor Seastrom and scenarist Frances Marion. Although critics differed in their reactions, Richard Watts, Jr., a reviewer for the *New York Tribune,* correctly assessed that the plot was secondary to the landscape and force of nature:

> *Atmosphere, through the unassailable pictorial resource of the screen, becomes essentially drama. The sand and the wind and the spell created by their endless presence in the life of the heroine provide the menace of the picture, and any savagery on the part of the people of the drama becomes of minor importance before the essential drama of a malignant nature.*[32]

The picture begins with the arrival of the heroine, Letty Mason, at a barren, windswept destination in Texas. She expects to find a home with her cousin, Bev, and his wife, Cora, but the harshness and cruelty of the landscape is matched by that of a jealous spouse. Cora is determined to drive Letty out of her house and in desperation, the friendless girl accepts a marriage proposal from their neighbor, Lige Hightower. Lars Hanson, the Swedish actor, gives a remarkable performance as Lige, the good-natured but boorish young cowboy who becomes the object of his bride's revulsion. Lige is angry and dispirited but promises to find enough money to send her away. When the unceasing winds begin to develop into a destructive "norther," Lige goes out to corral the wild horses driven by the windstorm so that he might earn some money.

Left by herself in the cabin, Letty stares in terror at the dark, billowing clouds as the winds increase in violence, and she begins to feel herself going mad. A blank, dazed stare becomes fixed in her eyes. The tragic events which follow form part of the nightmare unleashed by the wind. A man whom Letty had met on the train finds his way to the cabin and discovering her alone, violates her. In the aftermath, she shoots him and buries his corpse in the sand, but the wind begins to reveal the face and hand of a dead man. The horrified woman becomes unbalanced, wanders away, and disappears into the windstorm. At the insistence of the studio, Gish had to consent to an alternative happy ending in which Letty reconciles with Lige when he returns to the cabin. Unfortunately, this very inappropriate ending inverts the cinematic conception of the wind as a violent and destructive force linked with human tragedy.

The last film which Lillian Gish made for M-G-M, *The Enemy,* was a production set in a European background during World War I, but she disavows it as she does *Annie Laurie.* Gish never made a sixth film as her two year contract expired. After an interval, she signed with United Artists for $50,000 per film plus 50 percent of the profits. She made her first talkie, *The Swan,* retitled *One Romantic Night,* in 1929 and was disappointed with the result. The United Artists contract had not stipulated sound films, but Gish felt it wise to make at least one talkie before canceling the agreement. The silent era was over. The public reception of sound had been enthusiastic and undiscriminating. Gish could not reconcile herself to changes in technique required by sound, though her voice was more than adequate, and she decided to abandon films for the stage. She has remarked that at the time she ended her film career, she was bored with the type of roles she played. Gish had been a pioneer in the industry, but the golden age had passed and she knew it.

THE GISH IMAGE

Anita Loos once remarked about Lillian Gish, "Men were always marrying her in absentia." [33] James Branch Cabell waxed rhapsodic about her as Helen of Troy. Joseph Hergesheimer wrote in an article for *The American Mercury,* "You will be, like the April moon, a thing for all young men to dream about forever...." [34] Edward Wagenknecht observed that her outlines were "dreamlike, subdued" and that she seemed "to float on the screen like a remembered vision of Boticelli's women." [35] Mark Twain's biographer, Albert Bigelow Paine, wrote a saccharine volume about her life and work. Drama critic George Jean Nathan gave her a ring with an intaglio stone bearing his profile, squired her about for years, and pressed her to marry him but with no success. He himself had appraised, "The whole secret of the young woman's remarkably effective acting rests, as I have observed, in her... technique of playing always, as it were, behind a veil of silver chiffon...." [36] In real life, as on the screen, there remained an elusive and ineffable quality about Lillian Gish. She seemed always beyond reach and meant to be worshipped from afar.

The image of Lillian Gish still appeals but the feeling of nostalgia associated with it is apt because she belongs to the past. Louise Brooks, herself a silent screen star, charges in an interesting article, "Gish and Garbo: The Executive War on Stars," that M-G-M deliberately phased out Gish's career because she represented an ideal type of femininity which was no longer box-office. [37] *La Boheme* was premiered on Broadway in New York during the same week that *The Torrent,* an M-G-M feature starring an unknown Swedish actress, began its run. [38] *La Boheme* had been directed by King Vidor and co-starred John Gilbert. *The Torrent* was made by a lesser known director, Monta Bell, and co-starred Ricardo Cortez, a comical leading man. At the Embassy Theater, *La Boheme* drew an average crowd while *The Torrent* attracted large audiences to the Capitol. In terms of production costs, Lillian Gish's exclusive contract stipulated $400,000 a year while Greta Garbo earned only $16,000. Symbolically, *Anna Karenina,* a film which had been meant for Gish, was retitled *Love* and starred Greta Garbo. And Garbo inherited John Gilbert as a lover in both her screen and private life.

Although Brooks is quite perceptive in posing Gish and Garbo as opposite and successive screen types, the transition was not really so marked at the box-office. *La Boheme* received mixed reviews but news articles indicate that the film did quite well at both the Embassy and Capitol theaters in New York. As a special M-G-M production, *La Boheme* was premiered at the Embassy where top admission tickets cost two dollars. The simultaneous screening of *The Torrent* at the Capitol, which showed films at popular prices, excited considerable interest because critics and audience alike were impressed by the debut of Greta Garbo. The Capitol receipts totaled $68,000 at the end of the first week and the film was held over. But when *La Boheme* was screened at the Capitol later in the same year for a run at popular prices, it grossed $60,889.15 at the close of the first week.[39] Although Garbo was not well-paid as an unknown, in contrast to Gish who had been a star since the beginning of silent features, she went on a strike after her third feature and received a sizeable salary increase.

The critics were mostly enthusiastic about Garbo's debut whereas Gish's performance as Mimi drew some ridicule, and this reaction is a more telling sign than dollars and cents. The reviewers had heretofore been generous if not hyperbolic in their praise of Gish. But the New York *Sun* critic wrote:

> *The fair Lillian, it is safe to record, is the first convincing tubercular* Mimi *in history. Certainly, the operatic stage has never seen such a pictorially convincing consumptive. She goes through her usual screen tricks, however, including running around the room in a portrayal of hysteria, and blinking coyly at the camera in the manner of a frightened gazelle. She was best in the death scene.*
>
> *There is no denying, though, that she gave a striking and moving, if familiar performance.*[40]

This criticism, if rather harsh in referring to "screen tricks," was fairly accurate. As reflected by the bored tone of the reviewer, the Gish heroine had become all too familiar though it was undeniable that her acting was still superb. Louise Brooks' accusation that M-G-M deliberately ended Gish's career takes on substance in light of the actress' remarkable performance in *The Wind*. Although a reviewer for *Motion Picture Today* rightly observed "much in it reminiscent of former days," Gish displayed new dimensions as a screen actress. [41] The studio shelved the film for months, however, until a happy ending was appended. Brooks charges that this was an intentional maneuvre to deny Gish the first Oscar. If, in fact, M-G-M discovered that the standard Gish heroine was no longer an asset and actively sought to displace her, the popularity of both the "new woman" and talking pictures completed her eclipse.

The program distributed at the premiere of *The White Sister* in 1923 had paid tribute to Lillian Gish in a familiar vein by describing her as "a splendid example of American girlhood, at its best." [42] Although the movie audience still admired American girlhood, that girlhood was no longer synonymous with the qualities which Lillian Gish projected on the screen. Perhaps the very artistry with which she had portrayed the sentimental heroine had only succeeded in defining her limitations as a woman. She was at the height of her popularity during and shortly after the war and for a while competed successfully with more daring heroines, such as the vamp and the "new woman." As the Jazz Age progressed, however, the Victorian heroine became increasingly outmoded. The value structure of the world in which she functioned had begun to collapse. The popular image of woman changed and with it, concepts of morality based on woman's purity and innocence. The descent from the pedestal meant that woman's position would be less clearly defined, as were morals, but that was the cost of change.

Chapter II

AMERICA'S SWEETHEART: MILLION DOLLAR MARY

The girl who lived a Cinderella life on screen led a parallel existence in real life but with one exception: she created the magic herself through hard work and clever business deals. America's Sweetheart was born Gladys Marie Smith on April 8, 1894 in Toronto, Canada. The straitened circumstances of her family affected Mary Pickford's attitude towards money in all phases of her famous career, during which she made millions. Not without significance, her earliest recollections involve money:

> To make some extra money, Father worked all night in a local theater, pulling up scenery until he got big blisters....Mother told me this later; I don't remember it myself. But I do remember the first money he gave me: he was standing beside me telling me to open my hands, and into them he put the seventy-five cents he had earned that night. ...Of course I gave it to Mother, but with a sense of great pride. Another recognition of the early lure of money was the time my sister Lottie dropped a Canadian silver piece between the keys of Mother's upright piano. The thought of this buried treasure tormented me so that I was determined to break all the keys to retrieve the priceless coin. Grandma caught me going from the kitchen to the "parlor," with a look of high resolve on my face and a hammer in my hand. [1]

The Smith's impoverishment worsened after Gladys' father died in an accident and left her mother a young widow with three small children to support. As a child, Gladys was not unaware of the financial consequences of such a death in the family.

> *When Father died I realized, with a strange and frightening suddenness, that Mother was alone, and I decided that I had to do something about it.*
>
> *…"Mama," I said, "have you next month's rent, and money for the coal?"* [2]

To make ends meet, Mrs. Charlotte Smith decided to rent the master bedroom and by coincidence, her tenant was the stage manager of the Cummings Stock Company in Toronto. This man started Gladys Smith on the road to becoming Mary Pickford when he suggested that she and her younger sister Lottie appear on the stage. After that, Charlotte Smith actively began to promote her daughter's theatrical career and soon the whole family was on the road. Always, Gladys concerned herself about money. During one stay in New York, the Smiths economized by sharing a flat with another theatrical family, the Gishes. Lillian Gish recalls that Gladys took charge of the children and management of both households.

> *The combined housekeeping made for economy, and here, too, Gladys Smith was a leader and a force. Even the mothers listened to her advice. On the kitchen table, at night, with a grubby little pencil and a scrap of paper, she audited the accounts.* [3]

Gladys Smith was never one to wait until opportunity knocks, not even as a little girl. When she succeeded in securing an interview with David Belasco, the celebrated Broadway producer, she amused him with the following outburst:

> *"Well, you see, Mr. Belasco, I'm thirteen years old, and I think I'm at the crossroads of my life. I've got to make good between now and the time I'm twenty, and I have only seven years to do it in. Besides, I'm the father of my family and I've got to earn all the money I can."* [4]

Belasco rechristened Gladys Smith as Mary Pickford and gave her a role in *The Warrens of Virginia*, a play written by William deMille, whose younger brother Cecil also had a part in the production. The play opened on Broadway in November, 1907. There are conflicting Pickford statements about the rigorous economy which she practiced during its run, but the point is that she knew the value of a hard earned dollar.

> *During this Belasco engagement I lived on five dollars a week and often went for days before I would break a dollar bill. I walked to and from the theater in any weather; on matinee days it meant walking four miles.*[5]

After *The Warrens of Virginia* closed down, the family reserves became dangerously low.

> *As the weeks went by and our funds got lower,...the old sense of insecurity returned to plague us.*

> *...It was occasions like this that made me more resolved than ever that my family would someday know real security. I never for a moment doubted that I myself would ultimately provide it for them.*[6]

Mrs. Smith suggested to her daughter that she apply for work at the Biograph Studio to tide them over, though Mary felt it beneath her dignity as a Belasco actress to appear in flickers.

> *The following morning,...I decide[d] to walk from where we were living on West Seventeenth Street to Fourteenth Street, take a cross-town trolley, and in paying my fare ask the conductor for a transfer up Broadway. I had no intention of wasting a perfectly good nickel.*[7]

Accounts vary as to the manner in which Pickford's first salary as a movie actress was settled. On that eventful day, however, she did not emerge from the studio empty handed:

> *It had begun to rain earlier and by now it was coming down in buckets. ...I was wet through when I arrived at the theater in Brooklyn, as I had to walk several*

> blocks. *My brand-new high-heeled shoes were ruined,*
> *and so were my silk stockings. A $3.50 straw hat*
> *with a big dark blue satin bow was a sight for tears,*
> *and my beautiful blue $15 serge Easter suit was one*
> *wringing mess. ...Clutched in my hand was the wet*
> *five-dollar bill.* [8]

From the beginning of her career in films, Pickford was always angling for a raise. As Linda Arvidson recalled:

> *I know Mary brought a business head with her to*
> *Biograph. Mr. Griffith had told her if she'd be a good*
> *sport about doing what little unpleasant stunts the*
> *stories might call for, he would raise her salary.*

> *...Not a second did Mary demur, but obediently flopped*
> *into the river. The scene over, wet and dirty, the boys*
> *fished her out and rushed her, wrapped in a warm*
> *blanket, to the waiting automobile.*

> *...Mary's place in the car was between my husband and*
> *myself. Hardly were we comfortably settled,...before*
> *Mary...naively looked up into her director's face and*
> *sweetly reminded him of his promise. She got her raise.*
> *And I got the shock of my young life. That pretty*
> *little thing with yellow curls thinking of money like*
> *that!* [9]

And Pickford herself remembered:

> *...In a crowded subway train one day,...[her brother*
> *Jack] whispered, "Mary, if you don't promise to give*
> *me a dime I'm going to tell everybody in the car that*
> *you're the Biograph Girl." The threat sometimes rated*
> *fifteen cents, depending on the size of the crowd. It also*
> *gave me a peculiar idea of my own which prompted*
> *me to ask Mr. Griffith for a ten-dollar raise.*[10]

The star system, which would evolve with the career of Mary Pickford and revolutionize the motion picture industry, did not yet exist but the actress was beginning to weigh the worth of public recognition in dollars and cents. And she also found, as did other stage performers, that the movies provided a good source of income.

Late in 1910, Pickford left Biograph and signed with Carl Laemmle's Imp Company for $175 a week. Ads which proclaimed, "Little Mary is an Imp Now!" testified to the popularity of the studio's new acquisition. The following year, Pickford switched to Majestic for $275 a week. She returned to Biograph in 1912, reportedly at a reduced salary, but with a promise that her name would appear in connection with her work though films did not then contain credits. The progression of Mary Pickford towards movie stardom and financial success was interrupted, however, by a brief return to the stage. On July 25, 1911, William deMille had addressed a letter to Belasco:

>...*you remember that little girl, Mary Pickford...? I met her again a few weeks ago and the poor kid is actually thinking of taking up moving pictures. She says she can make a fairly good living at it but it does seem a shame.*

>...*So I suppose we'll have to say good bye to little Mary Pickford. She'll never be heard of again and I feel terribly sorry for her.* [11]

But Mary Pickford was not quite destined for theatrical oblivion yet. In 1912, she left Griffith permanently to accept the leading role in a Belasco production, *A Good Little Devil*. She occupied the coveted dressing room with a silver star on the door and after opening night, requested and got a raise in salary.

>*"My goal, Mr. Belasco, is to earn five hundred dollars a week by the time I am twenty," I announced.*

>*"That's a most excellent reason for you getting an additional twenty-five dollars," he said. "From now on your salary will be two hundred a week."* [12]

The critical and popular acclaim which greeted Mary Pickford upon her return to the stage did not escape Adolph Zukor, then embattled in the patent war. Zukor had become convinced that the future lay in feature films and began production with the Famous Players Company, later contracting to distribute his films through Paramount. When *A Good Little Devil* became a Broadway success, he negotiated with Belasco to purchase the play but really had his eye on the girl with the golden curls. Just why Pickford decided to abandon the stage and return to films is not clear. In her autobiography, she states that overnight, she experienced "a powerful yearning to be back in motion pictures."[13] James Card suggests in an article that Pickford returned to films when she realized that the crowds in the theater had really come to see "Little Mary" of the flickers.[14] Zukor relates in his own autobiography that he convinced Pickford she had a more lucrative future in films.[15] Whatever the reason--and money probably had a great deal to do with it--Pickford negotiated the first of her celebrated contracts with Zukor and achieved her goal before she was twenty.

> ...*Mary's price was five hundred dollars a week...a fantastic sum for any but a famous stage player--but I did not quibble. I knew her value for the future, and I expected to be paying her more than that before we were finished.*[16]

Pickford and Zukor established a compatible personal and professional relationship. The producer had a fatherly attitude towards his star, despite her metamorphosis from little girl into astute businesswoman during their many contract negotiations. In his autobiography, he paid her this tribute:

> *There is no doubt about her tremendous drive for success and cash-register nature of a segment of her brain. I am convinced that Mary could have risen to the top in United States Steel, if she had decided to be a Carnegie instead of a movie star.*[17]

Benjamin B. Hampton, author of *History of the American Film Industry,* was once involved in negotiations with both Pickford and Zukor and is one of the few film historians who recognizes the actress' importance (most ignore Pickford and devote pages instead to Chaplin):

> *Women's place in business has grown enormously in importance in the last three decades, but Mary Pickford*

is the only member of her sex who ever became the focal point in an entire industry.[18]

With her drive, ambition, and business acumen, Pickford would probably have been successful in whatever she undertook. But a career in United States Steel was not accessible to women whereas the motion picture industry was in its infancy. Even after the industry became concentrated under the control of Wall Street, film acting was still one of the few professions in which women could earn large salaries. Mary Pickford not only amassed a fortune as an actress, she was shrewd enough to organize her own corporation and enter the fields of production and distribution where the real profits lay.

On July 8, 1914, the *Rochester Times* pronounced:

> *Miss Pickford is the greatest drawing card in film world today, according to the exhibitors.*[19]

The film world knew it and so did Mary Pickford, who decided it was time to reopen negotiations with Zukor.

> *It was the summer of 1914 that I walked into Mr. Zukor's office to ask for my first raise in salary. I still had six months to go on my original contract, which called for five hundred dollars a week, and I had every intention of living up to it. I so explained to Mr. Zukor, adding, however, that I had received an offer of two thousand dollars a week from a rival company on the Coast.*[20]

According to Adolph Zukor:

> *I had voluntarily increased Mary's salary from five hundred to one thousand dollars a week. ...The box-office receipts showed that Mary's pictures justified the increase.*[21]

In addition to a raise in salary, Zukor had a special surprise for his star. Pickford recalls the moment in her autobiography:

> *As we talked over our tea, my eyes would catch the title*
> *of the film through the window of the restaurant. I soon*
> *began to wonder why Mr. Zukor didn't suggest leaving*
> *after we had finished our tea and talk. It began to get*
> *dark, and then suddenly I saw it, one of the most*
> *thrilling sights of my whole career: my name blazing*
> *on the marquee of the Fifth Avenue Theater!* [22]

It was a dream come true. But the Pickford family was still unaccustomed to affluence and remembered the struggle of earlier days. Both mother and daughter were still wary about the future of Mary Pickford in films.

The enormous success of *Tess of the Storm Country,* released in 1914, proved to be a turning point in the careers of both Mary Pickford and Zukor's Famous Players.

> *Mr. Zukor told me some years later that* Tess *saved*
> *him from bankruptcy; that in order to meet the pay*
> *roll he had borrowed on his life insurance and pawned*
> *his wife's diamond necklace. All I know is that after*
> *the release of* Tess *I was Mr. Zukor's fair-haired child.*[23]

But the fair-haired child could be difficult.

> *Now trouble with Mary Pickford began to develop. Her*
> *shoes pinched her feet. Her costumes did not fit right.*
> *The directors were making unreasonable demands. The*
> *stories offered her were no good. This was not Mary's*
> *true nature, I knew. It was Mary's way of opening*
> *salary negotiations.*
>
> *...Eventually Mary signed a new contract with Famous*
> *Players at $2,000 a week....* [24]

One aspect of the contract negotiations indicated that Pickford's mind was racing ahead, and she was already thinking in terms of a separate distribution outlet for her features.

> *It was...announced that Mary had been overruled in a*

demand for a clause in her contract providing that "all Pickford features must be sold at double the customary prices and that an exhibitor showing them must charge double admissions." This was paving the way for something, too.[25]

On February 6, 1915, Paramount issued an announcement, saying that: "Owing to the enormous salary which it has been necessary to pay Miss Pickford in order to secure her services, all future releases will be first released to big city theaters charging a minimum price of twenty-five cents."[26]

The star system meant that the days of the nickelodeon were over. The newspapers and fan magazines kept the public informed about "Our Mary's"contract negotiations and headlines constantly associated her name with figures.

The Highest Paid Woman in the World
She is Mary Pickford, the Adored Queen of the Screen Dramas, Who Receives a Salary of $104,000 a Year, and is Said to Have Refused Even a Higher Sum...[27]

The number of digits in Pickford's salary continued to increase. She was the greatest star in demand by exhibitors and the moviegoing public. Whoever held her under contract had the advantage in the industry. No one assessed the financial aspect of the situation better than Pickford herself.

Mary liked being queen. One of the best ways of proving top sovereignty was to possess the largest treasury. We startled the film world and the public too,...by agreeing on a salary of $104,000 a year. And then a group called Mutual hired Charlie Chaplin at just short of $13,000 a week.

Mary felt that her place on the throne was being usurped by a clown--and a relative newcomer at that. There was nothing to do except reopen our salary relations. Under the final terms, Mary was paid $10,000 *every Monday. This was an advance against half the profits of a "Mary Pickford Company" organized inside Famous Players. In addition, there was to be a bonus of $300,000, for signing, if and when her pictures earned it.*

The total guarantee was $1,040,000 for a two-year period. The million-dollar figure made headlines and Mary felt better for a while. [28]

The million dollar contract contained extras befitting the queen of motion pictures. Pickford's name was to be in the largest type and featured exclusively in advertisements of her movies. The contract stipulated construction of a Mary Pickford studio in New York and a special stage in California. Pickford's films were to be released through a new distributing organization, Artcraft. The star acquired a voice in the selection of stories and directors and in other aspects of production. The contract also provided for parlor car transportation on trips to and from the West coast and an automobile for services outside of greater New York. In addition, Pickford collected $40,000 for the period between May 29 and June 24 when she had not been on the payroll, ostensibly for reading scripts. Not devoid of humor, Zukor quipped:

"Mary sweetheart,....I don't have to diet. Every time I talk over a new contract with you and your mother I lose ten pounds." [29]

And Samuel Goldwyn, whom Pickford never liked, exclaimed as he gazed out of his office window and saw her on the way to work:

"Ten thousand dollars a week and she's walking to the set yet. She should be running!" [30]

In 1918, the Pickford-Zukor relationship finally came to an end because the star was determined to share a greater percentage of the profits from her pictures. A series of behind the scenes negotiations occurred, but this time Zukor could not outbid his competitors without jeopardizing his own company. And he faced the unending prospect of raising the ante because Pickford never stopped thinking in terms of dollars and cents.

...Adolph Zukor and I finally came to a parting of the ways. I was determined to find some way of distributing my films separately from the other motion pictures. My hope was to form an independent company.

"It's a dangerous step, Mary honey," Mr. Zukor said gravely when I first broached the subject to him. "You'll be out on your own, completely and absolutely."

"That's where I want to be, Mr. Zukor." [31]

Benjamin B. Hampton relates the following episode about Pickford's departure:

Still reluctant to allow First National to acquire Miss Pickford, Zukor tried one more plan.

"You've worked very hard for years," he told her. "Why don't you take a vacation? If you will stop making pictures for five years, I will give you $250,000."

"Oh, I couldn't do that, Mr. Zukor," she answered. "I love pictures, and I'm just a girl. I couldn't quit now." [32]

Mary Pickford proceeded to sign a contract with Zukor's greatest competitor, First National. The agreement stipulated an approximate sum of $250,000 each for three negatives with profits to be evenly divided between the actress and the company; the former's total net revenue was estimated between one and two million dollars a year. [33] But Pickford became dissatisfied with First National because her pictures supported a train of mediocre productions through the system of block booking. The star was still intent upon maximizing profit by organizing her own distribution outlet.

The conferences which, in 1919, preceded the forming of United Artists--meetings which included Chaplin, Fairbanks, D.W. Griffith, and Nathan Burke, the lawyer--were quietly dominated by Mary. She had then,

3. Mary Pickford

4.   Mary Pickford in *Rags*

*as she has now, the gift of intelligent listening, but
at the end of one of those thoughtful silences, her rather
high Canadian voice would announce, "I disagree with
you, gentlemen, and I will tell you why." It generally
turned out that she was right. The United Artists
Corporation was her idea, to start with.* [34]

The following chart, which approximates her earnings per picture,
illustrates Pickford's success in her venture as producer and
distributor: [35]

> *1912-1914: $40,000 to $60,000*
> *1914-1917 (Paramount): $125,000 to $150,000*
> *1917-1919 (Artcraft and First National): $300,000
> to $500,000*
> *1919-1924 (United Artists): $600,000 to $1,200,000*

In the decade after signing her first contract with Zukor, Mary Pickford
achieved the goal she had set herself as family breadwinner in
spectacular fashion. A touching footnote to the Cinderella story may be
read in the will of her mother, Charlotte Pickford, who left an estate of
$1,444,972.

> *"Hers, her heirs...forever, because whatever property I
> possessed at the time of my death has come to me
> through my association with my said daughter in her
> business and through her most unusual generosity to
> me."* [36]

Despite the fact that she and her second husband Douglas Fairbanks
became American royalty and ruled filmdom from their Pickfair estate,
Pickford still retained her old philosophy and habits about money:

> *"I am almost a fanatic on the subject of saving. I
> could not waste a dollar knowingly. I do not mean I
> believe in being stingy or in going without things that
> will add comfort or contentment, but I do believe that
> regardless of income everyone should save."* [37]

She had a great deal of integrity when it came to her work, however. In 1930, she burned the negative of one of her few talkies, *Secrets,* at a loss of $300,000 because she was dissatisfied with the result. Pickford became a star because she had always been one of her own best critics.

AMERICA'S SWEETHEART

Adolph Zukor stated in his autobiography, "There has never been anything just like the public adulation showered on Mary."[38] This adulation was the basis for Mary Pickford's reign as "America's Sweetheart" and the strength of her position at the bargaining table. In reviewing the scant literature about her career, James Card observed that emphasis has been upon her role in the evolution of the star system and her spectacular financial success, not upon analyzing the enormous popularity of her pictures.[39] According to Card, the nearest approach to a serious discussion of the Pickford films is in Richard Griffith's *The Movies.* Griffith describes her as a girl in "that misty mid-region between sexless childhood and buxom womanliness which seems to have had a strong and specific appeal to many American males of the early century."[40] In *The Celluloid Sacrifice,* Alexander Walker writes in a similar vein, "Pickford was assisted to stardom by the same idolizing of prepubertal girlhood which is so persistent and at times sinister a strain in Victorian popular sentiment."[41]

In order to understand Pickford's enormous popular appeal, an attempt should be made to pinpoint her audience. Lewis Jacobs states that she captivated the hearts of the working classes who identified with her Pollyanna outlook on life.[42] Card points out more specifically that Pickford had her sights trained on the family, especially women and children. Mary Pickford herself stated in an interview, "I am a woman's woman. My success has been due to the fact that women like the pictures in which I appear."[43] And she was shrewd enough to realize the implications this had in film production. According to Pickford, she was one of the first filmmakers in Hollywood to evolve the concept of a "woman's director," as opposed to directors who had a talent for working with male stars.[44]

Both Pickford and Gish began their film careers under D.W. Griffith, the director who idealized on screen the sentimental heroine of

41

nineteenth century sweetness-and-light literature. The Gish heroine exerted a powerful appeal to male fantasies as the child-woman with whom sexual relations were unthinkable or as the victim of lust. Mary Pickford was also a Victorian heroine but in an altogether different sense. Pickford's character undoubtedly exerted as strong an appeal to women as to men, if not more so, for she was perfectly capable of taking care of herself and did so with determination and good humor. A typical scene in *Daddy Long Legs* captures her reaction to correspondence from a publisher who rejects her first manuscript. She stands for a moment with bowed head and then characteristically throws the letter on the ground, stamps her foot, and walks off determined to write another. And she succeeds. [45]

With some exceptions, the Pickford screen personality was a lively and spirited young girl, if not a little hellion. This image may be traced back to Pickford's first successful feature, *Tess of the Storm Country*, in which she portrayed a squatter's daughter. The *Moving Picture World* reviewed *Tess* as "a story by a woman, of a woman, and for women"--"and for men too" was added as an afterthought. [46] According to Pickford, that film "was really the beginning of my career. Tess was a character completely separate from what I'd been doing." [47] The reviewer who described Tess as "inimitable, always doing the unexpected thing, yet always human, lovable; impulsive,....religious,... self sacrificing," neglected to mention that she was also a hellcat. [48]
A social conflict takes place in the story between Deacon Graves, a humorless and unsympathetic figure whose mansion overlooks the eyesore of a squatter's village, and the squatters themselves. The Deacon fails to evict the squatters but succeeds in passing a law which prohibits net fishing and thus deprives them of their livelihood. Tess leads the villagers in a fight against the Deacon, whom she berates during an encounter on the street, assaults one of the authorities sent to burn their nets, and suggests that the squatters resort to poaching.

In a later film, *Rags*, Pickford is a tomboy who rescues a dog being tormented by little boys, engages in fistcuffs with one of the bullies, scolds the rest, and pelts them with cans. She then enters a saloon where her drunken father is about to become involved in a barroom brawl, knocks his adversary to the ground, pushes up her sleeve, and turns on her hapless parent. To the general merriment of the by-standers, she verbally abuses him, shoves him out the door, and throws his hat after him. Having dealt thus with her father, she seizes a chair to take on all comers and the men scatter in different directions. In *Heart o' the Hills,* Pickford wields a rifle, leads the mountain folk in a fight against land speculators, and charges off on a night ride disguised in a Klan type outfit. When she is apprehended, her grandpa remarks, "I reckon if ye does a man's work, Mavie, ye jes naturally take a man's medicine." The Pickford heroine is at her tempestuous best in a costume drama, *Dorothy Vernon of Haddon Hall,* in which she made an attempt to escape from little girl roles. As a recalcitrant daughter who resists her father's efforts to marry her off to a cousin, Dorothy is locked in a room and forbidden any meals. During a stormy encounter, she overturns a tray brought in to entice her, as well as the table and chair, and throws her parent out while uttering a stream of abuse not the less effective for being unheard by the audience. The father, considerably rebuffed, mutters, "I wouldn't have that girl's temper for anything in the world."

The Pickford heroines in such other films as *A Poor Little Rich Girl, Rebecca of Sunnybrook Farm, Amarilly of Clothes Line Alley, Daddy Long Legs, Love Light, Little Lord Fauntleroy, Little Annie Rooney,* and *Sparrows* are spirited characters, often provoked by a sense of injustice and motivated by an attempt to bring happiness to others. In *Rebecca,* a Pickford classic, the girls in the neighborhood taunt Rebecca after her arrival in Riverboro as "Missy Poorhouse." With an angry look, she descends from her wagon to single out the most odious of the girls, Minnie Smellie, the Reverend's daughter. And without further ado, she chases her about, slaps her face, unties her sash, jerks the ribbons off her hair, and troops jauntily off. In *Little Lord Fauntleroy,* Pickford as Cedric, a courteous little boy who is not without spirit, bloodies the nose of a brat who refers to his beloved grandfather as an old fossil. Even in *A Poor Little Rich Girl,* a film in which the Pickford heroine is a subdued child tyrannized by servants and neglected by her parents, she hurls all her clothes out the window rather than give her best lace dress to an incorrigible monster named Susie May.

The Pickford heroine was spirited but she also had an ineffable, sweetness-and-light quality which captivated her audience. In an article titled "Why Does the World Love Mary?" Adela Rogers St. Johns conjectured, "People are hungry for that high and spiritual something that shines in Mary's face in its loveliest moments." [49]

This engaging aspect of the Pickford image is always present in her pictures but most appealingly in *Stella Maris,* a film in which she plays the dual role of a poor cockney girl and a wealthy one who is lame. As the crippled Stella, brought up in luxury and shielded from life's realities by a devoted uncle and aunt, she appears like a fairy princess. The sign above the room where she is confined reads, "The Court of Stella Maris/All unhappiness and world wisdom leave outside/Those without smiles need not enter." The famous Pickford curls are back-lighted and displayed to best advantage and she is costumed in white, lacy dresses. After a successful surgery, Stella is able to walk for the first time in her life. The brutal shock of discovering the sordid and ugly realities of life is mitigated in the end when her romance with the man she loves, John Risca, ends happily. The lovers are photographed in long shots set in a light and airy landscaped garden removed from the outside world. As Stella leans against John's shoulder, the camera moves back and they are frozen in the springtime of their romance.

Interestingly, the spirited and willful aspect of her screen personality is absent in one of the few adult roles which Pickford attempted, the part of Maggie Johnson in *My Best Girl.* [50] As the shop girl who falls in love with the millionaire boss's son, she is still the characteristic sweetness-and-light Pickford heroine, but she is also a woman who responds ardently to her lover's kisses. No childish temper tantrums here. Such antics would have interfered with the characterization of a mature woman. Significantly, *My Best Girl* was Mary Pickford's last silent film. Although the portrayal was interesting in that it revealed a mature but still recognizable Pickford, the indescribable charm of the little girl with the corkscrew curls was missing.

The winner of a *Photoplay* contest had once written, "I think that the public likes you best of all in the not-too-sad, orphan type of story. One which shows that kindness is a trait worth cultivating and that love is the greatest thing in the world." [51] The public never wanted "Our Mary" to grow up because she symbolized that magic world of child-hood, forever lost to adults, where there was always a pot of gold on the other side of the rainbow and all endings--since there had to be one--were happy ones. She had a way of jumping as she ran that captured the essence of girlhood in motion. And the classic Pickford films always ended on this side of the world of adulthood.

Adolph Zukor assiduously cultivated Mary Pickford's image as a little girl. She appeared in public chaperoned by her mother, rather than by her first husband, Owen Moore, whom she had secretly married during her Biograph days. Pickford herself considered as her greatest compliment a chance remark that she overheard when a little girl's mother tried to explain that the actress was an adult woman. The child responded, "Why, she can't be Mother. She plays like me, and she cries like me, and she's just as big as me."[52] Ironically, Mary Pickford never had a childhood in real life. She wrote in her autobiography, "I sometimes feel that my only real childhood was lived through the many children's roles I played, even into adulthood."[53] There was a curious, reverse side to Pickford's image as a little girl, however, in that she also displayed strong maternal instincts both on screen and in real life. She shouldered responsibilities rather staggering for her small frame and early age, but she did so as if it were instinctual. Lillian Gish reminisces about their childhood together: "We loved the Smiths, especially Gladys, who was like a little mother to us. There was never any question when she told us to do something. We did it."[54] Mary's sister Lottie stated in a *Photoplay* interview, "Our real mother wasn't the only one we had. Mary has always been 'Little Mother' to the whole family. She was constantly looking after our needs, though she was only one year older than I, or a bit more, and not so big! I always used to think that she imagined Jack and I were just her big dolls."[55]

Although she married three times, Pickford herself never had any children until she and her third husband, Charles Rogers, adopted a boy and a girl. But by then, her famous career was over and she had retired from the screen. In her autobiography, Pickford stated, "The longing for motherhood was to some extent filled by the little children I played on the screen. Through my professional creations, I became, in a sense, my own baby."[56] She was at one and the same time both mother and child. The appeal of her screen personality lay precisely in this peculiar fusion of maternal and little girl roles. And yet, if Pickford succeeded on screen by playing cherished feminine roles, she charted a different path as a pioneer in the film industry and a self-made millionaire.

To sum up, the Pickford heroine, part hellion and part sweetness and light, was particularly equipped to confront the catastrophes which life dealt her. This double aspect of her personality was captured in a scene in *Rebecca.* Upon arrival in Riverboro, she is quite a pretty picture as she sits on a bench with a parasol in one gloved hand and a bunch of flowers in the other. A few moments later, however, she has clambered up a tree and is not only enjoying the fruit but tossing a few to the little girl below. Absence of one or both parents marked the starting point of the Pickford heroine's journey through life, which usually ended prematurely on the brink of adulthood. The significance of the little girl on her own was not lost on the audience, neither adults nor children. Although the Pickford heroine was constantly up against the contagion of the adult world, she always triumphed as a girl and retained her ebullience, optimism, and sweetness. Significantly, she could not have exacted such a success as a mature woman confined by societal norms and expectations.

The absence of the father is symbolic but the little girl with the corkscrew curls has no mother either in such films as *Tess of the Storm Country, Rags, Stella Maris* (the aunt is a surrogate mother), *Pollyanna* (there is matronly Aunt Polly), *Daddy Long Legs, Suds, Love Light,* an early attempt to portray a mature role, *Little Annie Rooney,* and *Sparrows.* In *A Poor Little Rich Girl,* the mother is a social butterfly who neglects her daughter. In *Heart o' the Hills,* she is an ignorant mountain woman who is abusive and marries a brute. In *My Best Girl,* she is a selfish, hysterical, and inept woman who is constantly reaching for her smelling salts. The only positive maternal figure is the Irish washerwoman in *Amarilly of Clothes Line Alley,* who is a warm, good-natured, jovial matron.

In two films, *Rags* and *Little Lord Fauntleroy,* Pickford plays the dual role of mother and child. In *Rags,* the roles are successive because the mother dies in childbirth and Pickford also plays the daughter, but in *Little Lord Fauntleroy,* she portrays simultaneously both Cedric and his mother Dearest through stunning photographic tricks and her own marvelous acting ability. The character of Alice McCloud in *Rags* (Pickford as a brunette) is stereotyped and uninteresting. She rejects the suit of a wealthy, middle-aged banker, John Hardesty, and elopes instead with Paul Ferguson, a cashier in the banker's employ. Ferguson is a good-for-nothing who has been embezzling at the bank and escapes prosecution only because the banker is concerned about Alice's happiness. There is no happily-ever-after ending for Alice, however. She lives in poverty and dies in childbirth. While on her deathbed, she implores the women attending her, "She is all the glory I have ever known. Call my baby Glory!" Ferguson, stricken with grief, reacts, "Call that thing Glory? Better call it Rags--that's all it'll ever have!"

Pickford is more engaging in *Little Lord Fauntleroy* as Dearest, the mother who bravely faces the prospect of losing her son to his grandfather and an aristocratic title. The radiance and sweetness of Dearest is reflected in the charm of her little boy, Cedric, whose childish ways contrast, however, with her quiet dignity. Although *Little Lord Fauntleroy* was enormously popular, Pickford concluded that the dual role was a mistake. "We created a false situation. I was distressed at being separated from myself,...."[57] This was a startling remark. Mary Pickford saw herself as both mother and child, but the actual bifurcation of these roles on the screen was upsetting and made her feel schizophrenic.

Pickford plays interesting maternal-child roles in *Tess of the Storm Country, Daddy Long Legs,* and *Sparrows.* In *Tess,* she incurs the stigma of unwedded motherhood by adopting a baby and shielding the guilty woman. In *Daddy Long Legs,* she is a constant visitor in the orphanage sick room and nurses a child who dies in her arms. A similar scene occurs in *Sparrows,* in which she plays Mama Molly to a dozen unwanted children stranded on a child-farm in the swamps. *Love Light* is the one film in which the Pickford heroine conceives and gives birth to her own child. The film received mixed reviews and was never a favorite among her fans.[58] *Variety* commented, "Mary in motherhood is not Mary as the millions know--and want her."[59] The objection was probably not against Pickford in maternal guise but the portrayal of a mature woman who actually gives birth to a child. In doing so, she crossed the line separating adults from the world of childhood and violated her Peter Pan concept of womanhood.

Although Mary Pickford considered herself as the head of her own household, she could not very well attempt fatherly as well as maternal roles on the screen. The absence of the father, as opposed to that of the mother, is more significant in her films. The father is conspicuously absent in *Rebecca of Sunnybrook Farm, Stella Maris* (the uncle is a father surrogate), *Amarilly of Clothes Line Alley, Daddy Long Legs, Heart o' the Hills, Suds, Love Light, Little Lord Fauntleroy,* and

Sparrows. In *Rags* and *Little Annie Rooney,* the father is shot part way through the story and in *Pollyanna,* he is a self-sacrificing missionary who dies a premature death in the Ozarks. In Pickford films where the father is still alive, he has become an ineffectual character. The squatter in *Tess,* for example, is arrested for murder while poaching and though eventually cleared in court, spends the duration of the picture in jail. Paul Ferguson, the dishonest bank clerk in *Rags,* degenerates into a drunk and is shot during an attempted robbery. Aunt Miranda exclaims to her niece in *Rebecca,* ''You're too much like your mincin', shiftless father! He spent your mother's money and left her with seven children to provide for.'' The head of the household in *My Best Girl* is a comic and spineless figure who succeeds in asserting himself in an amusing outburst at the end of the film. In *A Poor Little Rich Girl,* Gwendolyn's father is a successful business man, but he is too busy making money to pay much attention to his love-starved daughter. And Sir George Vernon in *Dorothy Vernon of Haddon Hall,* finds his ill-tempered daughter every bit a match for himself. She succeeds in the end--with some assistance from the turn of events--in marrying the man of her choice.

The absence or ineptness of the father as head of the household was a fascinating part of the fantasy of revenge played out in nineteenth century sentimental fiction, written by women for women.[60] Since woman was imprisoned within the household, designated as her proper sphere, she exacted a price by excluding or emasculating the male. A man's home was not to be his castle. Although this may appear to be a trifling sop, the ''lady of the house'' found herself in control of not inconsiderable power, especially since the family was deemed the cornerstone of society. The Pickford heroine must have appealed to a generation of women who found it difficult to identify with either suffragists or flappers but lived their lives within domestic confines and knew, contrary to prevailing ideology, that they were not the weaker sex.

Still another aspect of Pickford's films must have appealed to the fantasies of women brought up to be dependent upon men. Although Pickford had to rely upon her own resources--and she had an infinite capacity for cheerfulness in the most dreadful situations as well as the determination to carry through--a Cinderella touch was added to the plot. At the end of adolescence, a transitional phase such as finishing school meant the transformation of the ragged tomboy into a charming young woman. Such promise of womanhood was achieved, however, at the expense of surrendering the freedom of the rebellious girl who refuses to conform to adult sex roles. At this point, the figure of a benefactor becomes crucial, not only in resolving the film's dilemma, but in steering the heroine towards the more constrained world of adulthood. Should a wealthy and handsome benefactor become a potential lover, there was a re-enactment of the child-parent in addition to a Cinderella style man-woman relationship.

Pickford's first successful feature, *Tess of the Storm Country*, is not quite a Cinderella story, but it contains the seeds. Tessibel Skinner is a ragged, dirty squatter girl. A neighbor informs her, "Tess, do ye know ye'd be a...pretty gal if ye'd keep clean!" and subjects her to a thorough scrubbing. As the story develops, Tess wins the devotion of Frederick, the Deacon's son and a divinity student. While together in the country one day, they seek shelter in her shack during a rainstorm but sleep in separate beds. Such exemplary behavior contrasts with that of Frederick's sister Teola, who is seduced by his friend and conceives an illegitimate child. After the child is born, Tess protects Teola's reputation by declaring that the "brat" belongs to her, and Frederick is duly horrified. As befit stories about illegitimacy at the time, both lovers and the child are killed off at the end. In a symbolic final scene, Tess remarks as she embraces her father while Frederick clutches her hand "I air Daddy's brat, but I air your squatter."

The transformation of the rambunctious tomboy into a lovely girl destined for the arms of a Prince Charming is more apparent in a later film, *Rags*. After Ferguson's ignominious death, the banker who once loved her mother adopts Rags and sends her away to a boarding school. She returns as Glory, the name her mother had chosen for her, and becomes the sweetheart of the banker's nephew. The Cinderella story is more developed in both *Rebecca of Sunnybrook Farm* and *Daddy Long Legs*, films which have become Pickford classics. In the earlier picture, Rebecca leaves her impoverished family and goes to live with dour maidenly aunts. Her girlish charm attracts the eye of Adam Ladd, a small town boy who has made good and returned to Riverboro with a fortune. When Rebecca graduates from finishing school a few years later, Ladd, whom she has dubbed Mr. Aladdin, is present for the ceremony and declares, "I'm glad I met the child--proud I know the girl--and longing to meet the woman!" After Rebecca returns to Riverboro that autumn, Adam reminds her of a promise to marry him when she grew up. She responds coyly, "I am grown up, Mr. Aladdin," but eludes his embrace and scampers off as he pursues her into a corner of the screen.

The most interesting variation of the Cinderella theme is in *Daddy Long Legs,* because it goes further than *Rebecca* in merging the persons of the lover, benefactor, and father figure. The childhood of Judy (Jerusha) Abbott, christened by the grim matron of an orphanage after names in a telephone book and on a tombstone, contrasts with the silver spoon existence of Angela Gwendolyn Rosalind Wyckoff. The children in the orphanage, which resembles a prison, are dressed alike in ugly gingham uniforms, severely disciplined, and unloved. As Judy explains to a sickly child, "A Mama is something which us orphants ain't got." Judy survives the bleak years with good humor and becomes involved in a series of amusing pranks. On "Blue Wednesday," the day of the trustees' visit, she is caught drawing a caricature of one of the self-righteous benefactors who demands, "Is this the way you show your gratitude...by impudence and rebellion?" Not all the trustees are smug, self-satisfied, and insensitive, however. Miss Prichard interests a new trustee to finance Judy's college education. Since her benefactor chooses to remain unknown, Judy writes to him dutifully each month as Daddy Long Legs. She is graduated from college with honors, gains an entree into society as a well-known author, and begins to repay Daddy Long Legs for the cost of her education.

During her years in college, Judy matures from a pigtailed orphan into a charming young girl. As Juliet in an outdoor performance of Shakespeare, she captivates both Jimmy McBride, a young Princeton man, and Jarvis Pendleton, the wealthy, distinguished, and middle-aged uncle of her best friend. At first, she laughingly dismisses the attentions of the older man, whom Jimmy refers to as "Foxy Grandpa." When she falls in love with him, however, she becomes ashamed of her foundling past and refuses a marriage proposal. Judy explains to Jimmy that he isn't grown-up enough and confides her feelings about Pendleton in a letter to Daddy Long Legs. Taking the initiative, she decides to confront her benefactor at last but is surprised and angry to learn upon arrival at his estate that Daddy Long Legs *is* Jarvis Pendleton. The final scene of the picture is symbolic. The audience is

50

able to view only the back of a high armchair in which Pendleton is seated. Judy is still incensed and resists his attentions when he pulls her onto his lap. She angrily kicks her heels. Then, as she is mollified, she begins to move her legs up and down in a slow, rhythmic fashion. The merging of lover and father figure couldn't have been more graphically illustrated.

A Cinderella ending is also quite probable in a sequel to a film such as *Sparrows*. This picture is mostly a tale of the escape of orphaned children from a child-farm located in a murky swamp and run by a dastardly villain named Grimes. In a typical Pickford happy ending, a wealthy young widower places his mansion at the disposal of Mama Molly and ten orphaned children. The audience may speculate that the din in the nursery will be amplified in the future by the addition of more babies. In still other Pickford films, there are interesting variations on the Cinderella theme. A wealthy Southern aristocrat in *Heart o' the Hills* adopts Mavis and sends her away to a boarding school. No longer the rifle-toting tomboy but an appealing young girl, she captures the attention of her benefactor's son, Gray Pendleton. But she points to the social gulf between them, "My people are not yours, Gray, nor yours mine--not in our generation." Returning to her mountain home in Kentucky, she marries instead her childhood sweetheart, Jason Honeycutt. A similar situation occurs in *Amarilly of Clothes Line Alley*. A wealthy society matron adopts Amarilly as a social experiment but is dismayed when her dissolute nephew, Gordon Phillips, falls in love with her. Amarilly resists the efforts to transform her into a debutante ("I don't want to be no lady--") and is unimpressed by high society ("I never knowed what a swell place Clothes Line Alley was, 'till they took me away from there."). As she previously explained to Gordon, "Grandma scrubbed...Ma scrubs...an' I LIKES scrubbin!!" In the end, she rejects Gordon's suit and returns to her family in Clothes Line Alley and to her childhood sweetheart, Terry McGown.

The Pickford heroine was said to have appealed to the working classes. Whether her story had a Cinderella touch, or whether she rejected a wealthy beau in favor of a childhood sweetheart, she captivated the masses that crowded into the theaters to see "Our Mary." In the case of the Cinderella stories, she appealed to their fantasies. And when she refused wealth in favor of a suitor from her own background, she repudiated the value of riches and showed where her loyalties were. A footnote to the Cinderella story may be observed in the star's last silent, *My Best Girl.* In this picture, Pickford attempted a mature role but she plays the part of a shop girl who wins the love of a millionaire's son. Although kindly benefactors appear in other films such as *A Poor Little Rich Girl, Pollyanna,* and *Little Lord Fauntleroy,* the Cinderella theme is absent since the heroine remains more or less a child throughout and is not transformed into a princess. This is also the case in pictures such as *Love Light* and *Dorothy Vernon of Haddon Hall* in which Pickford played mature as opposed to child roles throughout.

Although Mary Pickford made a few talkies and even won an Oscar for her performance in *Coquette,* a title which would have been unsuitable for her silents, an era came to an end when she walked into a beauty salon and emerged without the famous corkscrew curls. She was convinced that the curls had imprisoned her in little girl roles, and she wanted to develop her not inconsiderable talents as an actress. Besides, the star was in her thirties and although she had played child roles successfully for many years, eventually she would have to channel her career in a new direction or retire from the screen. As was typical of the heroines she played and the manner in which she lived her own life, once her mind was made up, she acted. But she had cause for regret later:

> *I sometimes wonder whether I had the right to cut off my hair. Were the choice ever given to me again, I am positive I would not do it....What I wasn't at all prepared for was the avalanche of criticism that overwhelmed me. You would have thought I had murdered someone, and perhaps I had, but only to give her successor a chance to live.* [61]

The little girl's adult successor did not survive on the screen for very long and so Mary Pickford's famous career came to an end.

Adela Rogers St. Johns conjectures in a *Photoplay* article, "Why Mary Pickford Bobbed *Her* Hair," that the star waited until after her mother's death to take such a drastic step. "To Charlotte Pickford, those curls were the symbol of the wonderful child and artistic genius she had given to the world."[62] The death of her mother, who had been the most influential person in her life, was undoubtedly traumatic and may have been the catalyst which impelled Pickford to cut her hair. But hair styles were changing with the times. Although the cutting of hair is Biblically associated with castration, for women in the twenties short hair had a reverse symbolism. It meant freedom. The actress herself was not unaware of this and observed in an article titled, "Please May I Bob My Hair?":

Today the tempo is different--faster. For better or worse, our behavior has entirely changed. We have sacrificed our dignity, but it has not been a dead loss, for we have gained freedom of thought and action. ...Short hair fits our new character as gracefully as long hair crowned the more dignified behavior of our ancestors.[63]

And yet, she had stated in an earlier interview, "My curls have become ...a symbol and I think that shorn of them, I should become almost as Samson after his unfortunate meeting with Delilah."[64] These statements reveal that Mary Pickford had become a captive of both the years passing and changing times. The cutting of her locks signified not so much a woman's attainment of maturity and freedom, but the destruction of a little girl endeared to the public as "Our Mary."

The Pickford heroine had become America's Sweetheart during the years before World War I and now the Jazz Age was beginning to burn itself out. The sweetheart symbolized the unsophisticated life style of days gone by, but she was to be cherished all the more for that. The public did not want "Our Mary" to grow up. She was symbolic of the magic world of childhood, and a disillusioned and confused America which had lost its innocence during its teens and twenties was reluctant to part with that symbol. At the same time, the movie audience, as well as the social climate, had begun to change and the flapper was enjoying a heyday. The Pickford heroine was definitely not among the new breed of women though in some ways, she had an inner strength which the flapper lacked. The shearing of the Pickford curls occurred a year or two after the introduction of talkies to the motion picture audience and a year before the stock market crash. There was a symbolic coinciding of revolutionary events--personal, filmic, and historic--which meant an end and a beginning. The romance between America's Sweetheart and her moviegoing public was over.

Chapter III

THE VAMPIRE

The idealization of woman so characteristic of Victorian sexuality had its obverse side in that rivaling archetypes were discernible in the pure Lily Maid and the sexually destructive Vampire. A significant coincidence emerges in the history of film in this respect: a month before the premiere of *The Birth of a Nation* in Los Angeles, the Fox Film Corporation released *A Fool There Was* in the East.[1] William Fox, an independent distributor and exhibitor, had successfully fought the monopoly of General Film and entered production to ensure his own film supply, thus becoming the first to consolidate all three branches of the industry. *A Fool There Was,* based on the Porter Emerson Browne play, in turn based on a Rudyard Kipling poem, "The Vampire," which had been inspired by a Philip Burne-Jones painting, was the first Fox hit.[2] Unlike *The Birth of a Nation,* the crude Fox film was not revolutionary in terms of film technique but it continued the Vampire tradition on screen.[3] Theda Bara's sensuality and destructiveness as a siren would rival the Griffith image of imperilled white womanhood epitomized by Lillian Gish.

Born Theodosia Goodman in Cincinnati, Ohio, Theda Bara was the first movie star to have a personality manufactured by the studio publicity department. Adela Rogers St. Johns credits the actress herself with the invention of her name and exotic background and the aplomb to carry off the hoax.[4] As frequently pointed out, Theda Bara was an anagram for Arab Death. Depending on the account, she was born on the sands of the Sahara or in the shadow of the pyramids--her parentage variously ascribed to a French painter, an Italian artist, or a desert sheik who had mated with an Egyptian princess, an Arab mistress, or a French actress. She had been weaned on serpents' blood, given in mystic marriage to the Sphinx, and fought over by wild, nomadic tribesmen. A domestic and less vivid account of her upbringing related that her schoolmates shunned her and accused her of being a witch. Whatever the mystery of her origins, Theda Bara was given credentials as a stage actress and reputedly performed at the Théâtre Antoine in Paris.

The publicity stories published about Theda Bara stressed the macabre. A news article reported that a despondent lover committed suicide in her dressing room by seizing a snake bracelet which contained an Italian potion. She was compared with Elizabeth Bathory, a fiendish woman who reputedly lived in Hungary in 1624 and daily slew six hundred girls to bathe in their blood. It was alleged that she was a believer in reincarnation who had lived a previous life as Carmen. Charles Dana Gibson reportedly did a study of her and concluded, "In her dark eyes lurks the lure of the Vamp; in her every sinuous movement there is a pantherish suggestion that is wonderfully evil...." A recipient of a newspaper interview casually observed that she lunched on raw beef and lettuce leaves. [5]

Studio publicity stunts were as comic and strained as the attempts to create an exotic personality in the fan magazines. The actress wore Arabian robes, pretended not to speak English, and was chauffeured in a white limousine attended by Nubian footmen--a spectacle which must have been greater than any on film. She gave audiences in black draped hotel suites pungent with the odor of incense and perfume. Studio portraits were sinister contrasts in dark and white revealing a vampirish woman or stilted poses in erotic costumes. Theda Bara starred in films titled *The Eternal Sin, The Blue Flame, The Soul of Buddha, Purgatory's Ivory Angel, Carmen, Destruction, Cleopatra, Salome, The Forbidden Path, Gold and the Woman, The Eternal Sappho, The Tiger Woman, Madame Du Barry, Her Double Life, The She-Devil, Her Greatest Love, The Rose of Blood, The Serpent*. Was the moviegoing public naive enough to believe that the actress was evil incarnate? Theda Bara herself was constantly surprised to find film-goers incredulous that she was human after all. [6]

The manufacturers of screen personalities later became more sophisticated in their fabrications, if not subtle in their methods. The case of

Theda Bara is arresting because it was a first attempt and therefore the cracks are more visible than papered over. The audience could not be *that* naive, and stories which approximated her more closely to the girl next door countered reports about her sinister origins. A *Photoplay* article stated that in actuality, Theda Bara was "a gentle, slightly melancholy, even timid creature" who regarded "love as a bit of a myth, passion as too often an oppression, and a career of high license with bridle and blinders off as something too shocking to contemplate...." The titles and subtitles of articles written about her were in the same vein: " 'Vamping' in Movies Suffices: This Star Prefers Normality in Real Life;" "Theda, Misunderstood Vampire: Theda Bara's Greatest Wish Is to Play the Part of a Sweet, Essentially Feminine Woman;" "The Real Theda Bara--She Loves Kiddies and Horses, Not Vampiring." The *Green Book* claimed that off screen, the actress was deeply religious and gave her time to charitable work but also purported that she had been born in the Sahara. Theda Bara herself was quoted as having said, "They refuse to believe that I, in real life, am not as I am in my screen life." [7] Despite the confused and confusing nature of the publicity, there was a consciousness on the part of both actress and public that the real and fabricated personalities were initially alike, but the line became blurred. The blurring of that line constituted the basis and powerful appeal of movie stardom.

A Fool There Was, the film which introduced Theda Bara as the Vampire, was as crude as the studio publicity about its star. As implied by its title, the picture is a morality tale. The characters are introduced according to their roles, The Husband, The Wife, The Wife's Sister, The Friend, The Vampire. The stereotyped triangular situation involving the lady in distress, the hero, and the villain is inverted. In this drama, the Husband, ensnared by an evil-designing temptress, abandons a dutiful wife. The Vampire and the Wife are symbols of the moral polarity of the masculine world. The Wife, with her child, represents the ethical and social order based upon marriage and the family. In contrast, the Vampire shadows forth the chaos, destruction, and death which ensue when man succumbs to instinct. As soon as John Schuyler abandons his wife and child and falls prey to the Vampire, his demise becomes predictable.

Although the seductress threatened the institutions of marriage and the family which constitute society's bedrock, the term "vampire" implied that her powers were supernatural or that she was, at the very least, inhuman. The Vampire did exert a hypnotic fascination for men, callously discarded her lovers when they were broken, and gloated. A male counterpart might be labelled a Don Juan or a Lothario, but his amorous and sexual qualities were not imputed to the occult. The unearthly element in the Vampire's makeup provided a key to understanding this particular female stereotype. In essence, the Vampire symbolized man's objectification of his fear and hatred of woman and the power she exerted through her sexuality. The construing of a woman's sexuality in terms of power was unfortunate but such as it was, women were denied that power when its source was ascribed to the supernatural. The Victorian ideal of womanhood contained female sexuality within the institutional framework of middle class marriage and the family. The virtuous wife posed no sexual threat and even protected man from his own excesses. This restraint functioned at some levels in society but also produced a morbid preoccupation with sexual license in the guise, for example, of a vampirish female.

The story of *A Fool There Was* is a melodrama of the Husband's increasing degeneration, paralleled by the ascendance of the Vampire. John Schuyler, lawyer, statesman, and millionaire reformer, is ensnared as he sets off on a diplomatic mission for the President. While he tarries abroad in a lush, tropical setting, he receives a letter from his devoted wife. The Vampire tears it up and flings it at him. The camera cuts to a family scene in a crude cinematic attempt to heighten contrast. Schuyler deteriorates into an alcoholic but still feels guilt and remorse about his family. The Vampire intrudes upon him as he is composing a cable to his wife and snatches up the piece of paper. As the demoralized lover becomes powerless, each futile effort to abandon the Vampire fastens him tighter within her grasp. The couple finally return to the States and Schuyler installs his paramour in a town house, but he has been reduced to a besotted drunk who grovels on his knees the moment she threatens to leave him. The Vampire has indeed become his mistress, for she is unfeeling and can substitute lovers at will. The film in fact parades a succession of cast-off lovers who shoot themselves or end up on Skid Row or in jail.

The Wife, in the meanwhile, has been long-suffering throughout and will not abandon her weak-willed and fallen husband. The Sister is more spirited and alludes to a double standard: "You men shield each

58

other's shameful sins. But were it a woman at fault, how quick you'd be to expose and condemn her." She suggests a divorce, but the Wife turns to a male Friend who advises her, "Your promise was 'till death do us part.' Stick, Kate, stick!" In an effort to save her husband from further ruin, the Wife goes to plead with him. She is about to lead him away--child that he has become--when the Vampire appears to assert her will in a contest. As a last resort, Kate decides to bring their child, but by then her husband is in such a drunken stupor that he is barely able to stand. The Vampire has only to make an appearance and slink down the stairs before Schuyler wavers and places his head on her breast. "The Fool was stripped to his foolish hide."

Wedged between his dutiful spouse and the Vampire, Schuyler is at the center of the drama but his character pales in comparison with either woman. As he degenerates into a spineless drunkard, his wife's moral stature increases and the Vampire gloats over yet another victim. The Wife may be construed as a maternal figure, but so can the Vampire by a stretch of the imagination. As described above, Schuyler rests his head on her bosom after he makes a faint hearted attempt to leave her. The attraction of the Vampire lay precisely in her ability to paralyze the male until he was left completely without will. The virginal heroine, on the other hand, required the male to act, whether he restrained his amorous impulse or was tempted to seduction and rape. In relation to an aggressive siren, the male affected the passive and masochistic posture usually ascribed to women. The desire to surrender to a sexually dominating woman was a negation of self and the resulting loss of control viewed as a spiralling descent into confusion, darkness, and death. The burden of guilt shifted, however, to the cruel and evil-designing temptress who emasculated the male. The imputation that the Vampire was so wicked and unfeeling as to be inhuman and the reference to supernatural powers almost negated the man's culpability. A reviewer for the New York *Morning Telegraph* wrote: "He [Edward Jose] makes Cuyler [sic] so likeable [sic]...that despite his degradation and utter loss of all self respect under the spell of the Vampire we are prone to condone than condemn. He is so obviously the victim of the woman...." [8]

Although the Vampire represented the full unleashing of the male's sexual instinct, she herself was always in control. She had not enough feeling to lose herself and was coldly calculating instead. It might even be construed that as a supernatural version of the whore, she was frigid. "The vampire is rarely the oversexed 'rag and bone and hank of hair' which Burne-Jones and Kipling painted and described. Far more likely is she to be the woman who gains amusement and gratification of power-love out of conquering masculine hearts. It is sport for her." [9] The pulverization of her victim ultimately meant his repose in death. The skulls and skeletons which were the accoutrements of her trade implied that her sexual nature had more than a touch of necrophilia. The Vampire originally emerged from the shadowy world of the living dead and survived on the blood of human victims. As for the psychology of the victim, Karen Horney asked in an essay titled "The Dread of Woman:" "Does the man feel, side by side with his desire to conquer, a secret longing for extinction in the act of reunion with the woman (mother)? Is it perhaps this longing that underlies the 'death instinct?' And is it his will to live that reacts to it with anxiety?" [10]

A Fool There Was touched off some intriguing discussions about the nature of woman. Comments indicated that the traditional, dualistic attitude towards woman was based upon a sliding scale rather than a simple dichotomy. The female sex was not basically good or bad. Rather, the bad woman was more of the same in reference to the good. The *Dramatic Mirror* opined, "The Vampire is a neurotic woman gone mad. She has enough sex attraction to supply a town full of normally pleasing women, and she uses it with prodigal freedom." [11] Another news article asserted:

> ...*she is merely a woman who has surrendered to impulses which thousands of better women have felt and sternly stifled. The purest and most unsullied characters among the world of women would admit, if they were candid, that occasionally insidious, insinuating thoughts of conquest over other women's husbands have crept into the back of their minds, to be stamped out only by definite and prompt effort and the exertion of self control necessary for goodness.* [12]

The good woman, it would appear, was not so very different from the bad. A degree of sexual will power revealed moral distinctions. If men really believed this, no wonder they revered and reviled women in the same breath. Should women succumb to sins of the flesh and tempt men to perdition, there was no hope for salvation.

The statements attributed to Theda Bara during her interviews were revealing about popular and stereotyped conceptions of woman. "To me the only love worth while is the old-fashioned love--the love of men who are chivalrous and gallant for the women who are pure and sweet;..."[13] In a previous interview, however, she remarked, "A vampire must never love...I have never loved, and if I ever fall under the spell of a man, I know that my power over men will be gone! Every woman must choose whether she will love or be loved. She cannot hope for both!"[14] The conclusion to be drawn from these statements, notwithstanding the traditional assertion that love is woman's invention, was that romantic love may not be altogether desirable. According to the classic Freudian interpretation, love was at variance with sex. The "pure and sweet" woman who loved and was loved experienced sexual restraint. Not only that, her emotions rendered her powerless vis-a-vis males. The woman was thus anesthetized by romantic love and easily manipulated because she fell under the sway of her lover.

In the same interview cited above, Theda Bara exonerated the Vampire's actions as part of the duel between the sexes:

> "...believe me, for every woman vamp there are ten men of the same...men who take everything from women--love, devotion, beauty, youth and give nothing in return! V stands for Vampire and it stands for Vengeance, too. The vampire that I play is the vengeance of my sex upon its exploiters. You see,...I have the face of a vampire, perhaps, but the heart of a 'feministe.' "[15]

The Vampire was more than a husband stealer and a home wrecker. She scored off against the opposite sex on behalf of the weaker one. At the very worst, feminists adopted the behavior of men in dealing with men.

The most extravagant statement attributed to Theda Bara with respect to vamping was its justification in Victorian terms. In "An Open Letter from Theda Bara to the Mayor of Cincinnati" regarding the screening of her pictures in that city, she explained:

> I have just as definite a place, just as high a mission

*in pictures as the best of your evangelists and the
most beloved of your local ministers. Through the silent
but expressive medium of the motion picture I am
saving hundreds of girls from social degradation and
wrong doing. ...Furthermore, I am reaching one million
persons each day....* [16]

The reference to the drawing power of the new medium was astute, but
a different interpretation of the statement would render it suspect. The
moviegoers went to see the Vampire because they could participate
vicariously in unrestrained wickedness and derive the satisfaction of
moralizing about it at the same time. As expressed by Theda Bara
herself, "The sad ending is sort of compensation for the woman whose
sense of justice would be outraged if sin were to triumph in the end, but
who nevertheless craves a little of its color and excitement...." [17]
This exercise in voyeurism and righteous indignation, fanned by
publicity stunts and stories, reenforced the stereotyped equation of
woman and sex with sin. The equation was a traditional male point of
view, but it caused ambiguity in women about themselves. Undoubtedly, there were not a few women in the audience who enjoyed the
spectacle of the husband completely undone, the faithful wife unrewarded, and the Vampire triumphant to the very end.

Although Theda Bara starred in approximately forty Fox features, her
career as a movie star did not carry over into the twenties. The vamp,
however, survived as a stock female character. Since bad women meant
good business, moviemakers focused on female archetypes associated
with sin, Biblical figures such as Eve and Salome and notorious
courtesans like Messalina and Lucretia Borgia. A few of the most
revealing conceptualizations of woman as temptress, in contrast to a
Vampire with supernatural powers, were drawn from the Bible. The
Biblical context meant that the woman would exert diminished
influence and act mostly as a temptation to sin. And God's retribution
would be swift.

The creation of the vamp image in its still rudimentary stage is visible
in an early Maurice Tourneur film, *Woman* (1918). The Museum of
Modern Art print is incomplete, but enough of its episodic structure is

intact to stereotype the content with respect to its characterization. The film portrays a gallery of wicked females, beginning with Eve who vamped Adam in the Garden of Eden, and ends by contrasting them with Nurse Edith Cavell. The point of view is condescending, almost contemptuous. In the opening scene, a man styled as a philosopher remains cooly aloof while his wife fumes in anger. After she exits, he consults a dictionary which defines woman as: "1. An adult female; 2. One of the female sex who has attained full growth or come to the years of discretion. There are many interesting varieties of the species, some beautiful and some grotesque." The film then portrays a few of the species, beginning with Genesis.

The characterization of Adam and Eve in the Garden of Eden is intriguing, if laughable. Although Eve appears as a well developed but childishly behaved woman, Adam is an evolutionary throwback who looks as if he wandered off the set of *Planet of the Apes*. The mother of mankind is a flirtatious blond who is puerile and sullen when she eats the apple and then literally crams it down Adam's throat. This characterization of Eve is ludicrous, but it is important in understanding man's conception of woman and evil. As the temptress who listened to Satan in committing the Original Sin, Eve condemned mankind to exclusion from Edenic paradise. Symbolically, the sinful woman has been described in snakelike imagery as if linked in compact with the devil, and her powers are formidable. The successors of a hapless Adam have fared no better though Eve was created from his rib as an afterthought to serve as his companion. According to Karen Horney, the very mode of Eve's creation is significant:

> First of all, woman's capacity to give birth is partly denied and partly devaluated: Eve was made of Adam's rib and a curse was put on her to bear children in sorrow. In the second place, by interpreting her tempting Adam to eat of the tree of knowledge as a sexual temptation, woman appears as the sexual temptress, who plunges man into misery. [18]

Although the Bible was a traditional source from which to derive characterizations of woman as temptress, the Alla Nazimova production of *Salome* (1922) was based on a translation of the Oscar Wilde play. Aubrey Beardsley's illustrations inspired the art nouveau sets and

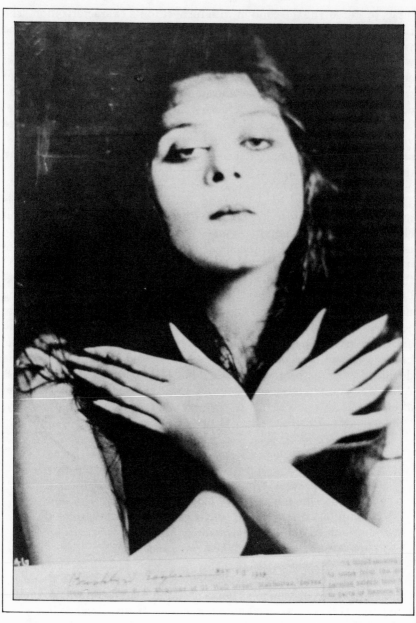

5. Theda Bara

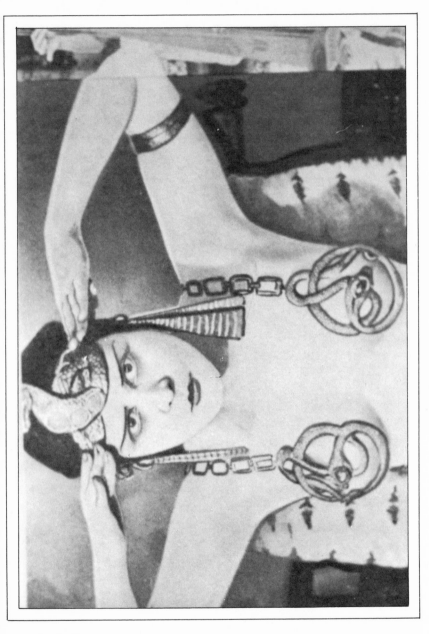

6. Theda Bara

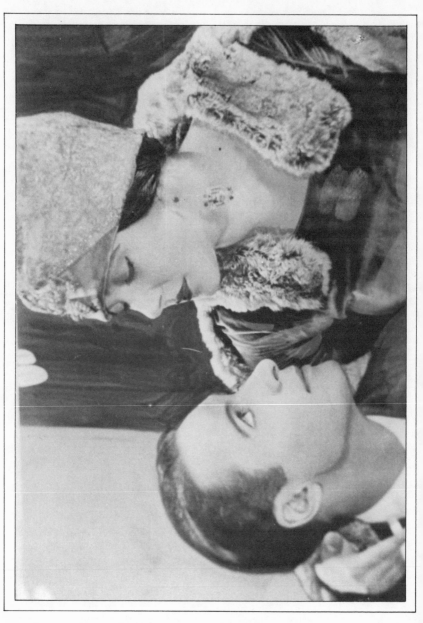

7.   Nita Naldi and Rod La Rocque in *The Ten Commandments*

8.   Greta Garbo and John Gilbert in *Flesh and the Devil*

9. An Impression of Garbo

10. Adam and Eve in the Garden of Eden in *Woman*

costumes designed by Natacha Rambova (Winifred Hudnut). As an effort to render the erotic nature of the play in cinematic terms, the picture was certainly unusual. *Salome* was labeled an art film and critics such as Robert Sherwood of *Life* wrote enthusiastic reviews. Unfortunately, it did not do well at the box office despite some initial publicity about the morality of its content. The National Board of Review gave its unqualified approval after a special screening in New York. The film was not offensive since the play's decadent atmosphere is conveyed by language and difficult to capture on the silent screen. Lack of audience appeal was understandable, however, since the movie was a stylized attempt to create a mood through costumes, sets, lighting, and specially composed music. The drama focuses upon the confrontation between Salome and Jokanaan, but there is scarcely any action and the characterization is too enigmatic to provoke interest in moviegoers weaned on cruder vampire films.

The silent screen adaptation of Oscar Wilde's *Salome* is a curiosity in light of Kate Millett's analysis of the play as a drama of homosexual guilt and desire.[19] Although it is impossible to dismiss Wilde, it is more fruitful to focus upon Nazimova's characterization. The actress is exotic in appearance but does not resemble Beardsley's voluptuous and sinister Salome. She has rather the slender body, flat chested appeal, and slim legs of a flapper. And she acts like a petulant and willful young girl rather than an imperious princess. Still, the drama of a confrontation with Jokanaan, the nocturnal mood of the film, and the use of titles lifted from the play create an image of the legendary Salome.

The story of the film proceeds in terms of the bizarre sexuality of the legend from incest to necrophilia. King Herod, who has slain his brother and married the widowed Herodias, now covets his beautiful stepdaughter Salome. The object of every man's desire, Salome is unmoved until her eyes fall upon Jokanaan, the one man whom she cannot possess. Assuming the aggressiveness of a male lover while Jokanaan is rendered impassive by both captivity and indifference, Salome lusts after him:

> *"I am amorous of thy body--suffer me to touch it."*
> *"It is thy Hair I am enamored of."*
> *"Suffer me to touch thy hair."*

"Suffer me to kiss thy mouth."
"I will kiss thy mouth. I love thee."
"I am athirst for thy body."
"I am hungry for thy body."
"Nothing but thy kiss can quench my passion."

At a climactic moment, a jealous Syrian guard who witnesses the scene stabs himself. Jokanaan recoils from Salome's touch and reviles her as the "daughter of adultery."

Salome is a devouring woman whose sexual appetites are unbounded, yet she has also been described as frigid. [20] The image of the devouring female is not incompatible with sexual frigidity, however, if the focus is upon the woman as Vampire. Nazimova stated, "Men regard vamping and love as two things as different as salesmanship and sincerity. As a matter of fact, a woman does her best vamping when she actually is in love; she puts her heart into her work, you might say." [21] The actress' definition of vamping does not make sense for characteristically, Salome would never love because that would mean surrender on her part. As a woman unviolated, she may in fact recoil from sexual encounter. She covets a man unresponsive to her allure and ensures that pose by demanding his decapitated head. The assertion of her sexual will is an act of castration. As for Jokanaan, he exacts his own vengeance since his impassivity seals not only his doom, but hers. In the final moments of the film, Salome carries the head of Jokanaan on a tray and then envelopes herself in the folds of her cloak. The summit of her desire having been achieved, she assumes a pose suggestive of death which is close at hand as the horrified king gives the signal.

The image of the temptress as drawn from the Bible illuminates the equation of woman and sexuality with sin but also the attenuation of such a woman's power. The temptress in Biblical context was an invitation to disaster in cosmic terms, not with specific reference to the sanctity of marriage. A great deal more was at stake. And God's vengeance was swift and terrible. The original Vampire had supernatural powers and escaped retribution. The fact that she battened upon her prey and never came to grief herself was part of her popular appeal. In the end, the virtuous wife was left with little besides her virtue and the erring husband completely devastated. During the twenties, the transition of the Vampire into a vamp meant the attrition of her strength and invulnerability. The vamp remained a stock character in the perennial story of a man caught between a good woman and bad, but her powers waned vis-a-vis the virtuous heroine. That is to say, the hero proved more resistant to her fatal allure or having succumbed, eluded her grasp in the end. Furthermore, the film industry's increasing sophistication in portraying the vamp as a woman meant a process of humanization which left her less deadly and dangerous.

The vamp in her crudest form, reminiscent of Theda Bara, was operating as late as 1922 in a film adaptation of Vicente Blasco Ibanez' novel, *Blood and Sand*. This film was a vehicle for Rudolph Valentino, who had achieved stardom the previous year, but the great Latin lover falls prey to Nita Naldi's vamp. The first encounter between the characters, Juan Gallardo, acclaimed bullfighter, and Dona Sol, widow of an ambassador and niece of a marquis, significantly occurs in the ring. Unlike Gallardo's bride, Carmen, who recites the rosary during a bullfight, Dona Sol thrills to the contest. She attracts Gallardo's eye and while he is taking a bow, tosses him a snake ring wrapped in her handkerchief. At her invitation, Gallardo begins to visit Dona Sol in her apartment, furnished in an opulent Moorish decor with drapes and divans. Although he resists in the beginning, Gallardo becomes enamored of Dona Sol and suffers from guilt. He confesses to a friend, "It is torture to love two women--There is no one like Carmen but the other woman--she is different." In an effort to save himself, Gallardo reviles Dona Sol as a "serpent from hell" and withdraws to his country estate at Rinconada, but the siren pursues and then humiliates him in the presence of his wife and mother. At the end of the film, Carmen, uneasy with fear, arrives at the ring during a bullfight to search for her husband. Gallardo has been gored and is being carried away while Dona Sol, bored and unconcerned, gazes at herself in a mirror. The dying bullfighter turns to his faithful wife and removing the snake ring implores, "My querida--forgive--I--I love only you." If only in death, he has escaped from the clutches of the temptress.

The stereotyped vamp described above reappears in the last two-thirds of *The Ten Commandments,* "the modern story," which introduces variations in the character of the husband and wife. Dan McTavish (Rod LaRocque) is as evil and unprincipled as the vamp while his wife, Mary (Leatrice Joy) is not completely the virtuous and martyred spouse. The vamp, played by Nita Naldi, is a woman of mysterious and evil origins. She arrives as a stowaway on a ship carrying a cargo of jute from Calcutta via the leper island of Molokai. The vamp, an unclean, diseased woman, emerges from a jute sack and stealthily slinks away into the darkness. She reappears months later as the exotic mistress of Dan McTavish. A friend warns him, "Go easy, Son! This Sally Lung is half French and half Chinese. The conbination of French perfume and Oriental incense is more dangerous than nitroglycerin!" Dan ignores this advice and goes to lunch with Sally, who has slinked into his office-- her eyes narrowed into slits--to announce that she has prepared a "Chinese Love-Drink 'Nygar-pay' distilled from a thousand lotus flowers!"

Dan's crooked world begins to collapse about him. In order to bribe a scandal sheet which threatens a ruinous disclosure, he appeals to Sally for funds but she is unsympathetic. As he is about to leave with her pearls, an extravagance from better days, Sally injects the last word. She shows him a newspaper article headlined, "BEAUTIFUL WOMAN FROM MOLOKAI LEPER ISLAND STILL ELUDES CAPUTRE," and gloats triumphantly but her victory is Pyrrhic. Dan shoots her with his gun and escapes as she calls out, "Danny dear--I'll tell the Devil, you won't be far behind."

As a variation, the sexual allure of the temptress did not always prove irresistible, especially if the hero was pure and incorruptible and had, moreover, a lily maiden as a prop. During the banquet scene in the epic film, *Ben Hur* (1927), Iras, "flower of the Nile" (Carmel Myers), tempts the young prince to reveal his carefully hidden identity on the eve of the great chariot race. The Egyptian woman is the paramour of Ben Hur's rival and hated enemy, Messala, and she is intent upon discovering his real name. The siren is always aggressively male by movie standards. When Ben Hur (Ramon Novarro) strides into the tent, the camera tilts across his body feet first as Iras scrutinizes her prey. [22] She invites him to sit next to her at the banquet table and when he observes the four racing horses brought inside, she purrs, "Flashing eyes and milk white bodies--Beauty to be tamed--Does it thrill you?" The prince yields momentarily to his fascination for the temptress and embraces her but then becomes disturbed. Iras taunts him by inquiring if he is as slow in racing as he is in love. At the point, Simonides, the faithful slave of the Hur family, enters with his blond daughter, Esther.

The portrayal of the vamp in more sophisticated, less caricatured, if not less symbolic terms is achieved in *Sunrise* (1927) and *Flesh and the Devil* (1927), both based on works by Hermann Sudermann. In *Sunrise,* the famous Murnau film, the vamp (Margaret Livingston) as the Woman from the City arrives in the country amidst a crowd of vacationers. [23] The audience first views her as she prepares to go out in the evening and entice a lover from hearth and home. She has dark bobbed hair, walks about the room in seductive lingerie, and smokes a cigarette. The visual image is sufficient to convey the immoral character of the woman. The camera tracks her movement as she walks to a nearby farmhouse and calls out to her lover. Inside, the man's wife, a blond and childlike woman (Janet Gaynor), is preparing dinner. The siren, always destructive of family life, thus intrudes upon the ritual of the evening meal. Unable to resist her call, the man (George O'Brien) goes out to the meadow to rendezvous with her. The somber lighting over a darkened landscape with full moon intimates a foreboding atmosphere. The temptress suggests that the man sell his farm and come to the city. When he inquires about his wife, she hints, "Couldn't she get drowned?" Enraged, the man attempts to strangle her but this violent outburst shades into sexual lust as the woman makes passionate advances. The lovers fall to the ground. [24] The posture of the couple, with the temptress cradling the man's head, suggests the woman's dominant role. Upon his return home, the man agonizes about the contemplated deed until the clutching figure of the seductress appears in a double exposure shot to dominate him. After this conflict, he rises and proposes to his unsuspecting wife that they take an excursion in their rowboat.

Although the introductory titles of *Sunrise* claim that the story is of "no place and every place," whether in the "city's turmoil" or under the "open sky on the farm," the temptress as the Woman from the City stereotypically contrasts with the farmer's wife, who is a child-woman. The siren and the wife as counterparts are personifications of good and evil. The wife eventually forgives her husband and reconciles with him inside a church after they symbolically witness a wedding ceremony and reaffirm their own vows. The characterization of the temptress as a woman who uses her sexuality to overpower her lover is related to Theda Bara's Vampire, but the Woman from the City appears truly evil in that she is not a caricature. Unlike the tragic end of *A Fool There Was,* the faith and goodness of the wife prevail as a new day begins and the temptress returns to the city alone. [25]

With the arrival of Greta Garbo on the Hollywood screen, the vamp metamorphosed from a caricature into a truly desirable and believable woman. The Swedish actress made a vivid impression on both viewers and critics in her first two American films, *The Torrent* and *The Temptress* (1926), melodramas devoid of interest but for her appearance. The reviewers enthusiastically described her as "quite unlike anybody else, " "highly individualist," "unusual, " an actress with "a manner of her own," and having "a peculiar type of beauty which sets her apart from others."[26] Garbo herself recognized that she was different: " 'They don't have a type like me out here,' she wrote home in 1926,....."[27] The uniqueness of Garbo as a screen personality was immediately perceived though not always definable. Critics then and now have attempted to comprehend her enigmatic appeal. According to Alexander Walker:

> ...the first impact Garbo made on Hollywood was a
> vividly physical one. When she was seen moving on the
> screen, her nature altered dramatically. Then her
> awkward proportions shifted into sensuous adjustment
> to each other, and gave the Americans a kind of animal
> movement they had never before seen in their own
> pictures. This was especially remarked on then--
> and still would be now--in the love scenes she played,
> where the almost male intensity of her attack was
> played off strongly against the feminine spirituality of
> her looks.[28]

Greta Garbo became a star with the release of her third M-G-M picture, *Flesh and the Devil* (1927).[29] The film featured both Garbo and Lars Hanson, handsome Swedish matinee idol, while John Gilbert received top billing. The combination of Garbo and Gilbert as lovers proved box-office, but the film really belonged to Garbo. *Flesh and the Devil* was a great commercial success. In New York, it ran for an unprecedented four weeks at the Capitol Theater where receipts jumped from $49,312 to $71,466 in the first week and shattered all previous theater records. The film was subsequently released at Loew's State Theater and continued to play to capacity crowds. The news had spread about the city that the picture had a "full-measure dose of sex appeal."[30] And critics gave it enthusiastic reviews.

About *Flesh and the Devil,* one reviewer noted, "it's a title which has 'box office' written all over it."[31] Halfway through the plot, a pastor clarifies its meaning when he lectures Leo Von Harden (John Gilbert) that the devil creates a woman beautiful enough to tempt the flesh if he cannot reach man through the spirit. The woman in this case has the curious name, Felicitas. The plot of *Flesh and the Devil* consists of a series of overlapping triangular relationships. Leo von Harden, a cadet in the Austrian army, returns home on furlough and is strongly attracted to a beautiful woman who alights from the same train. At the fashionable Stoltenhof ball, he seeks out the mysterious lady who proves not indifferent to his attentions. The unexpected return of the woman's husband, whose existence was unknown to Leo, disrupts their passionate love affair. A duel follows. The camera cuts to a shot of Felicitas trying on a black hat and veil in front of a mirror.

Since dueling is forbidden, a military court metes out punishment by advising Leo to enlist in the African service for five years. Upon his return, he is shocked to discover that his closest friend, Ulrich von Eltz (Lars Hanson), who still believes the duel was fought over cards, has married Felicitas. The triangular plot begins to repeat itself. Felicitas is determined to win back Leo's affection, takes the initiative in seducing him, and overcomes his scruples. She even convinces him that they should run away together but experiences a change of heart when Ulrich returns from a trip with an expensive bracelet. While toying with the bracelet, Felicitas becomes doubtful and then decides that she cannot abandon her luxuries. When Leo arrives, she tries to persuade him that it would be foolish to give up her position and wealth if they can continue as lovers. Ulrich discovers them together, and Felicitas accuses Leo of having forced his attentions upon her. Rather than disillusion his friend about his wife, Leo accepts a challenge to a duel. On the morning of the duel, Ulrich's sister Hertha appeals to Felicitas. Although unmoved at first, Felicitas becomes tormented and rushes across a frozen landscape towards the site of the duel, but the ice breaks beneath her weight and she drowns in the freezing water. At that very moment, Ulrich and Leo decide that they cannot shoot each other and freed from Felicitas' bewitching spell, reconcile as blood brothers.[32]

As Felicitas in *Flesh and the Devil,* Garbo proves irresistible to her lovers in the best vamp tradition, but her disturbing sexual allure could hardly be ascribed to supernatural powers. The pastor's sermonizing that a beautiful woman is an instrument of the devil and responsible for sins of the flesh becomes ludicrous in a film obsessed with extramarital sex. During their passionate love affairs, Leo and Felicitas betray her first husband and then Ulrich. If Leo had been in a position to marry Felicitas when she was unattached, the film would have come to an abrupt and early conclusion. And it might not have been such a box-office success. Furthermore, Felicitas may simply be viewed as an agent through whom Leo and Ulrich act out their repressed homoerotic attraction for each other.

As a vamp, Garbo displays continental sophistication and is not the dark, exotic, caricatured female with sinful past who repels as much as she fascinates. Felicitas is completely desirable but she does not come with strings unattached. She is in fact so desirable that she can manipulate men for her own purposes. She lacks a studied ruthlessness, however, has a certain impulsiveness about her, and this proves her undoing. In yielding to Hertha's emotional plea to stop the duel, Felicitas dies in performing the single good deed she attempts in the film. The siren perishes but the moral of the story is peculiar: in order to survive, a vamp must be cruel and indifferent at all times. The surrender to sentiment is as fatal for her as it is for her unfortunate lovers.

Irving Thalberg stated in an interview with Louella Parsons that Garbo had been reluctant to play the part of Felicitas because she did not like the character. [33] Although Garbo played the vamp in her first three American films, this was a reversal of the roles she had portrayed in Europe. In *The Saga of Gosta Berling* (1924) and *Joyless Street* (1925), she retained her virtue to the end though married to a silly fop in the first film and threatened with starvation in the second. The heroines in these films are interesting characterizations, but when Garbo played the role of a virtuous wife in her last M-G-M silent, *The Kiss* (1929), she lacked the fascination she exerted as a vamp. The virtuous heroine was an American screen type which proved incongruous with her sophisticated allure.

In discussing the vamp roles which Garbo played on the silent screen, Arnheim wrote about her unique characterization:

> *It seems very strange that this woman has been used as a vamp, the destructive, immoral, dangerous principle. It was strongly felt that a real human being was the natural antithesis to everything that was considered right and seemly and pleasing in American film stories. And so Greta Garbo was selected to upset the comfortable marriages of gentle dark-eyed girls, to drive hard-working men to fight duels, and at the end of the film to go to hell....* [34]

A critic for the *New York Evening Journal* who reviewed *Flesh and the Devil* observed, "She's not a movie vamp in the stereotyped sense of the word...." [35] Parker Tyler later wrote in a similar vein, "She carried on the disqualified Vamp tradition with a subtlety, distinction and horse-power that do stack fantastically if you stop to tote them up." [36]

Although there is an affinity between Theda Bara's Vampire and Greta Garbo as temptress, the bad woman ceased to be depicted in the blackest colors in the intervening decade between *A Fool There Was* and *Flesh and the Devil*. Filmmakers showed an increasing sophistication in portraying her psychological motivation as a woman though the effect was to replace a crude stereotype with another more worldly. Sex continued to be illicit but lost its sinister aspect and became more pleasurable in the person of Greta Garbo. The sensual woman still posed a dangerous temptation for man, however, and she had to be anesthetized to prevent the repeated collapse of male ethics, if not supremacy. The temptress herself had to be saved from damnation. The bad woman divorced from her supernatural powers ceased to act as evil incarnate and became subject to redemption through love.

Chapter IV

REELS OF REDEMPTION:
THE SENTIMENTAL HEROINE AND THE FALLEN WOMAN

The Victorian archetypes of virgin and vampire continued to exert popular appeal as silent screen heroines during the twenties, a decade symbolized by the flapper as the "new woman." Although the vampire became subject to redemption as the fallen woman, the sentimental heroine did not undergo any significant mutation but with character and role intact, became a stock figure in costume dramas or contemporary scenes. True, the popularity of such Victorian heroines as Lillian Gish and Mary Pickford began to wane in the mid-twenties but a rising new star, Janet Gaynor, won the first Oscar in 1927. Gaynor possessed neither Pickford's spunkiness nor the ethereal quality which characterized Gish, but like the Griffith protegees, she appealed to the audience as a child-woman.

The child-woman was the ideal feminine type projected by the Victorian ideology of the spheres of the sexes. According to this doctrine, the woman was restricted to the private or domestic sphere while man dealt with the cash nexus in the public sphere. If woman was condemned to ignorance in a state of perpetual childhood, she nevertheless had a significant maternal function to discharge by virtue of her superior moral nature. The home, in contrast to the masculine arena of the market place, became the repository of virtue and woman its guardian. Thus, if woman was confined to the sanctity of the home, she was protected from the evils of the outside world. Man operated on a double standard and suffered from moral schizophrenia. Woman became the projection of his guilt as well as the source of his redemption. As that astute foreign observer, Alexis de Tocqueville, had remarked:

> The Americans are, at the same time, a puritanical people and a commercial nation; their religious opinions, as well as their trading habits, consequently lead them to require much abnegation on the part of women, and a constant sacrifice of her pleasures to her duties,.... Thus, in the United States, the inexorable opinion of the public carefully circumscribes woman within the narrow circle of domestic interests and duties, and forbids her to step beyond it. [1]

This bifurcation of the world into separate compartments assigned to each sex on the basis of complementary functions could at the very least result in ethical dubiousness. Contradictions did exist in Victorian orthodoxy about the nature and spheres of the sexes. The female as spiritual guide became a redemptive agent--behind every morally upright man stood a woman. But was it possible for her to inspire man to achieve spiritual excellence unless he gave up the pursuits properly designated as being within his sphere? And how was the woman to remain untainted when her husband or father, fresh from the wheeling and dealing of the market place, crossed her threshold each evening? Wasn't the very fact that the male's earnings supported her pure and cloistered existence morally objectionable?

Despite these contradictions, the redemptive power of woman remained a cultural myth and was represented as a potent force on screen even during the Jazz Age. The adopted formula, evidence of the dream factory's own process of standardization, was as follows: virtuous heroine (preferably in distress) + rescuing hero - lecherous villain = a happy ending. This triangular situation necessitated the victimization of the child-woman and her dependence upon superior male strength for resolution of her dilemma. As a quid pro quo, the heroine might then exercise her spiritual power to reform the male character. She was both standard bearer and prize. Perfected in the celebrated Griffith-Gish films, this formula proved so popular it was duplicated ad nauseum, sometimes with an interesting variation but more often according to a banal script.

The triangular plot was best adapted to costume melodramas in which the heroine experienced physical danger and the hero and villain both operated on a sweeping scale. A good example is Universal's archetypal horror movie, *The Phantom of the Opera* (1925), in which a hideous and depraved creature (Lon Chaney) explains to Christine, the soprano whom he has abducted and installed in his subterranean quarters, "So that which is good within me, aroused by your purity, might plead your love." And, "If I am the Phantom, it is because man's hatred has made me so. If I should be saved, it is because your love redeems me." Although she has triumphed as Marguerite in *Faust,* Christine (Mary Philbin) proves deceptive rather than redemptive and conspires with a former lover (Norman Kerry) to escape. A Warner Brothers costume drama titled *Don Juan* (1926) has John Barrymore playing the title role as a rake who values no woman because no woman can resist him. But he is redeemed by the virginal qualities of Adriana della Varnese (played by Mary Astor in her pre-*Maltese Falcon* career), whose spirituality is contrasted with the cruel and debauched character of Lucrezia Borgia. [2] Instead of going to the devil, the Don is humbled by Adriana's chaste demeanor and declares as he kisses the hem of her gown, "You have given me a new faith--faith in the goodness of women--." An earlier Barrymore vehicle, *Beau Brummel* (1924), made a commentary about the fate of a man who is deprived of the inspiration that only a loving woman can provide him. As the greatest dandy in Europe, the Beau wastes his not inconsiderable talents in frivolousness and ends his life in exile in poverty and obscurity. For him, "things would have been different had I known the real tenderness of a woman," but unfortunately he lost his heroine at the beginning of the film and fell into dissoluteness.

A more contemporary and less dramatic depiction of the redemptive powers of the virginal heroine is provided by the popular Fox film, *Seventh Heaven* (1927), described by one critic as "a Matterhorn of Mush." [3] An unabashedly sentimental love story, it stars Janet Gaynor as an orphan named Diane who is rescued from a cruel, elder sister by Chico (Charles Farrell), a young man who works in the sewer. Although he spends his days in subterranean tunnels, Chico lives in a garret amidst the Paris rooftops with the stars and the heavens as a backdrop. A chaste, temporary living arrangement becomes a romantic involvement when Chico returns one day with a bouquet of flowers and a wedding dress. The marriage is postponed by sudden mobilization orders, however, and Chico marches off to war still an avowed atheist;

he is persuaded by Diane, however, to wear a religious medal and to give God one more chance. Four years later, Chico returns blinded but not without faith as he declares in a very determined manner, "Nothing can keep Chico blind for long."

A significant visual aspect of *Seventh Heaven* is the positioning of the heroine so that in fact she is the weaker sex. As the film begins, the audience views Diane lying prostrate on the floor after having been beaten by her drunken sister. She rises, staggers out the door, and leans against the wall of the building. As she pauses, the lighting emphasizes her pale features against a dark and shadowy background. When Chico emerges from a manhole to find her being strangled by her sister, she is left insensible on the cobblestones until he props her up against the wheel of an automobile. Arriving at his abode, Chico takes Diane by the hand and leads her up the stairs. Several scenes later when she poses for him in a wedding dress, he is struck by her beauty, lifts her off the floor, and seats her on his lap. In the film's most dramatic scene, Diane rejects the attentions of a colonel who holds her in a supportive position when she learns that her lover has been killed, but Chico makes a sudden appearance which causes her to swoon. Although blind, Chico manages to raise her from the floor but she sinks again. Altogether, Diane is repeatedly shown lying prone and helpless on the ground, leaning against walls or other objects, and held or carried by men in a supportive manner. Such poses visibly re-enforce the characterization of the heroine as a child-woman who may be redemptive but is also passive and without resources.

A film such as Universal's *The Mad Whirl* (1924) presents the modern day sentimental heroine more in the role of a spiritual guide rather than a victim. In fact, the contemporary male no longer had scope enough to scale fortress walls and decamp with the imperilled heroine. Deprived of the sweep of costume dramas, twentieth century man not only ceased to function as the rescuer but needed to be rescued from himself. In *The Mad Whirl*, May MacAvoy portrays a conventional heroine up against the Roaring Twenties. The movie contrasts the fast life of flappers, Fords, and gin fizz with the accepted values of prewar, rural America in the characters of Jack Harrington and Cathleen Gillis. Cathleen, the daughter of a stern teetotaller, entreats her lover to reform his dissipated life and finally berates him, "You're not a man-- You're running away. You're a coward!" This outburst goads Jack into seizing Cathleen and kissing her passionately. But as he advances a second time, she strikes him. Jack drops to his knees and swears, "Before God, Cathleen, I'm sorry. It wasn't I who kissed you! That man has gone--for good." And he pleads in tears, "If you'll only love me, Cathleen, I know I can keep my promise." The young woman disobeys her disapproving father and elopes with Jack. Although she is an inexperienced small-town girl, Cathleen proves strong-willed enough to triumph over both her father and lover.

An inexplicable aspect of pictures such as *The Mad Whirl* was that the heroine should be so enamored of a weak and lacklustre male, unless she had it in mind to engineer a Maggie-Jiggs marriage. But she still acted as a benign maternal figure. Cathleen's romantic feelings for Jack display the quality of a mother's unconditional love for her child. Admittedly she was in a favorable position to exercise influence over him, but theirs was not yet a naked power struggle. The shrill response to momism would come later. Significantly, the modern day sentimental heroine reformed man in terms of his personal shortcomings, but she no longer redeemed him in a profound religious sense. Such a change in emphasis was a mirror of the times. A further variation of plots revolving around the woman's role as reformer may be seen in an independent production, *What's Worth While* (1921). Directed by Lois Weber, one of the few successful women directors of the silent era, it starred a discovery named Claire Windsor (nee Ola Cronk), who later became a minor star in the M-G-M constellation. [4]   As a woman's film, it is certainly worth discussing.

The heroine of *What's Worth While* is an Eastern socialite, Phoebe, who falls in love with a rancher named Elton but is repulsed by his lack of breeding. In order to gain an entree into her world, Elton spends two years acquiring an education and social polish. A perverse Phoebe is still dissatisfied, however, and then realizes the source of her unhappiness. "That was it! He had been *her* superior--*her* master! And now they were equals. She had put him through the conventional mill which had ground out all the men she knew!" Elton's best friend, Rowen, is also perturbed by the transformation of the rough-hewn rancher into a sophisticated and urbane young man. "I left them laughing over Elton's analysis of the 'new woman.' Lord! When I think how he once reverenced women, I'm homesick for the man he used to be." The dilemma is resolved by their return to the ranch where Elton reverts to

11. Janet Gaynor and Charles Farrell in *Seventh Heaven*

12. John Barrymore and Mary Astor in *Don Juan*

13.   Mary Philbin and Norman Kerry in *The Phantom of the Opera*

14.   Gloria Swanson in *Sadie Thompson*

his crude Western speech and manners, not to mention his reverence for women. "A good woman's pretty close to the angels Ma'am, and I sure was humble and proud when you sought me out that night." The ending does have a twist as Phoebe overhears an exchange between Elton and Rowen. "Heaven willing, I believe she is in my world for good." "Yes--and Heaven help us if she ever suspects how it was accomplished." Phoebe has the last word, "And Heaven help me to keep you from ever suspecting that I suspect."

The American woman has symbolized the cultural refinements and restraints of civilization about which man has been ambivalent in response. *What's Worth While* implied that if a man acquired the cultivation of well-bred society, he lost his virility and hence his attraction to women. The woman, conversely, could remain on her pedestal if she represented genteel culture and did not attempt to elevate man. Contrary to popular notions, Lois Weber implied that it was not woman's function to refine man because this would obliterate the distinction between them. She sidestepped the question of evil by assuming that the difference between the sexes was not one of spiritual character but cultivated refinement. Such an attempt at a cultural rather than moral definition of the sexes appears liberal, but Weber also assumed that man in his primitive guise fascinated woman because he was closer to violence and could assert himself as master. The woman was not yet in danger of abuse because she was still worshipped as an ethereal being. At a later point in time, she would step down from the pedestal and become subject to defilement and brutal death.

THE FALLEN WOMAN

Although the sentimental heroine survived more or less intact during the Jazz Age, the vampire was neutralized as the fallen woman. Theda Bara's vampire was a caricature, but she was also a powerful and destructive female in league with the supernatural and glorified herself in terms of evil. The vampire was so threatening a woman that she had to be humbled. What better way than to convert her to a religion that obliterated the line between sacred and profane and made her susceptible to love? A creature who inspired madness in men, the vampire herself never felt emotion on any seismographic scale and thus remained invulnerable. As her successor, the vamp succumbed to romantic love and became subject to redemption.

88

Divested of her supernatural powers, the woman without virtue (virginity) came to resemble the virtuous heroine. She too was capable of great feeling and could inspire an undying love in return. As Greta Garbo declares in *A Woman of Affairs,* "How little you know of my kind of love." [5] The sensuality of such a woman dictated tragedy, however, for her passion could never be contained within a domestic melodrama. She was meant for a life of suffering, not a rose-covered cottage and domesticity. The sanctity of hearth and home would be imperilled if wives, in contrast to their male counterparts of the double standard, led sexually adventurous lives. Deprived of a happy ending, the bad woman fared badly. All was not fair in love as far as she was concerned. The vampire was better off waging war with the opposite sex because she was never victimized by love. The bad woman in love usually lost.

Ultimately, the scarlet woman was just as much a victim of circumstances, had just as little control over her life as the virtuous heroine. Since she was undeserving of marriage, the difference in their lives was a matter of marital bliss. This transformation of the vampire into a woman who was passionate but could not aspire to wifehood was very convenient for men. Rather than fear castration by a sexually devouring female, men could now enjoy the pleasures of illicit love and trust to the essential goodness of the whore with a heart of gold. The archetypal story of the courtesan was still Camille's. The virtuous whore, a fusion of the good woman and bad, was a contradiction in terms of man's moral dichotomy but a necessary accomplice in his sexual amours.

The process of disarming the vamp by rendering her a woman susceptible to love occurs in a film aptly titled *The Temptress* (1926) starring Greta Garbo. Originally under the direction of Mauritz Stiller, Garbo's discoverer and mentor, the picture was completed by Fred Niblo who received credit. Its heroine, a sophisticated, European beauty named Elena, is a vamp by reason of fate. Apart from a passion she conceives for an Argentine engineer named Manuel (Antonio Moreno), she registers little emotion as a succession of men lose their careers, fortunes, and even their lives in pursuit of her. She is not a satanic, blood-sucking vampire, however, since she is as much victimized by her hypnotic beauty as her legion of admirers. A naturalistic version of the vamp, Elena has been reduced to a passive pawn of circumstances so that she is doubly defenseless when she falls in love. In the end, she accepts her destiny as an ill-fated woman who unwittingly destroys men and gives up her Argentine lover. According to James Card, an alternative happy ending has Manuel single out Elena as his inspiration during a festive occasion celebrating the completion of an engineering project to which he has devoted his genius. [6]

The redemption of the sexually destructive vamp was not a psychologically realistic process but one advantageous to men. Ironically, it was accomplished at the cost of shifting the burden of sexual guilt back upon the male. When Manuel confronts Elena with a list of casualties she has wrought, she claims that her husband sold her to a banker because he was in debt, that men have never forsaken work and honor for her happiness but for her body--a rather bold assertion for the period. Elena's defense comes close to the truth but reverses the original assumption about the culpability of the vampire as opposed to her male victim. The siren is not to blame if her disquieting beauty represents a fulfillment of male erotic fantasies and in addition, she also suffers and is doomed as a result.

During the twenties, bad women deprived of the powerful stature of the vampire were reduced to disreputable glamour girls, prostitutes, mistresses or kept women, and adulterous wives. In *The Torrent* (1926), Garbo portrays a village girl who is thwarted in her quest for love and gains instead a notoriety resulting from her career as an operatic diva and a courtesan. [7] Years later, an encounter with her childhood sweetheart only serves to heighten the loss of their romantic ideals and the divergence of their lives. The final scene of the film marks the beginning of the legend of Garbo as the Sphinx. After her curtain calls, La Brunna, as she is known on stage, emerges alone from the theater and steps into a chauffeured limousine. The camera focuses on the prima donna as she is driven away from her spectators, but it is difficult to penetrate the thoughts behind that impassive face registering the unfathomable. Clarence Brown, who directed Garbo in both silent and sound features explained:

> *Garbo had something behind the eyes that you couldn't see until you photographed it in close-up. You could see thought. If she had to look at one person with jealousy, and another with love, she didn't have to change her expression. You could see it in her eyes as she looked from one to the other. And nobody else has been able to do that on the screen.* [8]

Although Hollywood specialized in melodramas which were propelled by studio formulas rather than the logic of character or event, *The Torrent* was especially ludicrous. The characterization of an opera singer who could have been redeemed by love and otherwise became a loose woman was absurd. As portrayed by Garbo, Leonora was a convincing woman in love, but the object of that love hardly merited such devotion let alone disenchantment. M-G-M could not have committed a worse casting blunder than to pose Garbo against their answer to Rudolph Valentino, a laughable and nondescript Latin lover named Ricardo Cortez. Garbo fared better in her second feature, *The Temptress*, when she played opposite Antonio Moreno. The Great Lover who teamed successfully with Garbo was not of Latin vintage, however, but an American idol named John Gilbert.

The storyline of another Garbo film, *A Woman of Affairs* (1928), is a variation of *The Torrent*, but the characters are developed with greater sophistication and reserved for a more tragic end. Childhood sweethearts Diana Merrick (Garbo's favorite silent role) and Neville Holderness (John Gilbert) cannot marry because Nev's father objects to the dissolute Merricks and desires a diplomatic career for his son. [9] As a result, Diana marries David Furness (John Mack Brown) but on their wedding night, he inexplicably commits suicide by jumping out of the hotel window. An inquest is held. To avoid disillusioning her brother Jeffrey, who idolized David, Diana lies and shocks her interrogators by stating that David died for "decency." She proceeds to live up to her ruined reputation by having a series of well-publicized affairs, and polite society shuns her as "the notorious Mrs. Furness." The mysterious circumstances of David's death are disclosed years later when Diana's friend Hugh confides to Neville, a diplomatic success now married to a socialite, that Diana lied to protect her brother. David was an embezzler and about to be arrested when he committed suicide. Diana's return to England after a lengthy absence proves disastrous as she and Neville are still in love. In the last sequence, she frustrates Nev's attempt to leave his wife and kills herself by crashing her automobile into a tree. She was not a woman without honor.

A Woman of Affairs provides an insight into screen morality during the reign of the Hays office. [10] The screenplay, written by Bess Meredyth after Michael Arlen's sensational best-seller, *The Green Hat*, was very much a laundered version. Almost any adaptation would have proved superior to the wordy, pretentious potboiler, and the film was definitely an improvement. Since the Hays office had decreed *The Green Hat* unfit to be dramatized, the title was changed to avoid any reference to the novel as were the names of the characters, and the plot tampered with. [11] For instance, Jeffrey's clean-cut idol ends his life in the novel after having to reveal to his bride a syphilitic affliction. Apparently, a criminal offense such as embezzling was a more acceptable motive for suicide than venereal disease. Also, Diana announces to the authorities in the film that her husband died for "decency" as opposed to "purity" --the language of the novel--a semantic shift to play down an unmistakable allusion. The Virginia censors found the film objectionable even after these changes and cut an explicit but well-played love scene between Garbo and Gilbert.

In the Garbo films, the woman who embarked on sexual adventure as a result of disillusionment in love destroyed her claim to marital happiness and sometimes came to grief in the last reel. A reverse situation occurs in *Sadie Thompson* (1928), a story about a prostitute who is redeemed by false religion and true love. Gloria Swanson Productions made a film version of the successful play *Rain*, based on the Somerset Maugham short story, despite the objections of the Hays office. [12] Changes were made to accomodate the censors. The movie was retitled *Sadie Thompson* and the minister's occupation altered so that he became a professional, fire-eating reformer instead. The gamble paid off, for the film received favorable reviews and Swanson demonstrated that she was an accomplished dramatic actress.

The plot of Maugham's short story has been frequently dramatized on stage and screen. Swanson's performance as Sadie, the prostitute who flees San Francisco police and finds herself marooned on a South Seas island, highlights the silent film version. She is a vulgar, gum-chewing floozy dressed in flashy clothes with broad-brimmed hat, beads, and feathered boa. Although she is vulnerable and alone, Sadie affects a cheerful, good-natured, and happy-go-lucky manner. She may be just the sort of woman to attract Sargeant Tim O'Hara, a shy but amiable and well-meaning chap who becomes serious about her--"them that kicks the highest settles down the hardest." She is exactly the sort of woman to antagonize a crusading island reformer, Mr. Davidson (Lionel Barrymore). Sadie is very spirited in her confrontations with

Davidson but the reformer holds the trump card. Afraid of being deported to San Francisco where she faces a prison term, Sadie loses spirit and turns to Davidson for religious comfort. Unfortunately, the last reel of the film which includes its version of the rape scene has been lost but according to the American Film Institute catalog, Sadie and Tim sail for Australia after Davidson's suicide. The happy ending, which is thematically illogical and pure Hollywood, was deleted from the later sound remakes starring Joan Crawford and Rita Hayworth.

In the twenties, the prostitute could still sail into the sunset towards the glow of Australian domesticity, especially after mistreatment by a professional reformer. The course of true love never did run smooth, but even a scarlet woman from San Francisco's red light district could hope. Since wedlock represented woman's salvation, marriage to the wrong man for the wrong reasons could spell disaster. The faithless wife was as much a threat to the bedrock institutions of marriage and the family as the vampire. Such boring from within the institutional framework could be excused momentarily in the cause of passion (for the sake of audience titillation) but could not go unpunished to the last reel. The fate of adulterous lovers, as in *The Four Horsemen of the Apocalypse,* was disastrous since motion picture morals dictated that infidelity lead to tragedy rather than divorce and remarriage.

In 1920, Marcus Loew, the owner of an impressive theater chain in America and Canada, decided to enter the field of production and acquired control of Metro Pictures. The studio was in financial difficulty at the time but a year later, a talented young woman named June Mathis put Metro in the black. Despite the studio's reluctance to churn out another war film, Richard Rowland, the corporation's president, bought the rights to the Ibanez best-seller, *The Four Horsemen of the Apocalypse.* June Mathis wrote the continuity, suggested Rex Ingram as the film's director, and launched the career of Rudolph Valentino as a screen idol by casting him in the lead. As the youthful libertine Julio Desnoyers, Valentino seduces Marguerite Laurier (Alice Terry), the attractive young wife of his father's middle-aged friend. The events of the first World War dictate rehabilitation, however as Julio dies in action and Marguerite dedicates her life (in a Red Cross uniform) to the care of her blinded husband.

A realistic portrayal of an erring woman can be attributed to director

Monta Bell, who gave Garbo her first Hollywood assignment in a pot-boiler but also made a reputedly autobiographical film, *Man, Woman and Sin* (1927). Despite its melodramatic title and stereotyped plot, the film's characterization is credible if not psychologically subtle. The story focuses upon an Oedipal relationship between Al Whitcomb (John Gilbert) and his mother which is disrupted when the young man falls in love with the wrong woman. Al has always brought his paycheck home to his mother, whom he fondly refers to as "my girl," for their dream is to save enough money to buy a house. As a man, he is a naive and inexperienced lightweight who is disillusioned by the glamorous society editor of a newspaper, played by stage actress Jeanne Eagels. Vera is amused by Al's earnest admiration and touched when he spends his savings to buy her a bracelet, but she has so many expensive bangles. She thoughtlessly encourages his infatuation though she is involved in a liaison with Mr. Bancroft, the newspaper's publisher. When the disillusioned, young lover discovers the nature of her relationship to Bancroft, he accidentally slays the publisher in a scuffle and flees. Vera commits perjury during the ensuing trial to save Bancroft's reputation and her own and labels Al a socialist. That is enough to convict the luckless, young man and the judge sentences him to death.

Vera is not so unscrupulous that she cannot in the end be prevailed upon to save Al. The *New York Times* critic described her as a "vascillating vampire."[13] She listens to the appeal of his anguished mother and consents to alter her testimony before an attorney. In the final scene of the film, Vera peers anxiously through the rear window of an automobile as she waits for Al to emerge from prison. The car drives off as Al walks down the street with his mother, who tries to cheer him with talk about the neighbors, the radio, and dinner. A critic for the New York *Sun* complained that the film "doesn't end. It merely stops."[14] In fact, the final scene is quite a propos. For Al, life with mother looms such as it always had, and Vera will undoubtedly return to her previous existence. At least Bell did not tamper with the psychological realism of the film by situating the vamp with her collection of costly bracelets in a cold water flat. Vera's portrayal remains an exception in the cycle of redeemed fallen woman and redemptive sentimental heroines who continued to grace the silent screen during the Jazz Age. Although these stereotyped heroines still commanded a large audience, the appearance of more contemporary types signalled a change in conventional perceptions of women. It remained to be seen whether the ''new woman'' of the twenties would serve as a non-traditional role model or was symptomatic of plus ça change.

Chapter V

THE WORKING GIRL: STATISTICS VS. CINDERELLA

Apart from the traditional archetypes of virgin and vamp, silent screen heroines were also cast as contemporary women living in early twentieth century America. The working girl appeared in a number of films, especially comedies, but the Cinderella story of the Hollywood shop girl was removed from the workaday reality of women as represented by government statistics. Such figures showed that the line between the traditional spheres of the sexes was being blurred by economic necessity. According to the *Report of the President's Research Committee on Social Trends,* the number of gainfully employed women over age sixteen between 1870 (the first year for which the Bureau of Census collected such data) and 1930 increased six-fold, compared to a less than four-fold increase in the female population of the same age. [1] This phenomenon of women entering the labor force in ever greater numbers, despite the Depression and job discrimination, would continue in future decades.

Significantly, what emerges in the early twentieth century mass consumption economy is a pattern of female employment still in existence today. Women, by virtue of sex, were locked into what are currently labeled "pink collar" jobs and still earn roughly 55 percent of men's wages. U.S. Department of Commerce figures show that trends in terms of occupational categories in the years 1910, 1920, and 1930 indicate that the number of women employed in agriculture declined though not spectacularly, while figures for women in manufacturing remained constant or showed a slight increase. The large scale employment of women in the factories was a socio-economic phenomenon of

96

the nineteenth century industrial revolution. The significant fact about the masses of women working in the early twentieth century was their increasing employment in areas such as transportation (usually as telephone operators), trade (usually as sales clerks), public services, professions (usually as teachers and nurses), domestic and personal service, and most dramatically in clerical occupations. [2]

The increasing percentage of women in the labor force, which by 1930 had climbed to 21.9 percent, and the types of employment available to them were both indicative of significant shifts in the American way of living. [3] In 1920, urban population figures outstripped rural, reduced to 48.6 percent for the first time. [4] What did city living mean for the American woman now removed from traditional farm life and her contributions to an agrarian economy? In an urban, mass consumption society, the purchase of bare necessities, not to mention luxury items (spurred by advertising and credit) meant that cash was all important. The American woman became a shopper, but the standard of her family's living came to depend not only upon her sagacity as consumer but her contribution as wage earner.

Significantly the number of women employed between 1910 and 1930 doubled, but the number of married women employed increased four-fold. [5] According to an article in the December 1, 1926 issue of *Survey,* which was devoted to the question of working women, statistics for the decade 1910-1920 showed that though the number of women employed in manufacturing and mechanical industries, trades, professional services, and clerical occupations increased, the proportion of married to single women constituting that increase was very great. For example, the number of unmarried women in the clerical field increased 141 percent but the figure for married women is a startling 209 percent. [6] Unquestionably women's wages were lower than men's, but their earnings must have contributed to the percent increase in per capita realized income from 6.4 in the years 1909-1913, to 8.1 in the years 1914-1918, to 11.8 in the years 1919-1923. The figure declined to 9.1 in the years 1924-1928 but the relative increase remained fairly constant. [7]

That so many married women were employed outside the home attracted the attention of sociological works such as *Recent Social Trends* and *Middletown,* whose authors weighed the impact of this

15. Clara Bow and Antonio Moreno in *It*

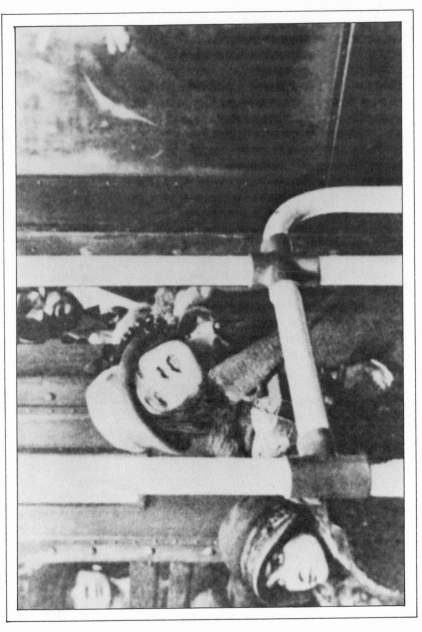

16. Gloria Swanson in *Manhandled*

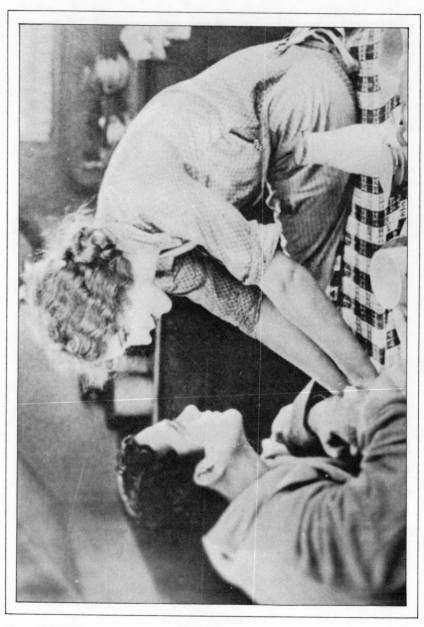

17. Mary Pickford and Charles Rogers in *My Best Girl*

18.   Laura La Plante, Pauline Frederick and Malcolm McGregor in
      Smouldering Fires

phenomenon upon marriage, family life, and the traditional role of women. The issue of *Survey* cited above was devoted to the problem of working mothers and child care. Apparently what was no longer at issue was the social propriety, if not desirability of married women working outside the home. That was now an economic necessity. But social attitudes lagged behind financial exigency. The Lynds found in their study of Middletown that "there is a widespread tendency to adhere to the view of a generation ago that the employment of married women involves an 'ethical problem.' "[8] A National Education Association study cited in *Recent Social Trends* concluded that school districts discriminated against married women in their hiring practices. [9] This finding was quite significant in view of the fact that teaching had traditionally been one of the few professions accessible to women.

Although debate during the twenties centered on wives and mothers who worked, the paychecks of employed women who were unmarried also figured within the context of the family's economic status. According to data collected by the Women's Bureau, 53.2 percent of 61,679 single women who worked in various occupational fields in the period 1888-1923 contributed all their earnings to their families. Thirty-seven and one half percent contributed a part and only 9.3 percent contributed nothing. As for professional women, a significant number of unmarried teachers and librarians also contributed to the support of their families. Apparently, large numbers of single as well as married women could not afford to remain idle, and a good percentage of their earnings constituted a portion of the family income. [10]

The portrayal of the working girl in silent films usually dispensed with the question of single women contributing to the support of their families or the problems of women employed after marriage. Predictably, the daily routine of women who worked out of economic need was relegated to a world beyond the silent screen. The work experience of the silent movie heroine, not to mention the length of the film, lasted only until her wedding day. And her employment served a purpose secondary to earning a living, for she usually met her future husband while on the job. Should Prince Charming chance to be the son of a millionaire, that fortuitous circumstance obviated the necessity for clerking at Macy's once the honeymoon was over.

Silent movie stars cast as working girls who had to earn their own living found themselves in an assortment of jobs, most of them true to life. Gloria Swanson portrays a bargain basement salesgirl in *Manhandled* (1924), a waitress who dreams about a glamorous career in *Stage Struck* (1925), and a chorus girl self-styled as an "artiste" in *Fine Manners* (1926). Evelyn Brent and Louise Brooks are sisters employed in Ginsburg Department Store in *Love 'em and Leave 'em* (1926). As *Irene* (1926), Colleen Moore demonstrates beds in a department store window, becomes a delivery girl, and fortunately enters a modeling career. In *Orchids and Ermine* (1926), she operates a switchboard in a Fifth Avenue hotel. Mary Pickford is a stock clerk in a five and dime as *My Best Girl* (1927). [11] In *It* (1927), Clara Bow sells lingerie over the counter at Waltham's, World's Largest Store, and she is a barber shop manucurist in *Mantrap* (1926). A Frank Capra silent, *That Certain Thing* (1928), features Viola Dana as a cigar counter salesgirl who later runs a successful box-lunch business. Mabel Normand arrives starry-eyed at a Hollywood studio in *The Extra Girl* (1923) and is promptly put to work in the wardrobe department. A beauty contest winner, Colleen Moore also arrives in tinsel town but successfully crashes the studio gates to become a star as *Ella Cinders* (1926). Marion Davies graduates from custard pie slapstick to movie stardom in *Show People* (1928).

This inventory of jobs available to women on celluloid was quite accurate even though there were no secretaries or clerk-typists in these particular comedies. As working girls, these heroines were all single and with a few exceptions emanated from a lower class background. For the most part they were not qualified to do much else than wait on tables or at the sales counter. In fact, the nature of their employment was not even important inasmuch as work represented a background for romance. But though silents were realistic in mirroring the job situation of most women, this reflection served the purposes of fantasy. Such realism allowed a moviegoer to identify with the heroine at a plausible starting point and then participate in daydreams of wish fulfillment with the unraveling of an implausible Cinderella story. An updated film version of the fairy tale dictated that the heroine be rescued from continued employment rather than domestic drudgery. Not too subtly, one of these working girl comedies was titled *Ella Cinders*. Predictably, the silent screen working girl usually married in such a fashion that she stepped into a cozy, rose-covered cottage or a palatial mansion.

The number of millionaires and rich men's sons floating on the movie marriage market was enough to turn the head of any young shop girl. Although scarcely knowledgeable about upper class amenities, the heroine bounded up the social ladder with just one marriage in the style of upward mobility approved for women. The appearance of an elegant, sophisticated, and well-bred rival served only to heighten the homespun charm and virtues of the working girl. Irene O'Dare, daughter of an Irish washerwoman, marries Don Marsh, a socialite's son and head of an electrical company. Pink Watson, a PBX operator who covets real orchids and ermine, wins the affection of an Oklahoma oil tycoon. Maggie Johnson becomes the best girl of Joe Merrill, son of a millionaire who owns a chain of five and dimes. Betty Lou Spence, saucy *It* girl, attracts Cyrus Waltham, whose father owns Waltham's department store. Tessie McGuire, wiser for having been manhandled by wealthy playboys, becomes engaged to an old sweetheart who has invented a gadget for the automotive industry and promises to support her in style. Chorus girl Orchid Murphy lacks fine manners but appeals to a debonair lover who divides his time between Park Avenue and South America. And Molly Kelly in *That Certain Thing* marries an heir, who, if temporarily estranged from his father, puts her culinary and his capitalistic talents to use.

Films in which the heroine achieved movie stardom ironically tended to denigrate the pursuit of fame and fortune in lieu of woman's true destiny. Ella Cinders exits from a motion picture career to marry a former boyfriend who is really a rich man's son in disguise. Sue Graham, the extra girl, finally obtains a screen test but gives up any prospects to marry a childhood sweetheart. Later she tells her husband as they screen her test for their son, "Dearest, to hear him call me mama means more than the greatest career I could ever have had." Peggy Pepper, the successful movie queen of *Show People*, walks out on an extravaganza marriage to her leading man and instead gives a fillip to the career of an ex-boyfriend with whom she is still in love. A woman's responsibility to encourage the employment prospects of her man is also dramatized in *Love 'em and Leave 'em, Stage Struck,* and *That Certain Thing*. The heroines in these films possess skills useful in joint ventures with their men but certainly do not upstage them. For example, Mame Walsh in *Love 'em and Leave 'em* encourages the prospects of her fiancee to become a window decorator even though it is obvious that she has more talent in that capacity.

For the silent screen working girl, employment was simply a detour en route to the altar. And to the extent that being on the job enhanced her marital prospects, an independent life style reenforced convention. The so-called "new woman" in these films could only be discerned in terms of personality and style, not economic independence. Even so, the conventional silent screen heroine as typified by Pickford's character in *My Best Girl* is an example. Despite her appearance in some flapper roles, Colleen Moore as Irene is a comic ingenue who cannot do anything right and is started in a modeling career by the man who loves her. The Swanson heroines in *Manhandled, Stage Struck,* and *Fine Manners* are more modern in temperament but incompetent in coping with their personal or professional problems. A new breed of woman is identifiable, however, in characters portrayed by "It Girl" Clara Bow and by Louise Brooks.

Although the flapper à la Fitzgerald was a leisure class phenomenon, mass production of women's apparel resulted in a feminine model accessible to more females. The Fitzgerald flapper's aggressive pattern of behavior became evident in a few of the working girl films. [12] Clara Bow as sexual predator, for instance, is a lower class type described as vivacious, pert, saucy, madcap, restless, rebellious, mischievous, and flirtatious. Vincent Canby right labeled her as the auteur of Paramount's famed film, *It.* A dichotomy between work and play is set up in the opening sequence of the movie which takes place in the office of Cyrus Waltham, Jr. (Antonio Moreno). The lettering on the office door reveals the fact that Jr. has only recently supplanted Sr. as head of the world's largest department store. Inside, his effeminate friend Monty, who is impervious to work and chatters about "it" (later defined by author Elinor Glyn as that "quality...which draws all others with its magnetic force"), is positioned so that he intermittently obscures a patriarchal bust to the right of the desk. Later as the two men walk about the main floor of the department store, Monty inspects a row of salesgirls, each standing next to a single, plastic, female leg thrust upside down into the air--a mise-en-scene that would provoke any Freudian analyst. According to Monty, the only salesgirl present who has "it" is Betty Lou Spence (Bow), but she has already set her sights on her wealthy and handsome boss. ("Sweet Santa Claus, give me him!") As the film progresses, she plots and schemes, utilizing "it" to full advantage, and finally extracts a proposal. The characteristic Bow heroine, whether a flapper or not, is in perpetual motion in pursuit of her man--almost any man. [13]

Although Bow was spunky and spirited, she was basically generous whereas Louise Brooks had a touch of the stereotyped vampire in her rather unique sensual appeal. In *Love 'em and Leave 'em,* she plays Janie Walsh, a spoiled brat who takes advantage of her older sister Mame's better nature and acquires everything she has, including her boyfriend Bill. When Janie loses the funds collected for the Welfare Dance, she has no compunction about shifting the blame and disgrace on to Mame. In the end, she discards Bill, flirts with a middle-aged department store manager, and drives off in a Rolls with the store owner himself. No doubt she is beginning a promising career. If Mame has been too indulgent in rearing her younger sister, she is in other respects competent and mature and proves to be no long-suffering martyr. As Janie becomes increasingly thoughtless, she reacts angrily and is probably relieved to be rid of her in the end. As for the man in contention between the two sisters, he is overshadowed by the un-scrupulousness of the one and the competence of the other. In a symbolic scene, Bill arrives to rescue Mame in her confrontation with a disreputable bookie about the Welfare Dance money lost by Janie. Not only do his pants fall to the floor as he stumbles into the room, his presence is rendered superfluous by Mame who has successfully trussed up the villain in a hide-a-bed.

Despite the fact that the silent screen working girl earned her own living for a time, she was conventional in that she usually married and became economically dependent upon a male. A film titled *The Eyes of Youth* (1919) made a blunt if rare observation in a scene when a discarded wife (Clara Kimball Young) exclaimed, "I came here to laugh at all these fool women who never stop to think that all they have depends on the whim of some man." Since women in these working girl films had little economic choice besides marriage, obviously the style and object of courtship assumed importance. And when it came to catching a husband, especially a well-heeled one, tactics changed with the heroine. A few "new women" were not the decorous types admired during the Victorian era but were aggressive in both a golddigging and a sexual sense. At times, plot devices such as the momentary reversal of a suitor's fortunes intruded to mitigate the heroine's predatory character and to prove that romance triumphs over money. Significantly, the male leads on screen were often overshadowed by the persona of well-known actresses as well as by their respective charac-terizations.

Within the context of these working girl movies, the blurred line between reality and screen fantasy becomes rather intriguing since moviegoers did receive mixed signals if attention is shifted to a level other than plot. The rise of the star system, a phenomenon associated with the spectacular career of Mary Pickford, was based upon erasing the line between screen image and everyday life. [14] Movie magazines early capitalized upon the public's curiosity and hunger for details about the lives of stars--a form of voyeurism which served as an extention of the film viewing experience itself. Since the viewer was led to identify with an actor or actress, stars provided powerful role models that defined socially accepted standards of behavior. Ironically the female stars who played shop girls intent on being rescued from work were successful, highly-paid, envied career women.

Among the facts publicized to fans about movie stars were the astronomical figures of their salaries. Pickford's legendary financial coups, for example, were progressively noted by the press. Although Pickford was an exceptionally astute businesswoman who had a cash-register brain and was the driving force behind United Artists, screen actresses did command sizeable salaries. When Gloria Swanson left Paramount, her last contract negotiations involved figures quoted as high as $20,000 a week. Colleen Moore collected $12,500 a week under the terms of her contract with First National while her rival, Clara Bow, earned $7,500 a week at Paramount. Comedienne Mabel Normand reportedly drew a salary of $10,000 a week at the height of her popularity. Laura La Plante, Universal's leading female star, was grossing $3,500 a week when she decided to abandon her film career. Viola Dana stated in an interview in the early twenties that she spent $50,000 on clothes alone one year. And the story goes that Marion Davies was able to hand William Randolph Hearst a million dollars when his empire suffered a setback in the thirties. [15]

For the movie actresses starring in these films about the working girl, conflict between marriage and a career did not preclude their marrying and often more than once. Gloria Swanson and Pauline Frederick married five times. Mary Pickford, Colleen Moore, Viola Dana, and Evelyn Brent married three times. Laura La Plante married twice. Mabel Normand, Louise Brooks, and Clara Bow married only once. Marion Davies did not marry until her famous thirty year liaison with Hearst ended with the publisher's death. [16] The fact that these actresses were successful career women who also married perhaps did not appear a contradiction because movie acting was an acceptable and envied profession for women. Should a woman succeed in what was regarded as purely a man's world, such as business and management, she incurred the risk of becoming unmarriageable. The lesson of a film titled *Smouldering Fires* (1924) was not to be taken lightly.

Unlike the working girl films which were comedies, *Smouldering Fires*, as evidenced by its title, was a heavy melodrama. Jane Vale, the female lead (Pauline Frederick), is a middle-aged career woman who has become President and General Manager of a clothing factory inherited from her father. In the opening sequence of the film, Jane is presiding over a business meeting. She has short, unwaved hair, dresses in a mannish suit with white shirt and tie, and makes emphatic gestures by pounding the table and jabbing her finger in the air. Jane's mottoes read, "Be Necessary to Others" and "Let No Man Be Necessary to You." She reproves a flirtatious, blond secretary by inquiring, "Do you girls ever think of anything but clothes and a man to lean on?" And she dominates the men on her staff, who ridicule her in private but dare not question her in public.

Vale's portrait is heavy-handed but it gets worse. Enter Robert Elliott (Malcolm McGregor), a young factory inspector whose direct and outspoken conduct impresses his boss. She promotes him to Assistant General Manager. Nothing is wrong with her usual business acumen, but Jane falls in love with her employee like any adoring young girl and Bobby is chivalrous enough to propose. The situation develops into a triangle when Jane's much young sister Dorothy (Laura La Plante) arrives from Bryn Mawr. A vivacious blond, Dorothy is almost immediately drawn to Bobby but alludes to "the first real happiness Jane has ever known--."

Smouldering Fires is a deadly film. According to the plot, a woman cannot successfully pursue a business career without losing her femininity (however defined) and becoming rather masculine. In effect, she becomes unloved. The film further implies that a forty year old woman already has one foot in the grave. When Jane and Bobby entertain guests one evening, some young couples engage in frenetic steps on the dance floor. Jane watches from the sidelines and exclaims in despair to her sister: "Oh darling! You're all so young--so young!"

Significantly the original print of *Smouldering Fires* was tinted in various colors to evoke moods, and this particular scene was dyed a deep red as was the final scene in which Jane yields her youthful husband to her sister. [17] As stressed by these scenes in red tint, Jane's predicament is shameful and embarassing. She ruined her life by succeeding as a career woman and then made a fool of herself over a younger man. Essentially, she failed as a woman. Vale's name is meaningful in more ways than one.

Jane Vale failed as a woman in the traditional sense but succeeded in quite another. That success, depicted in a different set of circumstances, did and still does provide women with alternative role models and life styles. As film historian Iris Barry wrote at the time, however haltingly, "We are beginning to realize that a woman who isn't well-- I mean who doesn't feel she is doing the best that's in her--inside marriage, is best out of it. But it's hard to get people to admit this, even if they believe it, for 'popular opinion' is against them...." [18] Jane Vale's success was mocked and her failure made glaringly evident. But one woman's failure could be another woman's success. And the marital state, for which Hollywood destined its heroines, was not a bed of roses but itself beset with problems and failures.

Chapter VI

"THE NEW WOMAN"

In "Echoes of the Jazz Age," F. Scott Fitzgerald commented about "the universal preoccupation with sex" which characterized the twenties. Accepted explanations for the hedonistic "eat, drink, and be merry" atmosphere, whether it was typical of the twenties or discernible earlier in the teens, stress the collapse of the Protestant ethic under the impact of accelerated industrialization and urbanization, prohibition, automobiles, movies, sex magazines, Freudianism, and postwar indulgence. [1] A celebrated revolution in manners and morals coincided with the advent of the "new woman," most typified by the flapper, who popularized a new style of femininity. The transition in feminine ideals from sentimental heroine to rebellious flapper was quite significant in that both were a reflection of the moral climate of an era. Since the image of womanhood upheld by society is a cultural byproduct of its mores and profoundly resistant to change, whenever change occurs, society is experiencing certain transformations as it was during World War I and its aftermath.

The ability of political and social reformers like the feminists to alter the popular concept of womanhood as a societal norm has been limited by existing conditions. Examples abound in the history of the feminist movement in the United States. The demand for political and legal equality, later channeled into the woman suffrage movement, was first articulated at the now famous Seneca Falls convention in 1848 but the Nineteenth Amendment was not ratified until 1920. Unfortunately, the decade following was labeled apolitical. According to Fitzgerald, "It was characteristic of the Jazz Age that it had no interest in politics at all." Gertrude Stein observed, "Politics and voting do not make a difference." [2] And with respect to the status of women, voting did not make a difference because it failed to challenge definitions of womanhood based on domesticity. [3] Change came from a source altogether different than the vote. As Virginia Woolf wrote in *A Room of One's Own*, "Of the two--the vote and the money--the money I own, seemed infinitely the more important." [4] Despite the fact that women were locked into undesirable and ill-paid work, a significant index to their changing status lay in their working numbers, not in their turnout at the polls. Unfortunately, there was a reverse side to the coin in a high mass consumption economy. As Malcolm Cowley observed at the close of the first World War, "To keep the factory wheels turning, a new domestic market had to be created. Industry and thrift were not longer adequate. There must be a new ethic that encouraged people to buy, a *consumption* ethic." [5] The woman as consumer and object of conspicuous consumption became the negative counterpart of the woman as wage earner.

F. Scott Fitzgerald declared that the ideal flapper was "lovely and expensive and about nineteen." [6] The flapper, like all feminine ideals, was in vogue among social classes that could afford her life style, though mass production of apparel made the ideal more democratic and accessible. The flapper's youthful, spirited, and impulsive manner suggested a party without end. Although the number of hours devoted to leisure and recreation had been increasing, the masses did work during the week unlike the rich in the movies. [7] Yet, the "consumption ethic" and increasing prosperity among certain elements in society had much to do with the feasibility of life construed as a permanent weekend. The flapper, petting in automobiles, dancing the charleston, and drinking from a hip flask, symbolized fun. She was part of a hedonistic life style that advertisers were making desirable for all America. Indeed, the projection of a woman's sex appeal to symbolize the pleasurable and inviting became a cliche.

The concept of fun was essential to the flapper because it determined her appearance and style. The flapper was a pal. And she dressed like one. The Victorian woman, encased in layers of petticoats beneath a dress requiring twenty-five yards of fabric and tight-lacing, could scarcely be active. In the early twenties, the uncorseted, long-waisted look came into vogue as skirts became shorter and eventually reached

111

just below the knees to reveal rolled up stockings. The flat-chested, slender, boyish look revolutionized the lingerie industry which manufacutred a combination girdle and hose supporter with a boyish brassiere top to replace the hourglass corset. The flapper gained considerable freedom of movement but at the cost of losing her right arm. Since clothes were so scant, the pocket ceased to be functional and women resorted to carrying pocketbooks. A cloche hat which enveloped bobbed hair completed the flapper's ensemble. [8] Thus outfitted, the flapper was ready to become man's playmate and companion but oddly enough, she resembled a male at a time when sexual mores were being questioned.

The flapper looked boyish and acted mannish. According to Victorian standards, women as moral superiors elevated men to the level of their pedestals. The flapper reversed gears and acted like a man, thus making herself more accessible to the opposite sex. She smoked, drank, and petted. But if women rebelled by behaving like rather than opposite men, their unconventional actions led to a conventional end. The flapper might have been sexually precocious but in fact, she was not really so distant from the sentimental heroine in terms of her goal. The social climate had changed so that less inhibited patterns of courtship were acceptable. As a rebellious type, the flapper was freer because she intended to marry. Quite accurately, an *Atlantic Monthly* writer observed that the flapper was "in the most interesting stage of the long and complex process of getting ready to love and be loved," and that she had not gone wrong despite the shattering of conventions. [9] Or as stated more bluntly by one college graduate, "I want to get married. That's all I want to do, and I can't...because I don't know how to pet." [10]

The emergence of the flapper as the "new woman" who was more sexually permissive was no accident. A study of mass periodical fiction during the years 1921-1940 concluded that the "local boy who makes good" ceased to be a model for men in favor of "the little man." [11] Curiously, the titans of industry had erected a gigantic complex which subtracted from the concept of maleness because its scale and complexity overshadowed man. As Henry Adams wrote with respect to the "dynamo," the average mind had succumbed already in 1850; it could no longer understand the problem in 1900." [12] Sociological studies of the American male character in the early twentieth century have stressed the impact of the "dynamo." According to C. Wright Mills, "the decline of the free entrepreneur and the rise of the dependent employee on the American scene has paralleled the rise of the little man in the American mind." [13] David Riesman et al. analyze the transition in the American male psyche from inner-direction to outer-direction in terms of the economic shift from an age of production to an age of consumption. Subject to the process of mechanization and standardization, "the other-directed man" discovered that sex was the "Last Frontier" and found sexual excitement a "defense against the threat of total apathy" and "reassurance that he is alive." [14] Consequently, the sexual needs of "the other-directed man" dictated a reversal of the Victorian doctrine that sex was evil and that women were asexual creatures. As Steven Marcus has observed in his brilliant study of Victorian pornography, "Women's idea of their own sexuality...is historically a response to what men want and demand that sexuality to be...." [15]

A liberalization of sexual attitudes among certain elements of the population during the Jazz Age does not imply that there was an instant and untroubled transition from Victorian inhibition to sexual nirvana. According to a study published by Dr. Robert L. Dickinson, noted obstetrician and gynecologist, and his associate, Lura Beam, eighty-seven women were observed during a two-year engagement period. Dickinson found that approximately one-fourth had coitus, another one-fourth experienced strong excitement and perhaps orgasm, and one-half admitted self excitation or showed its signs. The most interesting fact about the sexual experience of these women, however, was Dickinson's observation that the "characteristic coitus of these couples is brief and without the woman's orgasm: coitus may have been infrequent or repeated but climax does not exist in half the cases." [16] The "new woman" may have petted in order to catch a husband but the assumption that she was sexually accomplished (not to mention the expertise of her partner) was too facile.

According to a study of motion pictures which analyzed film releases of the twenties and early thirties, sex, love, and crime constituted the major themes of film productions, but sex and crime themes increased whereas love themes declined. The categories of sex and love were differentiated as follows:

113

Sex

1. emphasis upon living together without marriage.
2. loose living, impropriety known or implied; plot revolving around seduction, adultery, kept women; illegitimate children the central characters.
3. no sexual impropriety but sex is the theme; sex situations, "woman for sale" stuff.
4. bedroom farce, incidents are farcical, but it is a play on fringes of sexual impropriety.

Love

1. love against a background of thrills, suspense, melodrama.
2. courtship, love, flirtations, marital difficulties.
3. historical romance.
4. operetta type, colorful scenes, songs.
5. character portrayal--love interest present but not dominant.[17]

The industry's increased interest in sex and the paralleling diminished interest in love may very well relate to the type of heroine popularized on the screen. The sentimental Victorian heroine was meant to be worshipped from afar, but the "new woman" lead a more adventurous sex life. Appearing in silent productions of the twenties, socialites and flappers as a new breed of women defied social norms and lived precariously on the edge of scandal. But these heroines were basically conventional and after a brief experimentation with a freer life style committed themselves to marriage.[18]

In 1921, Paramount released a film adaptation of a sensational English novel, *The Sheik,* which had appeared in an American edition earlier that same year. As a best-seller in England it had enjoyed a *succès de scandale,* not the least because its author, E.M. Hull, was disclosed to be a woman. A semi-pornographic novel which deals in a sado-masochistic manner with rape fantasies, *The Sheik,* notwithstanding its title is the story of a woman. Its heroine, Diana Mayo, is a wealthy and aristocratic British socialite who has had an unconventional upbringing. As her name implies, Diana rides and hunts like a man but in matters of sex, her temperament is rather cold. She has never been kissed in her life because "It is one of the things I do not understand."[19] As for

114

marriage, that "women could submit to the degrading intimacy and fettered existence of married life filled her with scornful wonder." [20] Diana's conception of marriage is strangely primitive and this provides the clue to her personality. That which she disdains and fears is what she secretly desires.

After years of accompanying her brother Aubrey on various hunting trips all over the globe, Diana decides against his wishes upon a solo expedition in the desert. The huntress becomes the prey, however, for she is abducted and ravished by an Arabian sheik who imposes his will upon her.

> *She...fought until the unequal struggle had left her exhausted and helpless in his arms, until her whole body was one agonized ache from the brutal hands that forced her to compliance, until her courageous spirit was crushed by the realisation of her own powerlessness, and by the strange fear that the man himself had awakened in her,....*
>
> *...For the first time she had been made conscious of the inferiority of her sex. The training of years had broken down under the experience. ...she was made to feel acutely that she was a women,....* [21]

The sheik breaks her spirit and will to resist until Diana becomes his willing captive.

> *Quite suddenly she knew--knew that she loved him,.... ...she knew herself at last and knew the love that filled her, an overwhelming, passionate love that almost frightened her with its immensity and with the sudden hold it had laid upon her.* [22]

In a subplot with homosexual overtones, a visit from the Sheik's boyhood friend, Raoul Saint Hubert, produces a curious effect. Raoul, like so many men before him, is fascinated by Diana's beauty, falls in love with her, and arouses his friend's antipathy. Later, when a rival desert chieftan captures Diana for his harem, the Sheik realizes that he loves her and gallops off to her rescue. The heroine, subdued as she is,

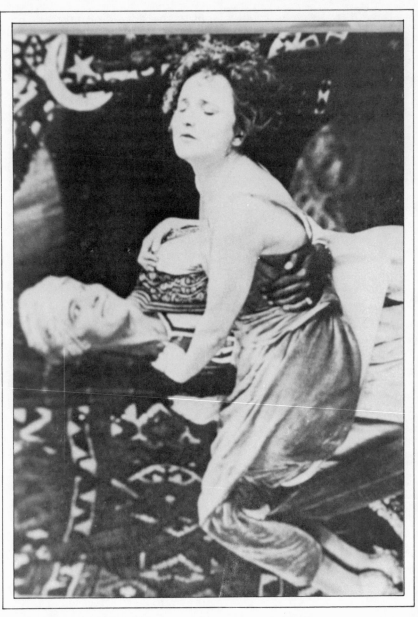

19. Rudolph Valentino and Agnes Ayres in *The Sheik*

20. Leatrice Joy in *Manslaughter*

117

21. Olive Thomas in *The Flapper*

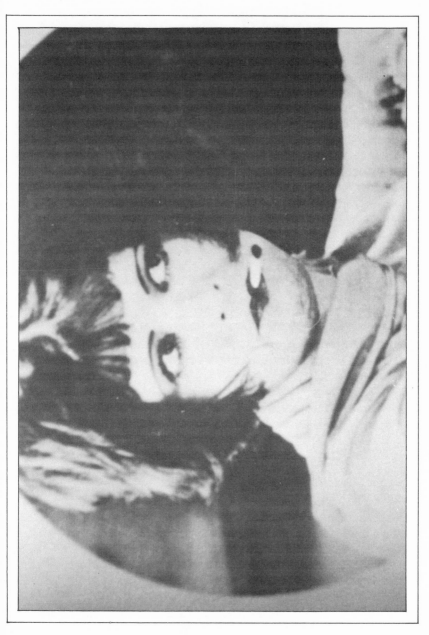

22. Clara Bow in *Dancing Mothers*

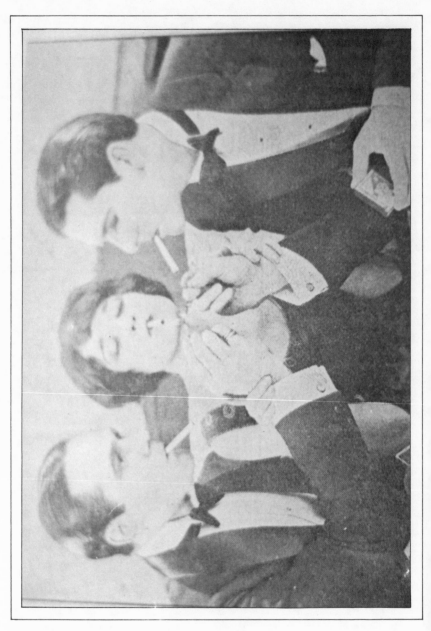

23. Eleanor Boardman in *Wine of Youth*

24.   Joan Crawford in *Our Dancing Daughters*

has her way after all and the improbable romance ends in marriage. As for the reader's anxieties about miscegenation (which provided a great deal of the excitement), there is the revelation that the Sheik is really the son of an English earl and a Spanish gentlewoman.

The film version of *The Sheik* tampered with both plot and characterization but the studio understandably retained the story's romantic trappings. Diana's unusual education and sexual frigidity are de-emphasized. An initial encounter between the haughty Englishwoman and her lustful Arab admirer occurs on the night before the expedition. Later, Diana (Agnes Ayres) wanders about her balcony and thrills to the singing of an unknown male voice. She is obviously carried away in romantic transport, a mood which the heroine of the novel would scarcely experience. After her abduction in the desert, Diana is not raped. Although the spicy dialogue was lifted from the best-seller ("Why have you brought me here?" "Are you not woman enough to know?"), the inaction was not. Valentino is not the brutal and unfeeling Sheik of the novel. Although he leers and makes advances while stalking about his tent, he would rather the woman be willing and so he waits. The situation is illogical in terms of the context but not with respect to movie censorship. Ads exploited the logic of the plot though the script did not adhere to it.

> SEE
> the heroine, disguised, invade the
> Bedouins' secret slave rites.
> SEE
> Sheik Ahmed raid her caravan
> and carry her off to his tent. [23]

According to Valentino's biographer, the decision to film *The Sheik* was made after an enthusiastic reading of the novel by Jesse Lasky's secretary, Jeane Cohan, and Julia Herne, a reader from the studio's story department. The women were convinced that their response would be shared by females all over America and so it was. [24] A nineteen year old college coed later recalled:

> *The first picture which stands out in my memory is "The Sheik" featuring Rudolph Valentino. I was at the impressionable and romantic age of 12 or 13 when*

I saw it, and I recall coming home that night and dreaming the entire picture over again; myself as the heroine being carried over the burning sands by an equally burning love. I could feel myself kissed in the way the Sheik had kissed the girl. [25]

The enigmatic character of Ahmed Ben Hassan portrayed by Valentino seized the imagination of women and appealed to their sexual fantasies. Significantly, the story is contrived on a romantic basis and set in an exotic desert locale. E.M. Hull welded together both the fantasy of a masterful lover who threatens rape and romantic love so that the titillation of the former was legitimized by the latter.

Diana Mayo, an assertive and independent woman brought up like a man, was strangely asexual until she became the willing victim of rape. So much for the "new woman's" sexual identity and freedom. In the movie sequel, *Son of the Sheik* (1926), Diana makes a brief appearance as the matronly mistress of a desert mansion. The inevitability of marriage could be construed as the climax of a Hollywood romance, but the author of *The Sheik* moved such action beyond the pale of social custom and culture. According to E.M. Hull, woman's strongest instinct was submission to a virile lover and no amount of education could root it out. Any attempt to redefine woman's nature was therefore doomed to frustration. Significantly, Diana's frigid temperament, which was rather Victorian, is altered by her forceful lover but she then becomes enslaved rather than liberated by her sexuality.

Cecil B. DeMille's *Manslaughter* (1922), adapted from a novel by Jeanie Macpherson, exploits the story of the rebellious socialite as only the director himself could. According to William K. Everson, *"Manslaughter* is a fairly representative example of DeMille's view of the intelligence of his audience." [26] Lydia Thorpe (Leatrice Joy) is an irresponsible socialite who speeds recklessly from one drunken party to another. By contrast, her maid Evans (Lois Wilson) worries about a sickly child living with her mother in a cheap flat. Desperate for money, Evans steals Lydia's jewels, is caught and sentenced to prison because her mistress overslept and did not appear in court on her behalf. But "the Great Auditor begins to balance Lydia's account." (The business-like metaphor is rather apt for the twenties as well as DeMille.) The speed-crazy socialite accidently kills a policeman during a reckless chase and is prosecuted in court by District Attorney Daniel O'Bannon, (Thomas Meighan), the man "who loves her for the Girl he thinks she could be--but not for the Girl she is." O'Bannon heatedly declares, "The over-civilized, mad young set of wasters--to which this defendent belongs--must be STOPPED! Or they will destroy the Nation--as Rome was destroyed, when Drunkenness and Pleasure drugged the Conscience of its Young!" Such courtroom rhetoric provides DeMille with a second opportunity to insert in the film his well-known flashbacks to sadomasochistic, bacchanalian orgies.

Lydia is condemned to the prison where Evans is already serving a sentence, but there she learns that "the worth-while things in Life, are Love and Service." During an emotional outburst, she affirms with her inmates, "Prison has meant to most of us--a *Life-Preserver!*" She emerges from prison a changed woman. While her friends celebrate on New Year's eve, Lydia and Evans distribute coffee and doughnuts in the slums. What a shock when she encounters O'Bannon in line! Tormented by having sent her to prison, Dan has deteriorated into an alcoholic. [27] Such an inexplicable lapse of character on his part allows Lydia to pose as the standard Victorian heroine and redeem the man she loves. O'Bannon was more interesting as the incorruptible D.A. who is both righteous and sadistic enough to send the woman he loves to jail. As for Lydia, DeMille's heroines turned saintly are boring imitations of Victorian stereotypes.

An actress like Greta Garbo could infuse life into stereotyped Hollywood heroines and dramatize the individual and social aspects of the socialite's rebellion. In *The Single Standard* (1929), a product of director John S. Robertson and his wife Josephine Lovett, Garbo was cast as an American in contrast to her continental vamp portrayals. The story, adapted by Lovett from an Adela Rogers St. Johns novel, upholds a single as opposed to a double standard for the sexes. Its heroine, Arden Stuart (Garbo), is contemptuous of the men in her circle who deceive their wives and seeks instead a relationship in which both parties would be free and equal. After a sexual encounter with a lover who warns her that she cannot assume a man's freedom, Arden becomes attracted to an intriguing prizefighter, sailor and artist named Packy Cannon (Nils Asther). She breakfasts with him on his yacht, the "All Alone," and without hesitation, decides to cast sail with him. The lovers enjoy months together on a romantic South Seas voyage but one day, Packy decides that their love has been so perfect it must be enshrined in memory. Although theirs is supposedly a relationship grounded upon freedom and equality, the heroine assents to this rather abrupt conclusion.

Arden returns to her previous social life, affects a carefree manner, and marries a persistent admirer, Tommy Hewlett (John Mack Brown). When Packy returns from the "fever haunted interior of China" to reclaim her, she has become the devoted mother of a young son. And though she is still in love with Packy, Arden decides that her life now belongs to her husband and child, not herself. One critic wrote, "The ending...is the only logical one and it should certainly compensate the censors for any embarrassment they may have suffered in La Garbo's more tempestuous moments earlier in the film." [28] Decidely unconventional in her sexual behavior before marriage, Arden concludes that the responsibilities of motherhood restrict her freedom. The "new woman" was individualistic but there were self-imposed as well as social limits to her actions.

During the middle and late twenties, the flapper with her distinctive dress and style came to symbolize the "new woman's" independence. The evolution of the flapper image in silent movies is quite instructive. An early film titled *The Flapper* (1919), based on a script by Frances Marion and starring Olive Thomas, is about the rebellious school girl exploits of Genevieve King. "Ginger" is an irrepressible teenager who is impatient to become a woman of the world and quips to her friends about experience, "I'm getting it as fast as I can." She fantasizes about romance and steals out of the dormitory at night to dance with Richard Channing, an appealing "older man." Later, she spends a weekend at a "wicked city" hotel where she experiments with cosmetics and attempts smoking, then returns home to pose before astonished friends and family as a sophisticated vamp. A few years later, Ginger as a rebellious coed type will mature into the recognizable flapper of the Jazz Age.

Clara Bow played flapper roles even before she became the "It Girl" under the aegis of Elinor Glyn in the late twenties. According to Fitzgerald in an interview titled "Has the Flapper Changed? F. Scott Fitzgerald Discusses the Cinema Descendants of the Type He Has Made So Well Known," Clara Bow was "the quintessence of what the term 'flapper' signified.... Pretty, impudent, superbly assured, as worldly wise, briefly clad and 'hard-boiled' as possible."[29] As Janet Oglethorpe in *Black Oxen* (1924), she is a willful and spoiled flapper who behaves disrespectfully towards her grandmother, an imperious old society matron, and eludes her baffled father.[30] When Lee Clavering, a family friend, remonstrates and threatens to spank her for impudence, she retorts, "Can I depend on that?" Janet smokes, drinks from a hip flask, and drives around with an irresponsible crowd. The ambition of her life is to extract a proposal from Lee, drama critic and would-be playwright who is cynical about women. She flirts at every opportunity, throws herself at him, attempts to compromise him by sneaking into his apartment. And in the end, though circumstances help, she makes good on her threat, "I'll get you yet, my Passionate Love."

In *The Plastic Age* (1925), Clara Bow plays a flapper more sophisticated and less juvenile than Janet but still very animated. As Cynthia Day, she is a "hotsy-totsy" who runs around with a fast college crowd and flirts with the attractive men on campus. She becomes the object of rivalry between two roommates, Hugh Carter (Donald Keith), a clean-cut track and football star who is naive, and Carl Peters (Gilbert Roland), campus Romeo. Carl becomes angry when Cynthia breaks a date with him to go to a big dance with his rival but later that same evening, Hugh discovers them seated together in a car. When the two young men begin to quarrel over her, Cynthia asserts, "I'll go with whomever I wish." Hugh's involvement with Cynthia has a disastrous effect on his grades and worse, his athletic performance. After a speak-easy raid, Cynthia herself breaks off with Hugh because she realizes that she is ruining him. The flapper's sincerity and sense of honor are attractive traits which may not always prove convenient but are ultimately rewarded. When he is graduated from college, Hugh reconciles with Cynthia (after an unbelievable football sequence which takes up a great deal of footage). Carl explains, "She's changed a great deal--quieter--not the same girl." As if to underscore the fact, Hugh seeks out Cynthia whereas previously in their relationship, she made all the moves including the decision to end it. The flapper without her rebelliousness becomes a rather subdued and conventional young girl, a perfect mate for the clean-cut youth who represents traditional American values.

Joan Crawford became a star after the release of an M-G-M box-office success called *Our Dancing Daughters* (1928). Critics described the film as the "Best of All Jazz Theme Films," "a story of the love of a modern girl," "a satire on fast-living wealthy people," "a white-hot story of gin, jazz, and naughtiness among the debutantes," "sizzling celluloid," and "effervescing with the spontaneity of youth" and "a laxness of morals." [31] Despite the reviewers' descriptions, which read like blurbs from exhibitors' posters, *Our Dancing Daughters* is really a morality tale about the behavior of three flappers reared in very different families. Diana Medford (Joan Crawford) has casual but affectionate relations with her parents whom she trusts and confides in. Beatrice (Dorothy Sebastian), Diana's sedate best friend, has been brought up by strict and disapproving parents. Diana's pretty spirited rival, Ann (Anita Page), has been raised to exploit her feminine appeal so that she will marry a rich man.

Although she refers to herself as "Diana the Dangerous" and behaves very much like the flapper (she smokes, drinks, dances the charleston until dawn, and flirts with men), Diana is basically an honest young woman who has an intense desire to "taste all of life." Unfortunately, her uninhibited behavior invites suspicion. Ben Blaine (John Mack Brown), an eligible bachelor, is instantly attracted to her but hesitates because "a man has to be sure of the girl he marries--." The young man is so naive that Ann traps him into marriage by reciting on cue, "I can't be daring--and free with love--I'm not 'a modern' but it's because I want a home--a husband and babies--and be worthy of them." Ann's mother was right when she predicted, "Diana's too free--in public. When it comes to marriage men are still old fashioned." The flapper's lack of inhibition, designed to entice a man into marriage, proves self defeating in this instance.

Unlike Diana and Ann, who are a study in contrasts, Beatrice has experienced sexual relations and even a certain degree of promiscuity in her past. She explains to her lover, "Before I met you Norman--before I knew anything about love--things happened--." The young man forgives and marries her, but should the audience receive the impression that Bea escapes punishment, her married life is troubled. Norman becomes jealous, is suspicious and tormented, and declares, "If you had only been mine--just mine." As for Ann, she pays the price for deception when she becomes drunk and tumbles down the stairs to her death. This accident solves the problem of Diana's virtue going unrewarded by leaving her free to marry Ben after a decent interval.

For all the publicity about it being another "flaming youth" picture, *Our Dancing Daughters* remains a very moral movie through the aid of plot contrivances. In some respects, it is a successful combination of an updated Victorian melodrama about the fallen woman and the flapper genre of the twenties. The preoccupation with a woman's virginity in a film about flappers in the Jazz Age is quite revealing. The male characters in the movie appear more obsessed about it than the women. As for extra-marital sex, that too is unthinkable. When Ben realizes that his wife is a spiteful liar, he regrets having lost the opportunity to marry Diana. But having played the game squarely from the start, Diana is not about to begin an affair with another woman's husband and she rebuffs an impulsive advance.

The character of Diana Medford, whose boldness was part of a genuine sense of values, was misunderstood by viewers as well as her lover in the film. In a study of college and senior high moviegoers, a sociologist found that:

> *Many adults in conversation with the author impressed upon him their judgment that this picture was harmful and would likely lead to immoral attitudes and thoughts in high-school boys and girls. These informants included a number of high-school teachers, an editor of an educational magazine, and two college professors. In the experience of a number of high-school boys and girls, however, the picture tended to emphasize other values.* [32]

As one senior high coed remarked, "In Joan Crawford the true spirit of the younger generation was shown. No matter what happened she played fair." [33] The film did shift the burden of blame upon the parents of the flappers, but the younger generation appear to have understood Diana better. She was an attractive combination of conventional moral behavior and flapper style vivacity.

A King Vidor film, *Wine of Youth* (1924), examined some basic problems about marriage and the generation gap but in a skittish manner veering off into conventional solutions. The movie was based on a Rachel Crother play, *Mary the Third*, whose treatment of the young people's revolt from a generational standpoint had enjoyed a theatrical success on Broadway. Unlike her grandmother and mother, the third Mary is a flapper who pretends to know everything and goes to wild parties where couples dance a frenetic charleston, drink, and neck. She declines to consider that her first preoccupation is marriage. The film's treatment of the flapper is dissimulating, however, since the plot begins and ends with the problem of choosing a husband.

Unable to decide between an aggressive suitor named Hal and a more conventional young man, Lynn Talbot, Mary wonders out loud if there is not a way to find out what a prospective husband is like before marriage. This question leads to an experiment in which Mary, Hal, and Lynn, together with her friend Tish and a beau named Max, decide to camp out unchaperoned. The hitch in the plan is that both suitors have to promise Mary not to make love to her during the outing. An angry scene erupts when Mary reveals the proposal to her family, but the young couples climb into separate cars and speed away, exulting in their freedom. The experiment sours that very night, however, as Tish, Max, and Hal become drunk and cavort in the water. Hal enters Mary's tent and creates a scene by attempting to make advances. Mary resorts to a ruse in order to get her friends to return home. Afterwards, she explains that they had no right to make their parents suffer and reconsiders the value of old-fashioned ideas. Although it is five o'clock in the morning, she asks Lynn, "What's intelligence got to do with love?" and having made her decision at last, embraces him.

Although she rebelled against convention, the movie flapper was basically honest and moral in contrast to the Fitzgerald flapper, who could be destructive in a careless manner. In a short story titled "The Jelly Bean" from *Six Tales of the Jazz Age,* written by Fitzgerald in collaboration with Zelda, the heroine has "left a trail of broken hearts from Atlanta to New Orleans," shoots craps with the boys, does crazy stunts, drinks straight from the bottle, and has "scars all over her reputation." [34] Unlike the movie flapper, Nancy Lamar's impulsive and irresponsible behavior is unrestrained by any sense of values. She is really adrift. And there is a hard edge to her personality undiluted by movie sentiment. She warns Jim Powell, the Jelly-bean, "Don't treat me like a girl,...I'm not like any girl *you* ever saw." [35] After a dissolute evening at the Country Club, she causes an uproar by eloping with a wealthy beau during a drunken spree. Jim's friend, Clark, muses the next day, "It's too bad....I don't mean the wedding--reckon that's all right, though I don't guess Nancy cared a darn about him. But it's a crime for a nice girl like that to hurt her family that way." [36] This is quite a contrast to the ending of *Wine of Youth* when Mary abandons an unconventional experiment out of consideration for her parents, if not personal discomfort.

The distinction between the movie flapper and the Fitzgerald flapper, attributable in part to film censorship, is very revealing. Without conventional morals and the romantic notion of marrying for love, the Fitzgerald flapper was freer but she lived in a void. So long as youth and beauty lasted, she could indulge a whim without giving much thought to the consequences. The movie flapper was caught in another pitfall, as implied by the circular plot of *Wine of Youth*, for she began married life in a way not unlike her mother before her. And significantly, she married uninteresting males less energetic and more conventional than herself. Whether the flapper married capriciously or for love, there was really not much else in life for her to do. As Clark muses in "The Jelly Bean," "Seems like all the best girls around here marry fellas and go off somewhere." [37]

The rebellious screen heroine usually married in the end with expectations that she would be supported, if not lavishly so, by her husband. According to William L. O'Neill, there was already in the twenties a loss of interest in careers on the part of women. The rate of increase of women in the professions declined as did the percentage of women enrolled in colleges. O'Neill attributes this decline in part to the realization among women that sex discrimination blocked their career prospects and to the difficulty of balancing professional and domestic duties. [38] The traditional role of wife and mother appealed to the young women who did not know what to do with their so-called freedom in the midst of a sexual revolution. A study of the Class of 1920 at Wellesley College revealed that contrary to myth, 69.8 percent of college women graduates married sooner or later in the decade and 53.3 percent became mothers. [39]

The flapper appeared on the scene when career women were becoming disenchanted with their prospects and feminists, having won the

130

suffrage, became diffused. The rebellion against social convention could not enlarge upon previous political and professional gains because the style of the revolt was so dissimilar and it occurred on an altogether different level. The sexual revolution was not always comprehensible to women reformers who were not immune to the Victorian concept of female sexuality. The flapper did not have much in common with either the suffragist or the professional woman who belonged to a previous age when effort on behalf of a cause counted for something. She was, like the rest of her generation, uninterested in reforms aimed at political gains or breaking new paths for women in the professions. So she fell back upon the cult of domesticity.

Chapter VII

SEX AND MARRIAGE IN THE JAZZ AGE

In the late teens and early twenties, directors such as Cecil B. DeMille, Erich von Stroheim, and Ernst Lubitsch began to portray romance after rather than as a prologue to the wedding. [1] Critics and moviegoers alike responded to this focus upon marital life, undoubtedly because these directors made films that dealt with the sexual aspect of marriage. Contrary to Victorian belief, romantic and sexual love were seen as interrelated and thus any decline in sentiment presented a problem for wives as well as husbands. The pictures of DeMille, Strohem, and Lubitsch implied that matrimony could be antithetical to romance and that making love last within marital bounds was problematic. As a rule, however, the Hollywood movie affirmed that romance in marriage was possible and left speculations about free love and companionate marriage to Greenwich Village intellectuals.

A great deal has been written about the influence of social changes in postwar America upon Cecil B. DeMille as a director and vice-versa. DeMille's older brother William, who followed him to Hollywood after a successful theatrical career, noted in retrospect that "the whole country was feeling the reaction, and young people were talking about the 'new freedom' and feeling a general sense of rebellion. ...C.B. discovered that the whole country was very much interested in 'sex appeal.'...He started a new era of stories; smart sophisticated comedy-dramas." [2] Cecil wrote in his autobiography, however, that he filmed *Old Wives for New,* the first of his sex comedies, after repeated urging from the New York office. As early as January, 1917, Jesse Lasky had signaled to him in a memorandum, "I am strongly of the opinion that

132

ou should get away from the spectacle stuff for one or two pictures and
ry to do modern stories of great human interest."[3] DeMille suc-
:eeded with *Old Wives for New* (1918) and in an adaptation of James
3arrie's *The Admirable Crichton,* rechristened *Male and Female*
1919), he struck upon the combination of "modern stories" and
'spectacle stuff" which became his trademark.

Old Wives for New was the result of a collaboration between Cecil B.
DeMille and his scenarist, Jeanie Macpherson, who wrote the scripts
for several of the director's bathtub and Biblical spectaculars.
According to DeMille himself:

> *Essentially,* Old Wives for New *is the story of the*
> *damage which a lazy and slovenly wife can do to her*
> *marriage. Sylvia Ashton, as Sophy Murdock, the wife,*
> *was wonderfully disgusting; it is not every actress who*
> *would take such a part or play it as realistically as*
> *she did. ...If it or the picture as a whole had any other*
> *purpose, it was not to suggest to husbands that they*
> *should get rid of slovenly wives, but to suggest to both*
> *wives and husbands that marriages, though prover-*
> *bially made in heaven, are woven on earth of many*
> *strands, among which such elementary things as*
> *cleanliness and good-housekeeping can be of great*
> *importance.*[4]

The film features some interesting novelties as well as the usual conventions. According to James Card, *Old Wives* is the only such
American picture which caricatures the mother.[5] The portrait of
Sophy Murdock as a corpulent, unkempt, and self-indulgent woman
contrasts with that of her husband, Charles, who is still dapper after
several years of marriage. Sophy spends most of her time in bed under
mounds of chocolates and funny papers, and the viewer is more apt to
identify to her as Charles' mother rather than wife. In fact, the two
children who enjoy a camaraderie with their father comment that he
could pass for an older brother.

Although DeMille protested that he was not suggesting husbands
discard their slovenly wives, there appeared to be no other recourse
when spouses deteriorated into Sophy Murdocks. Charles concludes

that it is degrading for two indifferent people to live together and suggests a divorce and division of community property. Sophy reacts angrily and then bursts into tears. She will have cause for more tantrums when she learns that her youthful husband has fallen in love with an attractive shopkeeper named Juliet Raeburn. A round of musical chairs played to wedding music enlivens the marital dilemma of *Old Wives*. Accepting the inevitability of divorce, Sophy threatens to name Juliet as the "other woman." To protect the reputation of the woman he loves, Charles becomes the conspicuous escort of a "loose woman" named Viola. Juliet, already distraught by Charles' frank revelation that he is a married man, is further distressed by his appearance as a wealthy playboy. When she learns the truth in the end, a wedding scene in romantic Venice is intercut with another—Sophy also remarries. It's *Old Wives for New*.

The Famous Players executives in New York had some cause for their initial concern about releasing *Old Wives*. Any censorship problem is sidestepped, however, with the legal and thus moral resolution of a double wedding. Also, there is the traditional bifurcation of females into girls who were marriageable and girls who were not. Juliet has already fallen in love with Charles when he discloses that he is a married man. She reacts quite properly by disappearing from his life—there is nothing he has the right to say or that she ought to hear. In contrast, Viola is a sexually promiscuous woman who can be bought. She is not a vamp without feeling, however, and elicits some audience sympathy because she is hurt by Charles' indifference. And Charles is using her for his own purposes. The moral questions in DeMille's overlapping triangles sometimes become unmanageable so that not all loose ends are neatly tied.

The cost of the film negative for *Old Wives* was $66,000. The picture grossed $380,000. [6] In Hollywood, the box-office success of a film dictated its reputation. The *Old Wives* formula was reversed in *Don't Change Your Husband* (1919), also written by Jeanie Macpherson. As the scene opens, Leila Porter (Gloria Swanson), an elegantly gowned and coiffeured young wife, is playing solitaire. Her husband James (Elliott Dexter), a businessman with an expanded waistline, smokes indifferently and buries his head in the papers. Leila notices the worn out shoes on his feet which he has carelessly thrust on her knitting. She is annoyed when he places his cigar on her playing cards and flicks the ashes on the floor. Still imbued with romantic sentiment, Leila hints about the next day but her husband has forgotten their wedding anniversary.

The scene is set for Leila's dissatisfaction with a humdrum marriage and her romantic interest in another man. Schuyler Van Sutpen (Lew Cody), an irresponsible ne'er-do-well who radiates charm, becomes the obliging "other man." Unlike Jim, Schuyler comments about the stylishness of Leila's gown, sends her flowers at the breakfast table, and recites Shakespeare. This self-styled Romeo appears to have no compunction about pursuing a married woman despite her initial rebuffs. Clearly, Leila would have nothing to do with him if Jim were not so indifferent. In real life, she might indulge in an affair but sexuality on screen, even during the pre-Hays office era, should be confined within marriage. Declaring that she can no longer stomach their "corned beef and cabbage existence," Leila discards her husband and acquires another. Unfortunately, Schuyler drinks, sells Leila's jewels during a financial crisis, and has an affair with a golddigging blond named Toodles. Jim, still at a loss over Leila's departure, visits the gym and emerges a spruce and fashionable man of forty. The previous situation reverses itself. A disenchanted Leila is now attracted to her handsome, former husband and he has no qualms about winning her back. The resolution of this triangle calls for another divorce and re-marriage. In the last scene, Leila is again playing solitaire as Jim dozes off while reading the papers but he has bought his bride a ring to celebrate their one month wedding anniversary. And that is all the difference.

Don't Change Your Husband cost $74,000 and earned $300,000. DeMille decided upon a further elaboration of its theme in *Why Change Your Wife?* (1920), which cost $130,000 but earned $1,000,000. [7] In this latest round of marital musical chairs, DeMille adapted a story by his brother William about "an exceeding prim and proper wife 'whose virtues are her only vices.' " [8] Robert Gordon (Thomas Meighan), the husband, is irked by the annoyances of living with a woman (Gloria Swanson) who does not allow him to shave in peace, disapproves of his wine cellar, and will not permit the dog in the house. But more than that, he is bored with Beth's dowdy appearance and her pursuit of high-brow culture. To make married life more exciting, Robert buys his wife a backless, transparent, and decollete negligee, precariously

135

suspended with beads and trimmed with fur. Anticipating its delivery that evening, he puts a foxtrot on the victrola but Beth objects to it as "awful, physical music." When the box arrives, she is annoyed and embarrasssed by having to pose in a negligee, rebuffs a passionate advance as proof of inebriation, and objects to her husband's "Oriental ideas." As in *Don't Change Your Husband,* this would be an understandable moment for a spouse to seek stimulation elsewhere, and Robert finds model Sally Clark (Bebe Daniels) a more sympathetic and alluring companion. "When a husband has had his faults constantly explained to him at home, he listens more easily to an old friend who tells him how wonderful he is." Beth reacts angrily when she learns about the "other woman" and sues for divorce in a fit of pique though she is still in love with Robert. Afterwards, she considers sacrificing her life to charity. While shopping for a new dress, however, she does a volte-face, discards the idea that a man wants his wife to be modest and decent, and orders her clothes made "sleeveless, backless, transparent, indecent."

Robert has, in the meanwhile, married Sally only to discover that "wives *will* be wives." She won't let him shave in peace either. And if Beth was too serious-minded, Sally is selfish and volatile. The two Mrs. Gordons meet at a fashionable resort and a few episodes later, fight over Robert in a literal, knock-down, drag-out battle of feminine fists. Sally opts for alimony. In the final scene, Beth descends the stairs in her negligee and puts a foxtrot on the record player while the servants move twin beds closer together. The title admonishes, "And now you know what every husband knows: that a man would rather have his wife for his sweetheart than any other woman--but ladies, if you would be your husband's sweetheart, you simply *must* learn to forget that you are his wife."[9]

DeMille's *Old Wives for New, Don't Change Your Husband,* and *Why Change Your Wife?* constitute an interesting trilogy about married life. The theme of each film has to do with legalized spouse swapping as a mode of sustaining romance in marriage. In *Don't Change Your Husband* and *Why Change Your Wife?* couples sexually maladjusted but still in love experience divorce and a second more dissatisfying marriage before they find happiness with each other. The resolution of their dilemma lies in the guilty party acquiring sex appeal and thus injecting a note of excitement into married life. This solution is unworkable in *Old Wives* because Sophy's unattractiveness is an irreversible condition. The husband and wife therefore divorce and acquire more suitable partners in a second and presumably more permanent arrangement.

According to DeMille, the trouble with marriage was that it became a humdrum existence quite the opposite of the preceding whirlwind courtship. The husband and wife therefore shared a responsibility to preserve romance by continuing to exert their sexual attraction for each other. DeMille's portrayal of a desirable marriage as an endless honeymoon stressed the importance of sexual compatibility but was also unrealistic. The intoxicated feeling which accentuates romantic love in its first stages is remembered with nostalgia because it is evanescent. The flow of romance may be later recaptured but it is impossible to sustain. A way to sustain it is to fall in and out of love repeatedly, and this is what DeMille's characters do when they divorce and remarry each other. Although this cinematic approach to the difficulty of protracting romance in married life proved workable screen fantasy, it was a contradiction of what people experienced in their lives. And perhaps this accounted for the strength of its appeal. As the writer of a magazine article observed at the time, "The reaction against the romantic conception of marriage is largely confined to the intellectuals...; there has been, as yet, no corresponding popular revolt against romantic doctrines." [10]

The movies could afford to indulge in fantasies of romance ad infinitum because time was frozen on celluloid. The married couples in *Don't Change Your Husband* and *Why Change Your Wife?* are significantly childless. Charles Murdock in *Old Wives* has two children but he passes for an older brother. So long as there is youth, it is possible to exchange spouses, relive romance, and avoid the real world of mature adult persons. The marital fantasy which pervades DeMille's celluloid world did have its realistic edge, however. The importance of sexual compatibility in married life was treated with candor, perhaps because sexual gratification was the key to the luxurious lives of the characters. Unfortunately, DeMille fixated and never explored this theme beyond the visual rendering of sex appeal. The equation of sexual attraction with elegance of dress was too simplistic. Still, the relationship between fashion's dictates and popular conceptions of women is a fascinating one. In the Griffith melodrama, *Way Down East,* Lillian

137

25.   Thomas Meighan, Babe Daniels, and Gloria Swanson in
      Why Change Your Wife?

26.   Gloria Swanson and Elliott Dexter in *Don't Change Your Husband*

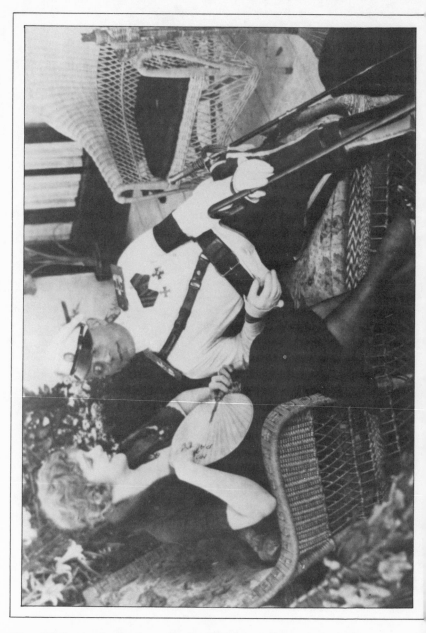

27. Erich von Stroheim and Miss Dupont in *Foolish Wives*

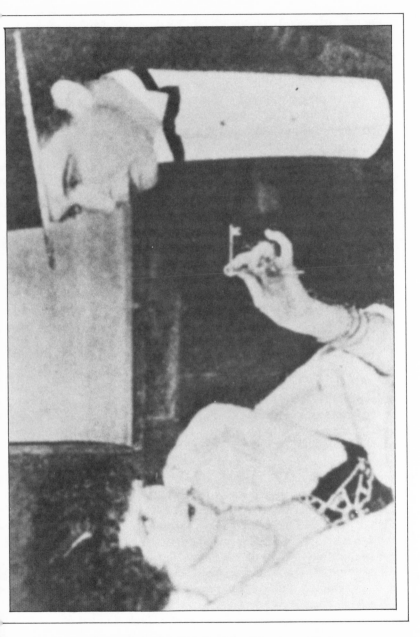

28. Marie Prevost and Monte Blue in *The Marriage Circle*

141

Gish is embarrassed to be costumed in a decollete evening gown for social affair. [11] By contrast, Gloria Swanson was the clothes horse pa excellence, both on and off the screen.

The role of Beth Gordon in *Why Change Your Wife?* is most revealin, as to what clothes can do for the woman. Beth is a conventional silen screen heroine made over into a fashion plate. She is modest, right minded, and cultured--that is, she is perfect as an ingenue durin, courtship but extremely dull as a mate. In reality, wives like Beth drov their husbands into the arms of more alluring women like Sally Clark and the double standard sanctioned such an arrangement. But DeMill poses his own solution--the transformation of Beth into a sexuall, desirable wife. Beth's conversion has some interesting implications. I exploiting her sex appeal, she becomes an object. In doing so wit style, she becomes an object of conspicuous consumption. In fairnes to DeMille, it should be noted that the male characters in his films notably Jim Porter in *Don't Change Your Husband,* undergo a simila change. As far as the heroine is concerned, the transformation elevate her out of domesticity and into the sexual arena on an active basis. Th physical brawl between Beth and Sally at the end of *Why Change You Wife?* is a logical consequence of the events. The sexual parity of thes movies implies that in some instances, women may have to misbehav like men.

The most flimsy aspect of the DeMille films about sex and marriag was the game of marital musical chairs. The game was necessary i sexual relations were to occur on a legitimate basis (for purposes o censorship) but was contrived and hypocritical. A startling aspect o these exchanges was the rapidity and ease with which they wer accomplished. Should a spouse appear en scene with onion on hi breath, that clearly was grounds for divorce. If divorce was taken so lightly, why not marriage? As William L. O'Neill has pointed out in hi study, divorce became increasingly acceptable once it was apparent that it functioned as a pressure valve to preserve, not destroy the insti- tution of marriage. [12] The circular pattern in the DeMille films provides an illustration. There is no final disillusionment about marriage and in fact, his characters think well enough of it to marry each other twice.

In 1919, the release of a film called *Blind Husbands* established Carl Laemmle's Universal as a major studio and Erich von Stroheim as a ranking new director. Stroheim delineated the characters who make up the triangle in his picture during an interview published shortly after the film's premiere:

> *The wife of my story loves her husband. ...She craves affection. She is sensitive to his apparent indifference, his unwitting rebuffs. He, in the supreme egoism of possession, his devotion to his work...forgets the man must always be the courtier.*
>
> *...the lover is a swanking, swaggering scion of militarism,...with all the absurd vanities; the ugly hypocrisies; the silly affectations of the kulturist. ...yet he succeeds in entangling a high bred wife who loves her husband. This only proves how hurt pride, stunted affection in a woman can poison her whole system. She too, becomes blind. She craves love. If she cannot get real love she accepts its substitute.* [13]

The setting of *Blind Husbands* is the village of Cortina on the Austro-Italian frontier where the peaks of the Monte Cristallo grace the skyline. [14] An Alpine mountaineer named Sepp entertains Robert Armstrong, an American doctor, and his sadly neglected wife Margaret. Armstrong's inattentiveness contrasts with the cavalier manners of a Prussian officer, Lieutenant von Steuben (Stroheim himself), and the blissful state of a honeymoon couple. Steuben, perceiving an opportunity, regales the forgotten wife with thoughtful gifts, attention, and romantic verbiage. "You were created for nothing else but love--love with its longing--its ecstasies." Margaret still loves her husband but yields just enough to the officer's persistent importuning to encourage him and is guilt stricken. A dream sequence during which Steuben points the finger of accusation at her expresses the agitated state of her mind. At this stage, the Prussian's chivalrous pursuit could easily deteriorate into rape were it not for the quiet intervention of Sepp, who, unlike the husband, is fully aware of the situation. When Armstrong's eyes are finally opened, he is more amenable to his friend's advice about marriage: "Little I know of the world--but one thing she needs: Love." As a horse drawn vehicle moves into the landscape, Margaret smiles and gazes tenderly at her husband when he makes an affectionate gesture by taking her hand.

The box-office and critical success of *Blind Husbands* influenced Laemmle to finance Stroheim's next picture, *Foolish Wives* (1922). The plot of *Foolish Wives* is another instance of American "innocents abroad" but in terms of its detail and sequence, the circumstances under which the film was made are significant. When production costs escalated, Laemmle exploited *Foolish Wives* as the first million dollar picture, and an electric sign to that effect was mounted in Times Square. With literally no end in sight, Irving Thalberg halted production by confiscating the cameras. Controversy then shifted from budget to the film's editing. Stroheim's thirty-two reel version was cut to twenty-four reels for the New York premiere, twelve reels for the road show, and ten reels for general release to the public. The censors in the various states where the film was screened also deleted scenes considered offensive.[15]

A plot summary of *Foolish Wives* attributed to Stroheim himself unravels the situation in the film as follows.[16] An American couple arrive in Monte Carlo and become acquainted with an unscrupulous Russian emigré adventurer, "Count" Sergius Karamzin (Stroheim), and his two accomplices, the "Princesses" Olga and Vera. The three Russian conspirators lure wealthy vacationers to the Count's villa where counterfeit money is circulated during gambling parties. A neglected and idle wife, Mrs. Hughes becomes the victim of Karamzin's cavalier ploys. The Count's attempt to seduce her is frustrated, however, by his much-abused maid, an unattractive but slavishly devoted woman whom he has previously exploited. Wracked by jealousy and despair, the maid retaliates by setting fire to the villa and then drowns herself. After the confusion caused by the fire, the authorities arrive and reveal the Princesses as women with criminal records. The Count in the meanwhile has retreated to an earlier scene, the abode of a counterfeiter named Ventucci, where the attraction is the old man's half-witted but nubile young daughter. In the end, Ventucci exacts a grim revenge by killing the intruder and dumping his body in the sewer.

Although the triangular plot and its resolution are similar in both *Blind Husbands* and *Foolish Wives*, the latter provoked controversy not only during its production but after its premiere. A *Photoplay* review deemed it "unfit for the family," and "a gruesome, morbid, unhealthy tale" (as if the two were synonymous). The same reviewer also

144

commented about "beautiful bits of acting" and "photography and decoration of unsurpassed appeal."[17] The New York *Sun* critic likewise praised the film as "a masterpiece of photography" but criticized the "decadent streak" in Stroheim's acting and directing.[18] The mixed response of these critics was understandable. The film does have compelling visual appeal and power. In an impressive sequence, for example, Count Karamzin visits Ventucci in a squalid neighborhood near Monte Carlo. The old counterfeiter confides that his dim-witted daughter is his only treasure and makes threatening gestures with a knife at the thought of any harm befalling her. The Count completes his business and proceeds outside where he pauses momentarily on a manhole cover. An iris is aptly used for the fade out on this scene. At the conclusion of the story, Ventucci surprises the Count during an attack on his daughter, kills him, and furtively drops his body down the manhole. Speculations about irony, poetic justice, and Freudian symbolism are in order.

The ambivalent reaction of film reviewers to *Foolish Wives* is understandable in that the character of Lieutenant von Steuben has been elaborated into the much more brutal and salacious Count Karamzin. Similarities exist in the men's decadent aristocratic breeding, their use of chivalry to disguise lust, and displays of cowardice in moments of danger. But Karamzin goes further than lecherous attempts to seduce the neglected wife of an American careerist. In *Foolish Wives,* he shares a villa with two mistresses, sadistically abuses an ignorant maid, and assaults a retarded young girl. Such graphically illustrated depravity was excessive for critics and censors alike. The moviegoers in New York responded by crowding the aisles of the Central Theater and subsequently the Capitol during a second run, but censorship problems elsewhere undoubtedly reduced profits. An article by *New York Times* critic Mordaunt Hall published in December, 1924, almost three years after the film's release, stated that Universal was then within $50,000 of breaking even on the film.[19]

Unlike DeMille's *Don't Change Your Husband* and *Why Change Your Wife?* Stroheim's second film was not a plot reversal of the first. The same marital situation in *Blind Husbands* is explored on a more opulent scale in *Foolish Wives* with the focus on the wife's naivete as opposed to her husband's indifference. The fault remains the same in either instance. A neglectful American husband is so preoccupied with his

145

own interests that his attractive, young wife falls prey to the attentions of a gallant but unscrupulous European. For what it was worth, the sexual parity which existed in DeMille's films was not a part of Stroheim's aristocratic world. Reversals in DeMille's sex comedies occurred because either husband or wife could be at fault and was required to undergo the transformation from dowdy to glamorous spouse. A visit to one's tailor or dressmaker injected romance into a humdrum marriage. The characterization of the sexes in Stroheim's pictures was more tradition-bound so that the result was a triangle instead of musical chairs.

Stroheim contended that women would not be tempted by the courtly behavior of an aristocrat if their dull American husbands were more gallant. Above all, the young wife was a passive and sentimental creature who craved thoughtful affection. The problem with this conception of woman's nature was that she easily became prey and defenseless victim, as evidenced by the fate of the American wives in *Blind Husbands* and *Foolish Wives*. Unfortunately, not all chivalrous men were ethical. And the emphasis upon romantic ritual, ascribed to the desires of women as well as man's instinct for pursuit, detracted from more relevant questions. The husband's character was surely more important than his conforming to a code of gallantry. And by Stroheim's own design, the cavalier aristocrat was always a heel and worse. The wives in Stroheim's pictures were thus victims of their own romantic notions, though admittedly the sexual disinterest of their husbands posed a marital problem.

Stroheim's conception of male and female sexuality was traditional to the extent that women were passive and did not initiate sexual activity. The American wives did give evidence of a sexual nature, however, in that they found their husbands lacking and were tempted into unwise flirtations. The American male, on the other hand, was curiously asexual while his European counterpart possessed a carnal appetite which descended to bestial levels. A sexually normal and healthy male was not among the cast of characters in either *Blind Husbands* or *Foolish Wives*. As for the women, the tendency to regard them in dualistic terms was based upon a conventional point of view. The wives flirted but retained their honor, even in the most desperate circumstances. Sexually active women in *Foolish Wives* were criminals masquerading as princesses and a lowly maid--females traditionally available to upper class men. For all the frank and sometimes brutal cinematic detailing of sexual passion, Stroheim was essentially conservative in his attitudes towards women. The heroines of his later films, such as *The Wedding March* and *Merry-Go-Round*, were Victorian in characterization and tragically victimized. [20]

The DeMille-Stroheim pictures that dealt with marital mishaps were filmed before the establishment of the industry's self-imposed censorship system under Will Hays in 1922. As a matter of fact, these films probably reenforced the arguments of censorship advocates who were always active on local and state levels and agitating for a nation-wide system. By the time that German director Ernst Lubitsch made his touch felt in Hollywood, motion picture studios, though not legally bound, generally respected the Hays code to satisfy the censorship boards existing in various states. That code specified:

> *The sanctity of the institution of marriage and the home shall be upheld. Pictures shall not infer that low forms of sex relationships are the accepted or common thing.*
>
> 1. Adultery, *sometimes necessary plot material, must not be explicitly treated or justified, or presented attractively.*
> 2. Scenes of passion *should not be introduced when not essential to the plot. In general, passion should be so treated that these scenes do not stimulate the lower and baser element.*
> 3. Seduction or Rape.
>   (*a*) *They should never be more than suggested, and only when essential for the plot, and even then never shown by explicit method.*
>   (*b*) *They are never the proper subject for comedy.*
> 4. Sex perversion *or any inference of it is forbidden.*
> 5. White slavery *shall not be treated.*
> 6. Miscegenation *is forbidden.*
> 7. Sex Hygiene *and venereal disease are not subjects for motion pictures.*
> 8. Scenes of actual childbirth, *in fact or in silhouette, are never to be presented.*
> 9. *Children's sex organs are never to be exposed.* [21]

Although movie makers tacitly subscribed to this code, films made after the organization of the Motion Picture Producers and Distributors of America under Hays were not necessarily more censored. Such motion pictures as *Sadie Thompson* and *A Woman of Affairs* were made over the objections of the Hays office and were successful because of or despite the controversy involved. [22]

In a tribute to Ernst Lubitsch written two decades after his death, his colleagues observed, "Sex and more sex was the motive for almost everything his characters did, but so adroitly did he handle his tours de amour, he never had a minute of censorship trouble in three decades of picture making."[23] The celebrated Lubitsch touch referred to a cinematic style with a deftness which evaded the censors. The director himself described that touch as "based on the theory that at least twice a day the most dignified human being is ridiculous."[24] And it first emerged in a much discussed picture called *The Marriage Circle* (1924).[25] The scene is Vienna, "still the city of laughter and light romance," which brings to mind the sparkling melodies of a Franz Lehar operetta. This Austrian capital is far removed from the Vienna of Stroheim's later films, *Merry-Go-Round* and *The Wedding March*, steeped in a grim atmosphere of decadence and brutality. Charlotte (Florence Vidor) and Franz Braun (Monte Blue) are ecstatic newlyweds very much in love who contrast with a disenchanted couple, Josef (Adolphe Menjou) and Mizzi Stock (Marie Prevost). Charlotte and Mizzi are best friends, but this does not preclude Mizzi from attempting to seduce Franz, perhaps out of jealousy of her friend's marital bliss. And though happily married, Franz is not above engaging in a flirtation until it threatens to ruin his marriage. Dr. Gustav Mueller (Creighton Hale), Franz' partner, provides a fifth wheel in the entanglement for he is hopelessly enamored of Charlotte. After a series of misunderstandings--not all of them unraveled--Gustav and Mizzi drive off together in consolation, leaving Charlotte and Franz happily reconciled and Josef with grounds for divorce.

According to Herman G. Weinberg, Lubitsch cast the woman as "sexual aggressor" in *The Marriage Circle* and films immediately following.[26] Mizzi is a cynic about romantic love and advises Charlotte, who speaks radiantly about "the perfect happiness of...married life," "You'll get over it in time!" And she intends to disenchant her friend by seducing Franz. The selfish, unscrupulous, and aggressive streak in her character contrasts not only with Charlotte's sweetness, (why are the two women friends?) but the personalities of the men involved in the pentagonal affair. Franz' vulnerability to a woman's charm leaves him prey to sexually aggressive females. Josef is rather deliciously amused by his wife's philandering. And Gustav is too blundering in his devotion to Charlotte and too willing to be consoled by Mizzi. In a scene close to the denouement of the film, Mizzi makes a distressing appeal to her husband, "Josef, I need love!" She then primps and arrays herself in her boudoir. This appears to be a case of a sexually mismatched marriage. Since Josef is unsatisfactory as a lover, Mizzi directs her energies elsewhere. The situation is an amusing reversal of standard Victorian bedroom values. The difference is that whereas traditionally men have been excused by the double standard, the woman as "sexual aggressor" is a "nasty carnal little creature." [27]

The films of DeMille, Stroheim, and Lubitsch, however different their styles and artistic merit, had in common the treatment of sex and married life among the very rich. Sexual gratification, within or without a marital framework, thus became associated in the minds of the viewer with riches. The luxurious surroundings of these pictures were deceptive, however, in that wealth is a constant given and not a cause for discord. The economics of marriage, let alone separation, were scarcely treated despite the fact that characters in the DeMille and Lubitsch pictures freely divorced each other. (Stroheim was more conservative and effected a reconciliation of his alienated couples.) When Beth Gordon goes on a shopping spree after her divorce in *Why Change Your Wife?* the viewer doesn't know if she is independently wealthy or collecting alimony. Judging from a remark made by the second Mrs. Gordon prior to *her* divorce, most probably Beth's extravagance is being charged to her ex-husband. The same assumption might be made about Mizzi, who drives off in a chauffeured automobile at the end of *The Marriage Circle.* In *Don't Change Your Husband*, Leila telephones her husband to ask if she might pay one hundred fifty dollars for a suit. It happens though that she has been aiding him through a financial setback by giving him the jewels bestowed upon her by her first husband. The economic dependence of wives upon husbands, whether married or divorced, does not for the most part affect their relations in these films. The husbands in the DeMille and Lubitsch movies were certainly generous with their money and never stooped to use it as leverage in domestic quarrels. In *Old Wives,* for example, Charles

Murdock suggests to his wife an equitable division of property when he contemplates divorce.

It is safe to speculate that in reality, money has often been a source of matrimonial discord in which the husband wielded an advantage. One woman writer claimed, "There is hardly a man who will never take advantage of his wife's economic dependence upon him or who will never assume that it gives him special prerogatives." [28] In fact, the husband did not even have to exploit this superiority on a conscious level. The woman, however, could scarcely delude herself about her circumstances. A young bride wrote in the twenties:

> After I had been married three months I awoke to the fact that all my money was gone, my purse was empty, and that not one word on the money subject had been spoken either by my husband or myself. ...I had no idea what to do and was beginning to think I had either married a very stingy or a very thoughtless man, when, observing the unusually solemn expression on my face, he anxiously inquired what was the matter. Without stopping to consider I blurted out the truth. He laughed, then said, remorsefully, "It never occurred to me. Of course you will need a little money," and handed me $10. [29]

This scene in real life calls to mind another in Sinclair Lewis' *Main Street* when Carol Kennicott declares to her husband:

> Yesterday, in front of a saloon, I heard a German farm-wife beg her husband for a quarter, to get a toy for the baby--and he refused. Just now I've heard Mrs. Dyer going through the same humiliation. And I--I'm in the same position! I have to beg you for money. Daily! I have just been informed that I couldn't have any sugar because I hadn't the money to pay for it! [30]

Later in her married life, Carol wields an advantage of her own during a domestic argument. She threatens, "I am perfectly well able to earn my own living. I will go at once, and you may get a divorce at your pleasure!" [31]

The economics which made divorce possible in reality, as well as its decreasing social stigma, led to dissatisfaction with marriages heretofore tolerated. [32] In their study of Middletown, the Lynds found that the rising divorce rate was not unrelated to the increasing numbers of women working outside the home. A Middletown attorney observed, "If a woman has ever worked at all she is much more likely to seek a divorce. It's the timid ones that have never worked who grin and bear marriage." Or as a divorced husband put it, "Why should a woman stay married if she don't like a man and can get a job?" [33] In short, a woman's independence had to be grounded upon a solid economic base. The possibility of divorce to end an unhappy marriage did not otherwise provide a viable alternative. As might be expected, the growing disenchantment with marriage led to a statutory change regarding the grounds upon which divorce was sought and granted. According to *Recent Social Trends*, "The most significant change in the legal cause for divorce has been the increase in the number of states (from 36 to 44 between 1905 and 1930) permitting absolute divorce because of cruelty...." [34] The Lynds also found that cruelty was the cause most often advanced for divorce but speculated, "It is impossible to say to what extent this charge is connected with the sex relation, but it seems probable that, in some cases at least, the connection is close." [35]

The Lynds' careful speculation raised some very interesting questions about sex in married life. At least in the DeMille films, the most frequent cause for divorce was a sexual complaint against the spouse. Sexual maladjustment, as in the marriage of Beth and Robert Gordon in *Why Change Your Wife?* undoubtedly existed in a period when the tendency to idealize women as spiritual beings persisted. A fascinating study about the sex lives of women by Dr. Robert L. Dickinson and Lura Beam reflected the persistence of a Victorian attitude despite an observed increase in sexual freedom among the younger generation. Beam was careful to note about her male colleague, whose medical records provided the data for their volumes, "The male tradition of woman is of a spiritual superiority, a questioned intellectual power and a physical handicap. The doctor clearly believed in the legend of spiritual superiority...." [36] Since the examining physician himself reflected prevailing masculine attitudes towards women, it was not surprising that he reached the following conclusion about the sex experience of married women. "Two out of every five women...had orgasm. ...Two more had never experienced it but rarely; or had lost a former capacity. The fifth woman had orgasm sometimes; she could not absolutely count on it; and sometimes got it by the secondary method of clitoris friction." [37] These medical findings lead one to speculate about the nature of the much publicized sexual revolution.

Unquestionably, the greatest single impetus to the liberalization of sexual mores and practice was birth control, a movement associated with the name of Margaret Sanger. The cause of birth control had been dramatized by her indictment in a U.S. District Court on August 25, 1914 for violation of the Comstock law which forbade the "mailing, interstate transportation, and importation of contraceptive materials and information." Twenty-two states had their own version of the federal statute, "little Comstock laws," and these regulations remained unaltered at the end of the twenties. Practitioners of the medical profession were quite as conservative as the legal. The American Medical Association advised abstinence as the only reliable form of contraception and the rhythm method as "free from criticism on religious and social grounds," though physicians disagreed about the predictability of a woman's fertile period. At the close of the decade, only thirteen of seventy-five highly rated medical schools gave regular courses in contraception though the public was resorting to methods such as coitus interruptus, suppositories, intravaginal and intrauterine pessaries, and condoms. [38]

Despite legal and medical setbacks sustained by the birth control movement, the average size of the American family had declined and remained relatively small since at least the turn of the century. According to a study of four Midwestern communities cited in *Recent Social Trends*, the average family size for the years 1900, 1920 and 1930 in farming areas was 4.21, 4.20, and 4.32, respectively, and in cities, 3.22, 3.12, and 2.85, respectively. [39] In their study of Middletown, the Lynds reached a conclusion which was characteristic of the birth control movement as a whole. Contraception had been accepted and effectively practiced by middle but not working class wives for some time. [40] Katherine B. Davis found in her study of one thousand women that 77 percent of university and college graduates expressed approval of voluntary parenthood and 76.48 percent did use contraceptives. Unfortunately, the number of women in the study who had less than a high school education was too few to warrant sound conclusions but the figures for them are 73.42 and 64.51 percent, respectively. [41]

152

The use of contraception at least among married couples in middle and upper income brackets raised questions about the nature of sexuality in a post-Freudian society. As Walter Lippman pointed out:

> ...when conception could be prevented, there was an end to the theory that woman submits to the embrace of the male only for purposes of procreation. She had to be persuaded to cooperate, and no possible reasons could be advanced except that the pleasure was reciprocal. ...She had, therefore, to give up the whole traditional theory which she may have only half-believed anyway, that sexual intercourse was an impure means to a noble end. [42]

The portrayal of couples who were not only romantically but sexually in love in the films of DeMille, Stroheim, and Lubitsch was an improvement over love stories in which the heroine was so asexual that the assertion of conjugal rights was not far from rape. The marital partners in the DeMille and Lubitsch movies certainly exercised their sexual prerogatives, while the wives in the Stroheim pictures were passive but willing. The existence of sexual compatibility was obviously not always the case on screen as in real life, but the very fact that it existed as a concept was evidence of a significant change in the traditional perception of woman.

Chapter VIII

THE UNCHARACTERISTIC HEROINE

The silent screen heroine was usually an accepted and recognizable type such as the virgin, vamp, or flapper who appeared in a standardized plot. Screen types, according to the Russian director, V.I. Pudovkin, were created at the expense of the richness in variety of human behavior and situations.[1] Critic Robert Warshow discussed this same question from a different perspective:

> *One goes to any individual example of the type with very definite expectations, and originality is to be welcomed only in the degree that it intensifies the expected experience without fundamentally altering it. ...It is only in an ultimate sense that the type appeals to its audience's experience of reality; much more immediately, it appeals to the previous experience of the type itself; it creates its own field of reference.[2]*

Although Warshow argued that the movie should be accepted as an "immediate experience" in itself, the complex interaction between film and reality poses some difficult problems. C. Wright Mills observed with respect to the type:

> *Manipulations by professional image-makers are effective because their audiences do not or cannot know personally all the people they want to talk about or be like, and because they have an unconscious need to*

154

*believe in certain types. In their need and inexperience,
such audiences snatch and hold to the glimpses of types
that are frozen into the language with which they see
the world.* [3]

As media critics have pointed out, the popular acceptance of types
can function to distort the viewer's perception and experience in
actuality. The Cinderella syndrome which persists in the psychology of
so many women is an example of the way in which "false images"
pervade and affect individual lives. Although a type conflicts with
reality at the same time that it serves as a guidebook to its interpretation, as Warshow points out, it also exists within its own frame of
reference. And that framework does not necessarily relate to real life.
Perhaps that is the reason why the type provides a deep source of
satisfaction for the moviegoer. As a medium for vicarious living in the
dark, the movies present types which are neither incomprehensible nor
arbitrary but satisfy expectations.

With respect to the screen image of woman during the silent era, the
popularity of certain types was a statement about the ways in which the
audience liked to perceive women. The experience of a senior high coed
was very revealing in this respect: "Goodness knows you learn plenty
about love from the movies. ...You see how the gold-digger systemat-
ically gets the poor fish in tow. You see how the...siren lands the man;
you meet the flapper; the good girl; 'n all the feminine types...." [4]
Screen types also provided women with role models, though not always
idealistic, upon which to pattern their lives. The single, most distinctive
trait which characterized these types as a whole was their absorption in
relationships with men. The movies projected an image of woman
always in relation to men and thus implied, whether or not the relationship was positive, that women had no sense of identity apart from men.

A few uncharacteristic heroines of the silent screen were unconventional enough to define themselves as women independent of men
and/or families and provided the "new woman" of the twenties with
some direction in her quest for an identity. The scarceness of their
numbers attested to the appeal and popularity of the feminine ideals
discussed in these chapters, as well as the effect of the motion picture
type in militating against novel characterizations. And insofar as film
was a mirror rather than a distortion of reality, the relative fewness of

these heroines testified to the inability or lack of desire on the part of women then to assert their so-called freedom. The uncharacteristic heroines of four films, *Miss Lulu Bett* (1921), *Black Oxen* (1924), *The Homemaker* (1925), and *Dancing Mothers* (1926), succeeded, each in her own way, in rejecting traditional roles to some extent and pursuing a more independent course of action.

Miss Lulu Bett, adapted by Clara Beranger from the Zona Gale novel and stage play and directed by her husband William deMille, was an unusual film because it is a simple and realistic story about a plain, unmarried woman. Unfortunately, the films of William deMille, who focused upon the human situations of ordinary people in contrast to Cecil's spectaculars, have not survived or are not available for viewing. [5] The *Variety* critic described *Miss Lulu Bett* as a "first rate, nonsensational" film but criticized the adaptation for its distortion of the psychology of the characters. [6] The characterization of the Deacon family is flawed by stereotyping and oversimplification but is not ruinous to the plot. The father, Dwight, is an unreasonable and insensitive tyrant; the mother, Ina, who is also Lulu's sister, is self-indulgent and lazy; Ma Bett, the mother-in-law, is a grumbling old woman; the two daughters, Monona and Diana, are both spoiled. The entire family exploits Lulu, who has become servant and household drudge, by constantly reminding her that she has a roof over her head and remains on sufferance.

Miss Lulu Bett is the story of a timid and quiet spinster's rebellion against the tyranny of a selfish family and her effort to make a life apart for herself. The plot with its contrivances is not entirely satisfactory, but Lois Wilson's portrayal of Lulu deserved the excellent reviews it attracted. The *New York Times* critic wrote, "Never before...has she been quite so clear and convincing as she is in the role of Lulu Bett." [7]
The unhappy spinster first attempts to escape from the household by way of marriage to Dwight's brother, Ninian, but is horrified to discover that he has previously been married to a woman who abandoned him years ago. Since the fate of Ninian's first wife is unknown, Lulu faces the dismal prospect of returning home.

Lulu's return provokes both consternation that the family name will be disgraced by bigamy and relief that a servant need not be hired. The family convinces her to swallow her pride and say nothing about her eason for leaving Ninian. Unfortunately, the neighbors begin to gossip and treat her as a fallen woman. The local school teacher, Neil Cornish, becomes angry about the malicious rumors and befriends Lulu. Their friendship deepens, but Lulu continues to wear her wedding ring despite uncertainty about her marital status. In the meanwhile, the elder daughter Diana, equally unhappy with family life, persuades her boyfriend to elope. Neil and Lulu pursue the couple to the train station where Lulu convinces Diana that she is acting rashly. "It don't pay to marry just to get away--I know," she counsels. Unfortunately, Dwight misconstrues the situation by assuming that Lulu was about to decamp with Neil and berates her as an ingrate unworthy of remaining under the same roof with "innocent children." A hypocrite, he then magnanimously forgives her because it becomes apparent to all that Lulu's departure would mean the loss of a servant. Such a transparent act finally provokes the heroine's anger and she expresses her pent up emotions by overturning pots and pans and breaking dishes. She exclaims, *"You* can't forgive *me!"* And pushing Dwight, she cries out, "I hate you! I hate your house! I wouldn't stay in it--I'm through!" Some time later, Lulu receives a letter from Ninian, who informs her about his discovery that his previous wife is still alive. As a paraphrase of the Declaration of Independence, the closing title reads, "Her new job in the village bakery assures Lulu of Life and Liberty and now she timidly ventures in Pursuit of Happiness." Not really so timid, Lulu seeks out Neil by going to the school house.

Although *Miss Lulu Bett* ends on the familiar note of marriage (the title is significant), enough negative aspects of married and family life have been depicted to give the audience something to reflect about. [8] The situation of a spinster dependent upon her family in small town circumstances must have been unhappy for countless women but as Lulu learns, marriage as an escape is senseless. Even had the marriage to Ninian proved legal, she would have found herself indebted to him. She has to rebel against an intolerable family situation and develop her own resources as a person. This is especially difficult for a woman like Lulu who has been schooled in passivity and oppressed for so long, but she manages to find work in the local bakery. That job meant self-reliance based upon economic security and as a woman surer of herself, she takes the initiative and approaches Neil. It should be noted that the plot resolution of the novel is not as forceful since Neil (a music man with poor prospects rather than a respectable school teacher) proposes to

Lulu as she is about to leave town in search of employment. The film version is less subtle in detailing Lulu's character but stronger in outlining her rebellion and quest for independence.

The Homemaker, a Universal production directed by King Baggot and adapted by Mary O'Hara from a novel by Dorothy Canfield, is similar to the deMille film in that it too deals with the problem of a woman's identity in relation to her family. The woman in this case is not a spinster, however, but a wife and mother. As a matter of fact, the movie begins with a scene which typically constitutes the Hollywood happy ending, newlyweds emerging from a church. Thirteen years later, Eva Knapp (Alice Joyce) is on her knees scrubbing the floor. She hopes that as soon as her husband Lester receives a promotion and raise, they will be able to afford domestic help and a new house. Meanwhile, she manages to stretch his eighteen hundred dollars a year income to support their three children. All the neighbors comment on her competence as a housewife and one of them remarks, "It's a pity to see such an efficient woman tied to such a useless man...." Eva is understandably discontented and frustrated, for housewifery means an endless round of "sewing, scrimping, and scrubbing," and her negative feelings affect the children.

Family troubles worsen when Lester fails to receive the anticipated promotion because Spencer Willing, the new managing director, is stressing efficiency, not seniority. The blow is a bitter disappointment to Eva and she breaks into tears of frustration. The worst is yet to happen, however. Lester is dismissed from his job. And during a fire, he deliberately plunges off the roof so that he might leave Eva and the children his life insurance policy. But "Lester proved a bungler even at dying" and becomes a paralytic confined to a wheel chair. This accident results in a complete role reversal. Lester stays home and proves to be a better parent because his fanciful and dreamy nature endears him to the children, previously constrained by Eva's qualities as a martinet. Eva approaches Mr. Willing for a job and becomes so adept in the sales department that she earns three thousand dollars a year plus a bonus on sales. [9] A title reads, "Eva, encouraged by joy in her work, brought joy home." She is more relaxed and begins to enjoy her children.

The Homemaker is an extraordinary film, but the moviemakers also adopted a weak plot contrivance from the novel to point out the impossibility of sustaining a role reversal in normal circumstances. While Lester dozes in his wheel chair one evening, Eva notices an involuntary movement of his leg. She is stunned and torn between conflicting emotions but writes a note to Dr. Merritt, the family physician. After she retires for the night, Lester awakens to find the curtain in his daughter's room has caught fire and unconsciously rises to prevent disaster. Although he exults, Lester begins to ponder the meaning of his recovery and its effect upon his wife and children. Dr. Merritt arrives to examine his patient and an anxious little boy confronts him outside. Stevie demands to know what will happen if "fadder" gets well. The doctor, who has previously remarked that Eva "always was the better man of the two," replies, "He'll go to work and your mother'll stay home where she belongs." The child becomes dejected. Inside, Lester pleads with his doctor that it is better for the happiness of his wife and children if he were to remain an invalid. Dr. Merritt is outraged that a patient should willingly confine himself to a wheel chair for life but agrees to the deception and reassures Eva, who is apprehensive, that Lester is incurable.

The Homemaker ends with an interesting question, "Who is the homemaker? Is it the one who stays home, or the one who goes forth to battle?" A more provocative title would have redefined these roles or their assignment on the traditional basis of sex alone. A role reversal in marriage is considered radical even today and is certainly contrary to the norm.[10] Such a reversal occurs in the film only under unusual circumstances after the father has been incapacitated as breadwinner. *The Homemaker* does portray on a realistic basis, however, the dilemma of the frustrated housewife whose talents are going to waste. A woman like Eva functions better as wife and mother when she has an outlet during the day for her creative energies. Eva's characterization in itself qualifies *The Homemaker* as a unique film and replete with implications about woman's traditional life pattern. Also interesting is the father's ability to relate to his children so well that he succeeds better than his wife in this capacity. The assumption that child rearing is naturally the woman's responsibility and what she does best thus becomes as questionable as the man's function to earn the bread and butter. As an atypical film, *The Homemaker* reenforces James Monaco's point that the cinema provides such powerful psychological role models that those roles for which there are no paradigms are difficult to conceive, much less act out. [11]

Although an exhibitor's sheet boasted that *The Homemaker* was "one of those pictures guaranteed to make great, big exhibitors break down and cry for joy," a New York reviewer was more perceptive in observing that the film was "a serious effort at domestic naturalism. There will be a certain number of people who will think it splendid in a quiet and yet forceful way. They do not promise, however, to be numerous enough to make the picture a real box office attraction." The exhibitor's sheet further gives evidence of a lack of comprehension about the film. It declares, "No, it can't be characterized as a 'woman's picture.' It will get the men, and hold them, too, for it has a powerful appeal to the masculine emotions and viewpoint." [12] Of course, the object of an exhibitor's service is to sell the film, but very few men then or now would willingly identify with Lester Knapp. The situation in the film was realistic in that it depicted a husband and wife dissatisfied with and inept in their traditional roles. But it was unrealistic in its mode of sustaining a successful role reversal. A film such as *The Homemaker* was unique in terms of questioning established social norms and setting up alternative models, but this was hardly calculated to become popular mass entertainment. A less static picture which was better dramatized may have been more successful, but the theme and characterizations did not conform to audience expectation.

Contrary to the myth of the happy Hollywood ending, *The Homemaker* suggests that a traditional marriage, at least in this one instance, frustrates rather than fulfills a woman. In *Dancing Mothers,* a film based on the stage play by Edgar Selwyn and Edmund Goulding and directed by Herbert Brenon, the heroine also finds marriage and motherhood lacking but ventures upon a solution other than role reversal. Alice Joyce plays Ethel Westcourt, an attractive woman who gave up a successful stage career when she married. She finds herself increasingly alone as her philandering husband and her teenage daughter Kitten (Clara Bow) lead a twenties style night life. Not until she decides to go on the nightclub circuit herself does Ethel discover that her husband's evening business engagement is named Irma and that her impetuous daughter is chasing Gerald Naughton (Conway Tearle), a reputed ladies' man. Concerned about her daughter rather than her husband, from whom she becomes immediately estranged,

Ethel poses as a French woman to disrupt Naughton's relationship with Kit. As a matter of fact, Gerald regards Kit as a troublesome child, and the situation becomes ironical when he falls in love with Ethel. "For the first time in my life," he confides to a former girlfriend, "I'm sincere with a woman."

The turning point and climax of *Dancing Mothers* occur in an emotional scene at Gerald's apartment where Ethel has been invited to dine. Kitten intrudes, is horrified to discover that Gerald has been making love to her mother, and reacts with sarcasm and bitter accusations. When her father arrives on the scene as an irate parent, Kit reveals that Gerald has made amorous advances to her mother. Ethel comments that the family reunion marks the first evening they have spent together in a while. After announcing to his wife that she may consider herself free from that moment, Hugh Westcourt angrily departs with his daughter. When Ethel leaves a few moments later, Gerald gazes down into the street and observes two cars pulling away in opposite directions.

Ethel decides to begin life anew and go abroad, but she becomes the object of everyone's pleas. Gerald pleads his love and desire to marry her. Although she is grateful to him for having exposed the selfishness of her husband and daughter, Ethel feels that unfortunate events have intruded and preclude a relationship. She rejects his appeal though not without regret. When Hugh points out her conjugal responsibilities in a righteous manner, she retorts that he has already given her her freedom. "My duty now is to myself." Kit entreats her as a daughter who still needs "Mummy's" care, but Ethel realizes that she is being selfish as usual. She kisses her daughter good-bye, shakes hands with her husband, and walks out the door--a scene which calls to mind Nora's exit in Ibsen's *A Doll's House*.

Dancing Mothers ends with a question mark. The husband and daughter are presented in such an unsympathetic light that the viewer appreciates Ethel's dilemma and may not be inclined to censure her final act. Still, it was a radical exit on her part. Undoubtedly, there are numberless women with ungrateful spouses and children who would be reluctant to take such an extreme step, although the fact that Ethel's daughter was nearing maturity makes the decision easier. Ethel also declines the alternative of beginning life anew with Gerald though at the moment it posed an attractive possibility. She would rather begin again on her own, for as she perceives, that is her duty to herself. And it is the choice which requires the most courage. Assuming that she is financially independent--and such an exit would scarcely be possible otherwise--the viewer wonders what sort of life Ethel will pursue after her voyage abroad. The film raises a question not easily resolved: what else is there in life for a woman besides marriage and motherhood, especially if the experience has been less than rewarding?

According to one film review, Paramount filmed an alternative ending to *Dancing Mothers* in which Ethel presumably reconciles with her wayward husband and daughter. The reviewer wrote that the dilemma presented by Ethel's serious involvement with Gerald would be obviated by the "alternate happy ending" (happy for whom?) for "regular audiences outside the bigger towns...."[13] Such an ending is a typical studio maneuver to hedge bets and to blur and make meaningless the controversial issues raised by the film. Unfortunately, there is no material available that would indicate to what extent the alternative ending was used and in what locales. The reviewer's distinction between urban and non-urban audiences, however, points to a social consciousness about geographical differences in values and life styles. But the description of the alternate ending as the "happy" one implies a complete lack of appreciation of Ethel's dilemma as a woman. Mordaunt Hall of the *New York Times* commented about the film's strong closing scene as compensation for the narrative's previous failings but ventured no remark about the social implications of such a conclusion.[14]

Black Oxen, an independent film made by producer-director Frank Lloyd and released through First National, also concludes with the heroine's rejection of a traditional role and a trip to Europe, but her future in relation to the past is more clearly defined.[15] Adapted by Lloyd and Mary O'Hara (who also adapted *The Homemaker*) from the best-selling novel by Gertrude Atherton, *Black Oxen* is the story of a rejuvenated beauty, the Countess Marie Zattiany, nee Mary Ogden (Corinne Griffith). She had been celebrated in her youth for her brilliance and charm, married an Austrian count, and become a figure on the European diplomatic scene. After World War I, she participates in plans for the reconstruction of Austria but the illnesses of old age plague her. At this point, she agrees to a treatment devised by a physician who restores her beauty and the vitality of youth.

The reappearance of the former Mary Ogden in New York, where she is consulting her legal advisor about the liquidation of her American properties, confounds the elite circles in which she once moved. As in the past when she was the reigning beauty of her day, Mary attracts considerable attention from several male admirers. She reacts with genuine feeling, however, to Lee Clavering, a brilliant critic and budding playwright who presses her to stay in New York and marry him. But the arrival of Count Hohenauer, a former lover, resolves her dilemma since he forcefully argues that she is not a woman who can be satisfied by love alone. The combination of her genius for statesmanship, her restored beauty, and the prestige of his family name will serve as the basis for exercising considerable power in Austria. She might decide instead to become the wife of an American writer, but what would be left when the infatuation dies? In the closing scene of *Black Oxen,* Mary enters a stateroom on board a ship bound for Europe and is received in a manner befitting the regal Countess Zattiany.

Mary Ogden's decision to reject an attractive suitor and devote her life to a political career was certainly unusual. Perhaps the ending was inevitable because Corrine Griffith played a rejuvenated beauty with a past full of romantic and political intrigue. In effect, Mary's future could be interpreted as the usual fate of a fallen woman rather than the result of an extraordinary decision. The film had more subtle implications, however, because Mary received the unique opportunity to live her life over and chose a different route the second time. She has already lived through the disillusionment of marriage and several love affairs, including a serious attachment to Count Hohenauer. And undoubtedly, she has experienced the ebb of romantic love as she has the fading of her own beauty. With the lessons of the past before her, she decides to avoid a repetition of her first life. Novelist Gertrude Atherton wrote in the picture's press book:

> It was not so much the originality of the theme that appealed to me,...but the opportunity in feminine psychology such as no novelist had ever had before. The old mind in the young brain. The vitalities and the external loveliness of youth and the terrible sophistications of fifty-eight worldly years. A memory crowded with lovers and disillusions and that final revolt against sex that comes to a woman who has lived too hard.[16]

29. Corinne Griffith in *Black Oxen*

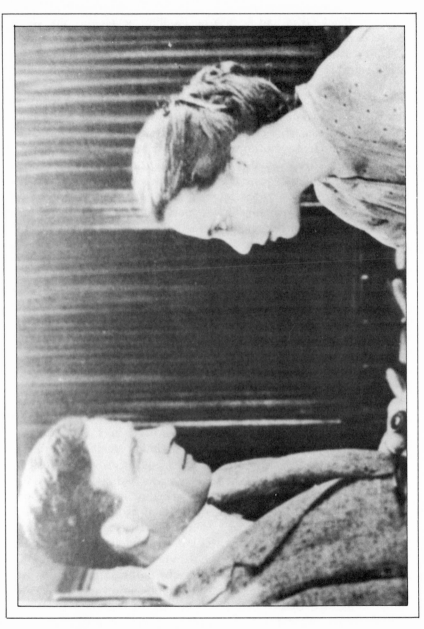

30. Lois Wilson in *Miss Lulu Bett*

Although *Black Oxen* had been a best-selling novel, the film version opened to mixed reviews and only did moderately well at the box-office. A *Variety* critic wrote, "It's a 50-50 break they'll eat it up if it isn't over their heads." [17] Ads exploited the unusual theme about an elderly woman's rejuvenation into a sexually desirable creature, but Clara Bow as the Countess' flapper rival may have had more audience appeal. The motivations of a sophisticated woman who was operating in a complex situation with past and present compounded were more difficult to appreciate. The film, whose title was lifted from a W.B. Yeats poem in which the years are likened to oxen treading the world, was certainly unusual in that it devalued the significance of love in a woman's psychology. According to the novel, "No woman had ever lived who was more completely disillusioned, more satiated, more scornful of that age-old dream of human happiness,..... ...Only the savages and the ignorant masses understood "love" for the transitory and functional thing it was...." [18] Assuredly, the woman in question was gifted and had a rare opportunity to exercise options, but that was all the more to the point. As Stendhal wrote in his inimitable style, "Do people really suggest that Madame Roland and Mistress Hutchinson spend their time in tending a little Bengal rose-bush?" And he asserted that a woman would become man's rival instead of companion "as soon as you have abolished love by law." [19]

The four heroines portrayed in these films were exceptions to the usual silent screen types because they attempted to redefine their identities and not necessarily in relation to men or to families. The women were certainly very different personalities and lived in a wide range of contrasting backgrounds. Lulu Bett is a timid, small-town spinster; Eva Knapp a frustrated, lower middle class housewife; Ethel Westcourt a glamorous and wealthy married woman who had been on the stage; and Mary Ogden a former New York socialite wedded to European royalty. Admittedly, there is a fantastic element in the stories about Mary Ogden's rejuvenation and Eva Knapp's successful role reversal. The problems which these four women confronted about the female personality and role, however, were decidedly real. The resolution of Lulu Bett, who asserts her independence by finding a modest job, was the most credible. But the posing of careers as an alternative or a complement to marriage and the portrayal of marriage itself as a negative choice were contrary to the usual happy ending. Unfortunately, research material about the production of these movies is scant, and it is difficult to speculate as to why the films were made in the first place. All four were adaptations of popular novels and stage dramas rather than original stories written for the screen, and this in itself is an interesting fact. Also interesting is the number of women writers involved in the screen adaptations or the originals. Possibly, there were other silent film adaptations, even original screenplays, as significant as these four in terms of the portrayal of women. The ratio, however, of unconventional to typed characterizations in the scores of film viewed for this study is so meager that it is safe to speculate the exceptions were few.

Chapter IX

CONCLUSION

During the teens and twenties, a significant change occurred in the screen image of woman so that feminine ideals which belonged to the previous Victorian era coexisted with more contemporary models. The continued appeal of the sentimental heroine was evidence that a type associated with the nineteenth century possessed attributes still identified as essentially feminine. According to the Victorian ideology of the spheres of the sexes, woman's place was in the home. As man's moral superior, she safeguarded the domestic sphere from corruption and inspired him to achieve spiritual excellence. The delicacy of her nature required, however, that the male should protect and shelter her from the cares of the external world. This differentiation between the Victorian male and female was extended to their sexual nature. Since the woman was an ethereal creature, she was also asexual. Sex was the ultimate evil from which she should be protected. As a quid pro quo, the virtuous woman's antiseptic nature prohibited and thus saved man from indulging in harmful excess. Ironically, women in the Victorian era continued to suffer a slow death through repeated pregnancies and died in large numbers as a result of childbirth. [1] Frigidity became an instinct for survival in an age both ignorant and condemnatory of birth control.

The characterization of the ideal Victorian woman had its counterpart in the temptress. Steven Marcus points out in his study of Victorian pornography that women were fantasized as possessing an endless capacity for and enjoyment of sex. [2] Such fantasies raised provocative questions because they ran counter to accepted social and cultural beliefs. Apparently, the asexual and virtuous woman was not above suspicion. Any wonder then that woman, characterized as passive and dependent, was restricted to the home? Or that she was weighted down with the obligation to save man from his appetites within the confines of marriage? The temptress, on the other hand, was a sexually devouring woman who consumed man but in doing so, eased his burden of guilt and responsibility. Whether the woman was virginal or impure, she was the one who bore the onus of man's incapacity or unwillingness to deal with his sexuality.

The silent screen actresses who best represented the Victorian tradition were Lillian Gish and Mary Pickford, on the one hand, and Theda Bara, on the other. Gish epitomized the child-woman who functioned as both victim and redeemer in the moral drama enacted by males. Pickford executed a reversal of Victorian orthodoxy by displaying courage and independence in a style calculated to overcome obstacles in a fatherless world. A great deal of Pickford's appeal lay in her refusal to enter the world of grownups with its prescribed sex roles. The obverse side of the pubescent Gish-Pickford heroine was the sexually alluring and devastating temptress. As a vampire, she was so overwhelming that her reign was short-lived and her successor, the vamp, was reduced to the status of a fallen woman. The vamp was even redeemed by love for a man in much the same way that the sentimental heroine's devotion saved him. Although a woman's love generated considerable redemptive power, in either case, it rendered her powerless in the grip of emotion. The Vampire remained invulnerable because she was immune to romantic love.

During the Jazz Age, the Victorian image of woman coexisted with contemporary types such as the working girl and the "new woman." Essentially, woman's sexual nature was redefined but in such a way that her domestic role was largely unquestioned. It was now acceptable for the young woman of the twenties to rebel against social convention before marriage, but marry she did. And that meant the assumption of woman's traditional function in the home. The essence then of the changing screen image of woman during the teens and twenties was her maturation into a sexual being. This transition has largely been ascribed to postwar developments in motion even before the war, especially the acceptance of the "consumption ethic" with both its conservative and non-traditional effects. The sexual sell linked in the minds of the public an updated and liberated concept of female sexuality with a hedonistic life style based upon acquisition of material goods.

Corresponding to changes in the image of woman and undoubtedly acting as an impetus was a shift in the popular image of the male. "The little man" became a familiar figure in a mechanized and standardized society which signalled the end of the era of rugged individualism. King Vidor's portrayal of a character aptly named John in his famous film, *The Crowd* (1928), is the story of an insignificant but hopeful individual overwhelmed by urban size and complexity. Significantly, the woman in the film emerges as the stronger character. Vidor's characterization, though cinematically detailed in an impressive fashion, was not unusual. In flapper films, for example, the "new woman," who both resembled and acted like a man, effects a role reversal and becomes the aggressive and reckless pursuer vis à vis lackluster males. Furthermore, in a few of the silent era's best-known films about male camaraderie and barracks life, there is an unmistakable current of homosexuality. Antagonism between males caused by rivalry for the same woman is resolved in undying friendship in such films as *What Price Glory* (1926), *Wings* (1927), *Flesh and the Devil* (1927), and *A Girl in Every Port*. [3] Of course, there was a reverse side to male characterizations in twenties film in that superheroic males like Fairbanks, Valentino, and Barrymore rescued damsels in distress. Interestingly, these films were melodramatic period pieces often set in faraway times and exotic locales.

Although the film industry both mirrored and reenforced changes in social perceptions about female sexuality during the Jazz Age, it was dishonest in its version of the working girl. She was modern in the sense that she earned her own living for a period of time, but she was still a victim of the Cinderella syndrome. [4] Needless to say, in movies as opposed to real life, the Cinderella story came true. According to the happy ending formula which typified most films (whether the heroine was a working girl or not), the woman realized her fate through Prince Charming rather than assume the onerous burden of becoming an entity in her own right. Any exceptions such as the character of Ethel Westcourt in *Dancing Mothers* were a distinct minority. Ethel walks into uncertainty when she rejects the traditional role of wife and mother and a new romance as well, but she confronts the obligation she s to search for her own identity. The film's open-ended conclusion ntrasts with evasion of reality as the usual screen resolution of a nplex life dilemma.

a fantasy, the Cinderella tale was apppealing because it satisfied emotional need on the part of women for whom there was no such t but who daydreamed about it. Undoubtedly, there was a negative d harmful element in the process of layering reality with movie make-lieve. And such fantasies reenforced the stereotyped image of the man who defined herself principally through a romantic attachment men. But there was, to be positive, a refreshing quality of innocence the transparent wish fulfillment of these films. As a reflection of ciety, the silent picture evinced a certain tone as well as narrative d charaterization. The silent movie era, described as the cinema's e of innocence, was sometimes naive and mirrored a quality in the nerican scene during the twenties which has provoked nostalgia. at decade evokes memories of such disparate events as the Red are and flag pole sitting, the Monkey Trial and bathtub gin. The vies of the period were ingenuous to the extent that life's realities re erased and its complexities unwound by the happy ending. The ference in attitude towards women between movies then and movies w, which focus a great deal upon sexual and physical brutality, is a asure of the changes which have taken place in our fantasy and real es.

NOTES

Chapter I

1 Robert M. Henderson, *D.W. Griffith: His Life and Work* (Ne
York: Oxford University Press, 1972), pp. 112-14.

2 *Ibid.*, pp. 42, 57; James Card, "The Films of Mary Pickford,
Image, VIII (December, 1959), 187.

3 Lillian Gish with Ann Pinchot, *The Movies, Mr. Griffith and M*
(New York: Avon Books, 1970), p. 35.

4 Henderson, pp. 115, 173-74, 190-91.

5 Gish, p. 102.

6 Arthur Lennig, *The Silent Voice* (Albany, New York: Facult
Student Assn. of the State University of New York at Albany, 1960
p. 22.

7 Parker Tyler, *The Hollywood Hallucination* (New York: Creativ
Age Press, 1944), pp. 78-81.

8 *Fighting a Vicious Film: Protest Against The Birth of a Natio*
(Boston: Boston Branch of the N.A.A.C.P., 1915) quoted in *Focus c*
D.W. Griffith, ed. Harry M. Geduld (Englewood Cliffs, New Jerse
Prentice-Hall, Inc., 1971), p. 94.

9 I saw *The Birth of a Nation* at a public screening in 1972 atten
ed mostly by film students. The audience was so affected by the pictu
that it burst into cheers when the Klan rode to the rescue at the en
The impact of the film must have been even greater among uneducat
audiences more than half a century ago.

10 Seymour Stern lists the sources which Griffith consulted
"Griffith: I--The Birth of a Nation," *Film Culture,* No. 36 (Sprin
Summer, 1965). According to Stern, "Griffith quoted material on th
Ku Klux Klan...[from Wilson's *A History of the American Peopl*
"Reunion and Nationalization"] in the introductory subtitles of Pa

Two of the film. Beginning in December, 1915, because of the public interest aroused by Griffith's citation of the work as an authoritative source..., the Chicago Daily News instituted a serialized publication of the book.'' (p. 35.) Griffith also used Original Ku Klux Klan Documents, Propaganda Hand Bills, Specimen Notices and Terror Warnings supplied by Thomas Dixon, Jr., author of fictional works titled *The Clansman* and *The Leopard's Spots,* which inspired the film. (pp. 34-36.) Stern writes that "both Thomas Dixon, Jr. and Henry B. Walthall...came of families whose earlier members had been Klansmen...and from Dixon and Walthall Griffith received the most veracious possible advice on Klan organization, regalia, ritual, and terror.'' (p. 36.) Stern further records that Dixon attended Johns Hopkins during the years when Wilson was a graduate student at that university, 1883-1885. (p. 75.)

The controversy and furor caused by *The Birth of a Nation* undoubtedly contributed to its commercial success. The fund raising efforts for the film resulted in a total budget of $110,000, but eventually it grossed more than $48,000,000. (Robert M. Henderson, *D.W. Griffith,* New York: Oxford University Press, 1972, pp. 148-49, 161.)

[11] Gish, p. 221.

[12] Henderson, p. 204. Since figures for film receipts vary, sources will be cited.

[13] Lillian Gish papers, Box 16, Library of Congress, Washington, D.C. (Library hereafter cited as LC).

[14] The figures for the rights to the play and cost of scenario are cited in Henderson (p. 215). The estimate for the film's earnings is found in the Lillian Gish papers, Box 1, LC.

[15] Henderson, p. 223.

[16] Griffith desired to secure insurance for the principal players in the film, but the only person who passed the insurance company's physical examination was Lillian Gish.

[17] Gish, p. 210.

[18] Henderson, p. 220.

[19] Gish, p. 248.

[20] Henderson, pp. 238-39, 259-67. Colleen Moore states in her autobiography, *Silent Star* (Garden City, New York: Doubleday & Co., Inc., 1968): "Lillian told me once that Griffith asked her to marry him, but she would not say why she refused him.... Whatever happened between them, Griffith soon began courting...Carol Dempster.... More

significant in the long run, he began giving Carol Dempster starring roles--roles that should have gone to Lillian." (p. 68.)

I have seen three films which Griffith made with Dempster in the lead: *Dream Street* (1921), *Isn't Life Wonderful* (1924), and *Sally of th[e] Sawdust* (1925). Significantly, the themes of rape and victimization ar[e] absent. That formula worked only too well with Gish, and Griffith deserves credit for discerning her peculiar appeal as a heroine[.] Dempster was certainly not a Gish type. There is a brief shot of her as [a] seductive woman amidst the crowd at the trial in *Orphans of the Storm*[.] The role she played in *Dream Street,* Gypsy Fair, is a contradiction as i[s] the character's name. She is convincing as a tease and a flirtatious gi[rl] who registers alarm when her lover becomes aggressive, but her mora[l] istic poses do not suit her. John H. Door suggested in an article title[d] "A Retrospective of the Griffith Era" (*Los Angeles Times Calenda[r]* June 13, 1971) that Dempster represented Griffith's changing worl[d] view in the twenties, when he came to see life less in terms of good [v] evil and more in terms of ambiguity.

21 Romano Tozzi, "Lillian Gish," *Films in Review* (Decembe[r] 1962), 587 (in Lillian Gish clipping file, Academy of Motion Picture Ar[t] and Sciences, Los Angeles; Academy hereafter cited as AMPAS[).]

22 Albert Bigelow Paine, *Life and Lillian Gish* (New Yor[k] Macmillan Co., 1932), p. 191.

23 *The White Sister,* non-catalogued scrapbook, Library for t[he] Performing Arts, Lincoln Center, New York (Library hereafter cited [as] LPA).

24 Seymour Peck, "Then and Now: Lillian Gish," *New York Tim[es] Magazine* (April 17, 1960; in the Lillian Gish clipping file, AMPA[S]

25 King Vidor, *A Tree Is a Tree* (New York: Harcourt, Brace, [&] Co., 1952), p. 131.

26 Gish, p. 280.

27 Telephone conversation with Lillian Gish, New York, Octob[er] 21, 1972.

28 While speaking before a theater arts seminar at U.C.L.A. [on] November 26, 1968, Gish referred to the story as "good, strong me[lo] drama" as well as a record of historical interest.

29 Gish quotes the *Sun* critic in her autobiography (p. 290). Alb[ert] Bigelow Paine related that after a private screening of the film so[me] years later, Gish remarked, "I was too immature to play the part. S[he] was a woman. I looked just like a child." (p. 231.)

The Scarlet Letter, non-catalogued scrapbook, LPA.

Gish, p. 292.

The Wind, non-catalogued scrapbook, LPA.

Arthur Mayer, "Lillian Gish," New York Times (June 8, 1969; ian Gish clipping file, AMPAS).

Joseph Hergesheimer, "Lillian Gish," The American Mercury, I , 1924), 397-402.

Edward Wagenknecht, The Movies in the Age of Innocence York: Ballantine Books, 1962), p. 243.

Quoted in Paine, p. 208.

Louise Brooks, "Gish and Garbo: The Executive War on Stars," and Sound, XXVIII (Winter, 1958-1959), 13-17.

The Torrent, see also Chapter V.

La Boheme, non-catalogued scrapbook; The Torrent, non-gued scrapbook, LPA.

La Boheme, non-catalogued scrapbook, LPA.

The Wind, non-catalogued scrapbook, LPA.

The White Sister, program for the World's Premiere at the -fourth Street Theater in New York, September 5, 1923, LPA.

NOTES

Chapter II

1 Mary Pickford, *Sunshine and Shadow* (Garden City, New Yor Doubleday & Co., 1955), p. 31.

2 *Ibid.*, p. 42.

3 Albert Bigelow Paine, *Life and Lillian Gish* (New York: T Macmillan Co., 1932), p. 34.

4 Pickford, p. 93.

5 Mary Pickford, "My Own Story," *Ladies' Home Journal* (Ju 1923; in Mary Pickford clipping file, Library for the Performing Ar Lincoln Center, New York; Library hereafter cited as LPA).

6 Pickford, *Sunshine and Shadow*, p. 101.

7 *Ibid.*, pp. 102-03.

8 *Ibid.*, p. 110.

9 Mrs. D.W. Griffith (Linda Arvidson), *When the Movies We Young* (New York: Dover Publications, Inc., 1969), p. 106.

10 Pickford, *Sunshine and Shadow*, pp. 122-23.

11 Letter from William deMille to David Belasco, Merriewald Pa New York, July 25, 1911 (in William deMille papers, New York Pub Library, New York City).

12 Pickford, *Sunshine and Shadow*, p. 157.

13 *Ibid.*, p. 159.

14 James Card, "The Films of Mary Pickford," *Image*, V December, 1959), 179.

15 Adolph Zukor, *The Public Is Never Wrong* (New York: G Putnam's Sons, 1953), p. 97.

16 *Ibid.*, p. 99.

17 *Ibid.*, p. 110.

[18] Benjamin B. Hampton, *History of the American Film Industry* (New York: Dover Publications, Inc., 1970), p. 190.

[19] Mary Pickford scrapbook, Robinson Locke Collection, LPA.

[20] Pickford, *Sunshine and Shadow*, p. 163.

[21] Zukor, pp. 114-15.

[22] Pickford, *Sunshine and Shadow*, pp. 163-64.

[23] *Ibid.*, p. 165.

[24] Zukor, pp. 129-30.

[25] Terry Ramsaye, *A Million and One Nights*, 2 vols., (New York: Simon & Schuster, 1926), II, 709.

[26] *Ibid.*, p. 710.

[27] Mary Pickford scrapbook, Robinson Locke Collection, LPA.

[28] Zukor, p. 176.

[29] Pickford, *Sunshine and Shadow*, p. 171.

[30] *Ibid.*, p. 177.

[31] *Ibid.*, p. 185.

[32] Hampton, pp. 195-96.

[33] *Ibid.*, p. 192.

[34] Margaret Case Harriman, "Profiles," *The New Yorker* (April 7,), 29-33.

[35] Hampton, p. 234.

[36] Mary Pickford clipping file, LPA.

[37] Pickford, *Ladies Home Journal* (July, 1923; in Mary Pickford clipping file, LPA).

[38] Zukor, p. 171.

[39] Card, 172-87.

[40] Richard Griffith and Arthur Mayer, *The Movies* (New York: Bonanza Books, 1957), p. 57.

[41] Alexander Walker, *The Celluloid Sacrifice* (New York: Hawthorne Books, Inc., 1966), p. 43.

[42] Lewis Jacobs, *The Rise of American Film* (New York: Teachers College Press, Columbia University, 1939), p. 265.

[43] Mary Pickford scrapbook, Robinson Locke Collection, LPA.

[44] Jack Spears, *Hollywood: The Golden Era* (New York: A.S. Barnes & Co., 1971), p. 181.

[45] The following analysis of Pickford films is based on sixteen features which constitute about half of the extant collection of the star's best features at the Library of Congress and at George Eastman House, including her best-known classics. These are *Tess of the Storm Country* (1914), *Rags* (1915), *A Poor Little Rich Girl* (1917), *Rebecca of*

Sunnybrook Farm (1917), *Stella Maris* (1917), *Amarilly of Clothes Li* *Alley* (1918), *Daddy Long Legs* (1919), *Heart o' the Hills* (1919 *Pollyanna* (1920), *Suds* (1920), *Love Light* (1921), *Little Lord Fauntler* (1921), *Dorothy Vernon of Haddon Hall* (1924), *Little Annie Roon* (1925), *Sparrows* (1926), and *My Best Girl* (1927).

46 Mary Pickford scrapbook, Robinson Locke Collection, LP.

47 Brownlow, p. 146. Significantly, *Tess* was the only picture whi Pickford ever remade.

48 Mary Pickford scrapbook, Robinson Locke Collection, LP.

49 Adela Rogers St. Johns, "Why Does the World Love Mary" *Photoplay*, XXI (December, 1929), 110.

50 *My Best Girl*, see also Chapter V.

51 "Mary Pickford Awards," *Photoplay*, XXIX (October, 192 109.

52 Mary Pickford scrapbook, Robinson Locke Collection, LP

53 Pickford, *Sunshine and Shadow*, p. 237.

54 Lillian Gish, *The Movies, Mr. Griffith and Me* (New Yo Avon Books, 1970), p. 20.

55 Julian Johnson, "Mary Pickford: Herself and Her Career *Photoplay*, VIII (November, 1951), 61.

56 Pickford, *Sunshine and Shadow*, pp. 350-51.

57 Mary Pickford scrapbook, Robinson Locke Collection, LP

58 Pickford did make a screen version of *Madame Butterfly* in 19 but it too was not well received by her public. I have not seen the fil

59 Mary Pickford clipping file, LPA.

60 Helen Papashvily's *All the Happy Endings* (New York: Harp & Bros., 1956) is an excellent work about sentimental novels and t women who wrote them.

61 Pickford, *Sunshine and Shadow*, pp. 293-95.

62 Adela Rogers St. Johns, "Why Mary Pickford Bobbed *F* Hair," *Photoplay*, XXXIV (September, 1928), 33, 128-29.

63 Mary Pickford, "Please May I Bob My Hair?" *Liberty* (Ju 1928; in Mary Pickford clipping file, Academy of Motion Picture A and Sciences, Los Angeles.)

64 Clare Boothe Brokaw, "Mary Pickford: The End of an Era (in Mary Pickford clipping file, LPA).

NOTES

Chapter III

[1] The Dark Lady in American literature could be a magnificent
roine such as a Cora or a Zenobia, but on the Hollywood screen, the
mpire was nothing more than a caricature.

[2] "The Vampire" by Rudyard Kipling, 1897.

A fool there was and he made his prayer
(Even as you and I!)
To a rag and a bone and a hank of hair
(We called her the woman who did not care)
But the fool he called her his lady fair--
(Even as you and I!)

Oh, the years we waste and the tears we waste
And the work of our head and hand
Belong to the woman who did not know
(And now we know that she never could know)
And did not understand!

A fool there was his goods he spent
(Even as you and I!)
Honour and faith and a sure intent
(And it wasn't the least what the lady meant)
(Even as you and I!)

Oh, the toil we lost and the spoil we lost
And the excellent things we planned
Belong to the woman who didn't know why

(And now we know that she never knew why)
And did not understand!

The fool was stripped to his foolish hide
(Even as you and I!)
Which she might have seen when she threw him aside--
(But it isn't on record the lady tried)
So some of him lived but most of him died--
(Even as you and I!)

And it isn't the shame and it isn't the blame
That sings like a white-hot brand--
It's coming to know that she never knew why
(Seeing, at last, she could never know why)
And never could understand!

3 A Kalem film titled *The Vampire* (1913) featured Bert French and Alice Eis in their famous "Vampire Dance." This extraordinary dance sequence depicts a young man ensnared by a seductive woman, whose sinuous movements suggest a serpent rather than a vampire. A young man in the audience viewing the dance understands that he is witnessing a parable of his own moral decline. Since he came to the city, he has abandoned his country sweetheart for a sophisticated woman who is both exploitive and heartless. All ends well, however.

4 Theda Bara clipping file, Library for the Performing Arts, Lincoln Center, New York (Library hereafter cited as LPA).

5 Theda Bara scrapbook, Robinson Locke Collection, LPA.

6 This description of Theda Bara's publicity is based upon materials in the Theda Bara clipping files and scrapbooks at the LPA; Edward Wagenknecht's *The Movies in the Age of Innocence* (New York: Ballantine Books, 1962), pp. 169-170; Lewis Jacobs' *The Rise of the American Film* (New York: Columbia University, Teachers' College Press, 1939), pp. 266-67; Arthur Mayer's and Richard Griffith's *The Movies* (New York: Bonanza Books, 1957), pp. 66-69; Alexander Walker's *The Celluloid Sacrifice* (New York: Hawthorne Books, Inc., 1966), pp. 19-27.

7 The articles cited are in the Theda Bara scrapbooks, Robinson Locke Collection, LPA.

8 Theda Bara, non-catalogued scrapbook, LPA.

9 Theda Bara scrapbook, Robinson Locke Collection, LPA.

10 Karen Horney, *Feminine Psychology* (New York: W.W. Norton & Co., 1967), pp. 138-39.

Theda Bara scrapbooks, Robinson Locke Collection, LPA.

Ibid.

Ibid.

Ibid.

Ibid.

Ibid.

Ibid.

Horney, p. 112.

Kate Millett, *Sexual Politics* (Garden City, New York: leday & Co., 1970), pp. 152-56.

Jose Ortega y Gasset, *On Love* (Cleveland: Meridian Books, , pp. 159-65.

Salome, non-catalogued scrapbook, LPA.

According to Kevin Brownlow, director Fred Niblo told Carmel s, who played Iras, to find "the most exciting headdress ever seen e screen." She came up with a white silk wig. (*The Parades Gone* Jew York: Ballantine Books, 1968, p. 461.) Ramon Novarro, who ast as Ben Hur, came already equipped for the role. The actor told g Thalberg, "You know what I can do, Irving. And if you're ed about my legs--you saw them in *Where the Pavement Ends.* 's nothing wrong with them." (Bob Thomas, *Thalberg,* Garden New York: Doubleday & Co., 1969, p. 71.)

For material on *Sunrise,* see *Quarterly Review of Film Studies,* Judley Andrew (Pleasantville, New York: Redgrave Publishing Vol. II, No. 3 (August, 1977).

The censorship board in Maryland cut the scene in which the e reclines and the man embraces the woman as she wriggles to ined dance music. (Morris L. Ernst and Pare Lorentz, *Censored,* York: Jonathan Cape and Harrison Smith, 1930, p. 38.)

Andrew Sarris makes an interesting comment about *Sunrise* by ng the theme of the vampire to Murnau's classic film about ıla, *Nosferatu.* (*Sunrise* clipping file, LPA.)

These clippings are in non-catalogued scrapbooks containing ws of *The Torrent, The Temptress,* and *Flesh and the Devil,* LPA.

Alexander Walker, *The Celluloid Sacrifice* (New York: Hawthorn s, 1966), p. 97.

Ibid., p. 66.

Flesh and the Devil, see also Conclusion.

Flesh and the Devil clipping file, LPA.

Flesh and the Devil, non-catalogued scrapbook, LPA.

[32] According to director Clarence Brown, the studio ordered him t shoot a happy ending. (Kevin Brownlow, *The Parades Gone By*, Ne York: Ballantine Books, Inc., 1968, p. 170.) If so, the film's conclusio would have entirely different implications with respect to the characte of the vamp and the friendship between the two men. The selection of happy or tragic ending for the film probably depended upon th exhibitor.

[33] *Flesh and the Devil*, non-catalogued scrapbook, LPA.

[34] Rudolph Arnheim, *Films*, trans. by L.M. Sieveking and Ian F.R Morrow (London: Faber & Faber, Ltd., 1933), p. 183.

[35] *Flesh and the Devil*, non-catalogued scrapbook, LPA.

[36] Parker Tyler, "The Garbo Image" in Michael Conway's *Th Films of Greta Garbo* (New York: The Citadel Press, 1968), p. 12

NOTES

Chapter IV

1 Alexis de Tocqueville, *Democracy in America,* trans. Henry eves (2 vols.; New York: A.B. Barnes & Co., 1863), II, 212.

2 In praising Mary Astor's performance, John Barrymore narked, "In these roles of the virginal heroines, virtue is its own ward." (*Don Juan* clipping file, Library for the Performing Arts, acoln Center, New York; Library hereafter cited as LPA). According Jack Warner in his *My First Hundred Years in Hollywood* (New rk: Random House, 1964), Barrymore originally protested the sting of Mary Astor as his leading lady: " 'Mary Astor!' he snapped. clod alongside of my winkie [Delores Costello].' " (p. 168.)

3 *Seventh Heaven,* non-catalogued scrapbook, LPA. The film was the ten best list of other critics.

4 According to Claire Windsor, Lois Weber was successful enough a director to maintain her own motion picture studio and thus ntrolled every step in the production of her films. Interview with aire Windsor, Los Angeles, August 2, 1971.

5 *A Woman of Affairs* is discussed later in this chapter.

6 Conversation with James Card, Rochester, New York, vember, 1972.

7 *The Torrent,* see also Chapter I.

8 Kevin Brownlow, *The Parades Gone By* (New York: Ballantine oks, 1968), p. 169.

9 Mordaunt Hall, *New York Times* (March 24, 1929), George C. att in *Spellbound in Darkness* (2 vols.; Rochester, New York: iversity of Rochester, 1966), II, 400.

10 Unfortunately, films were subject to censorship in a way that

novels, magazines, and stage plays were not. The states could and
exercise censorship through boards which previewed films and
undesirable scenes or changed offensive titles, but there was always
movement afoot to effect a national system of censorship under t
interstate commerce clause. The moviemakers disarmed this mov
ment by fighting fire with fire and submitted to a form of self-impos
censorship. As early as 1909, a committee of motion picture produce
agreed to a form of supervision under the National Board of Cens
ship, later the National Board of Review. But this body came incre
ingly under attack from outspoken individuals and organizations su
as the General Federation of Women's Clubs, who claimed it was t
liberal. The industry's formation of the Motion Picture Producers a
Distributors of America under Will Hays in 1922 was a more success
effort to mollify critics and avert restrictive legislation.

[11] Morris L. Ernst and Pare Lorentz, *Censored* (New Yo
Jonathan Cape & Harrison Smith, 1930), pp. 17-18.

[12] *Ibid.*, p. 7.

[13] *Man, Woman and Sin,* non-catalogued scrapbook, LPA.

[14] *Ibid.*

NOTES

Chapter V

1 Report of the President's Research Committee on Social Trends, cent Social Trends in the United States (New York: McGraw-Hill Co., 33), pp. 711-12.

2 United States Department of Commerce, Statistical Abstract of United States (Washington: Government Printing Office, 1916), . 243-54; Statistical Abstract (1924), p. 57; Statistical Abstract (1933), 67.

3 Recent Social Trends, p. 713.

4 William E. Leuchtenberg, The Perils of Prosperity (Chicago: iversity of Chicago Press, 1958), p. 225.

5 Recent Social Trends, p. 715.

6 Mary Ross, "Shall We Join the Gentlemen?" Survey, LVII cember 1, 1926), 265-66.

7 Recent Social Trends, p. 229.

8 Robert S. Lynd and Helen Merrell Lynd, Middletown, (New k: Harcourt, Brace, & World, Inc., 1929), p. 26.

9 Recent Social Trends, pp. 715-16.

10 Robert L. Dickinson and Lura Beam, The Single Woman: A dical Study in Sex Education (New York: Reynal & Hitchcock, Inc., 4), p. 351.

11 My Best Girl, see also Chapter II.

12 The movie flapper, unlike Fitzgerald's models, was for reasons censorship if nothing else, quite spirited in behavior but very contional in her moral standards. See The Plastic Age, Our Dancing ighters, Our Modern Maidens, Wine of Youth. For a further discus- of the Fitzgerald flapper and flapper films, as well as Zelda gerald as a model, see Chapter VI.

[13] Despite her being dubbed the "It Girl" after *It*, Clara Bow played flapper roles proper in films such as *Black Oxen, The Plastic Age,* and *Dancing Mothers,* all dated prior to *It.*

[14] Mary Pickford, see also Chapter II.

[15] Clipping files and scrapbooks, (non-catalogued), listed under names of the stars, Library for the Performing Arts, Lincoln Center New York City and Academy of Motion Picture Arts and Sciences, Los Angeles.

[16] *Ibid.*

[17] Kevin Brownlow, *The Parades Gone By* (New York: Ballantine Books, 1968), p. 330.

[18] Iris Barry, *Let's Go to the Movies* (New York: Payson & Clarke Ltd., 1926), p. 65.

NOTES

Chapter VI

[1] The Fitzgerald quote is taken from his essay about the twenties, ~~hoes~~ of the Jazz Age," *Scribner's*, XV (November, 1931), 459-65. A ~~dard~~ description of the twenties is journalist Frederick Lewis ~~n's~~ *Only Yesterday* (New York:Bantam Books, 1959; copyrighted in ~~)~~, whose kaleidoscopic style reminds the reader of a newsreel. Also ~~able~~ is journalist Mark Sullivan's multi-volume history, *Our Times* ~~York~~: Charles Scribner's Sons, c. 1926). William E. Leuchtenburg ~~ents~~ a concise historical survey with a comprehensive biblio-~~hical~~ essay in *Perils of Prosperity* (Chicago: University of Chicago ~~s~~, 1958). Literary critic Malcolm Cowly describes the Greenwich ~~ge~~ revolt against puritanism in *The Exile's Return* (New York: Viking Press, 1951; copyrighted in 1934). Sociological tracts ~~de~~ *Recent Social Trends in the United States* (New York: McGraw-Book Co., Inc., 1933), a report by a presidential research com-~~ee~~. Also insightful is *The Lonely Crowd* (New York: Doubleday ~~hor~~ Books, 1950) by David Riesman et al. John McGovern argues ~~vincingly~~ that the sexual revolution began in the teens rather than ~~twenties~~ in an article titled "The American Woman's Pre World ~~I~~ Freedom in Manners and Morals," *Journal of American History*, September, 1968, 315-33.

[2] Leuchtenberg, p. 83. The Fitzgerald remark is from his essay, ~~hoes~~ of the Jazz Age."

[3] See William L. O'Neill, *Everyone Was Brave* (Chicago: ~~drangle~~ Books, 1969), Chapter 9.

[4] Virginia Woolf, *A Room of One's Own* (New York: Harcourt, ~~ce~~ & World, Inc., 1929), p. 37.

187

5 Cowley, p. 62.

6 Leuchtenberg, p. 172.

7 According to the Lynds (*Middletown,* New York: Harcou Brace & World, Inc., 1929), "The lessening of the number of ho spent daily in getting a living and in home-making and the alm universal habit of the Saturday half-holiday...make leisure a m generally accepted part of every day.... ...Its more striking aspe relate to the coming of inventions, the automobile, the movies, radio...." (p. 226.)

8 Carrie A. Hall, *From Hoopskirts to Nudity* (Caldwell, Ida The Caxton Printers, Ltd., 1946).

9 G. Stanley Hall, "Flapper Americana Novissima, *Atlar Monthly,* CXXIX (June 22, 1922), 776-78.

10 Eleanor Rowland Wembridge, "Petting and the Campus *Survey,* LIV (July 1, 1925), 393.

11 Patricke Johns Heine and Hans G. Gerth, "Values in Ma Periodical Fiction, 1921-1940," *The Popular Arts,* eds. Berna Rosenberg and David White Manning (Glencoe, Ill.: The Free Pre 1957), pp. 226-34.

12 Henry Adams, *The Education of Henry Adams* (Bost Houghton Mifflin Co., 1961; copyrighted in 1918), p. 496.

13 C. Wright Mills, *White Collar* (New York: Oxford Univers Press, 1956), pp. xii-xiv.

14 David Riesman et al., *The Lonely Crowd* (Garden City, N York: Doubleday & Co., 1950), pp. 106, 173.

15 Steven Marcus, *The Other Victorians* (New York: Basic Book Inc., 1964), p. 113.

16 Robert L. Dickinson and Lura Beam, *The Single Woman: Medical Study in Sex Education* (New York: Reynal & Hitchcock, In 1934), pp. 101, 145. A later study conducted by Lewis M. Term indicated that 63.1 percent of 777 wives who responded to questionair "disclaimed premarital sexual experience," but the figure for wom born in 1910 or later was 31.7 percent in comparison to 86.5 percent f women born before 1890. (*Psychological Factors in Marital Happines* New York: McGraw-Hill Book Co., 1938, pp. 320-21.) Dr. Gilbert V Tassel Hamilton's study of one hundred New York City wives co cluded that 54 percent of the women born in 1891 or later had no sexu experience prior to marriage, whereas the figure for women bo between 1886 and 1890 was 80 percent. (*A Research in Marriage,* Ne York: Albert and Charles Boni, Inc., 1929, p. 383.) These studies va

ieir figures with respect to the percentage of women who were
ns at marriage but indicate that their numbers were decreasing
time.

17 Edgar Dale, *The Content of Motion Pictures* (New York: The
millan Co., 1935), p. 19. This study was based upon an extensive
ysis of the themes of five hundred films released in 1920, five
lred released in 1925, and five hundred released in 1930. Forty
s from among those released in 1929, 1930, and 1931 were analyzed
reater depth. The investigator relied upon *Harrison Reports,* a
wing service for exhibitors, which furnished a short synopsis of
lot and commented upon the film's box-office value. I have found
the synopsis of a plot can be very misleading, especially because
ywood filmmakers had devious ways of dealing with themes of sex
morality.

18 Although film historians such as Lewis Jacobs (*The Rise of
rican Film,* New York: Columbia University, Teachers College
s, 1939) reel off titles such as *The Smart Set, Our Dancing
ghters, Darling of the Rich, Wildness of Youth, The Plastic Age,
y Business, Has the World Gone Mad?, Why Be Good?, Madness
uth, The Jazz Age,* and *Children of Divorce* to indicate that filmic
s abounded, most if not all of these titles are misleading. One has
to view the film to ascertain this. The number of flapper films
able for viewing is actually quite small, but the characterization of
ers in such films as *Our Dancing Daughters* and *The Plastic Age* is
ithout a moral.

19 E.M. Hull, *The Sheik* (Boston: Small, Maynard & Co., 1921),
.

20 *Ibid.,* p. 35.

21 *Ibid.,* pp. 60, 91-92.

22 *Ibid.,* p. 133.

23 Irving Shulman, *Valentino* (New York: Trident Press, 1967),
5.

24 *Ibid.,* pp. 161-62.

25 Herbert Blumer, *Movies and Conduct* (New York: Macmillan
1933), p. 16.

26 Kevin Brownlow, *The Parades Gone By* (New York: Ballantine
s, 1968), p. 210.

27 Lois Wilson has commented that although the film was a great
ing vehicle for Leatrice Joy, the characterization of O'Bannon and
plot were not very credible. (Interview with Lois Wilson, New

189

York, November 24, 1972.) DeMille portrays prison life in a m[...] realistic fashion in his last silent, *The Godless Girl* (1928).

28 *The Single Standard,* non-catalogued scrapbook, Library for [...] Performing Arts, Lincoln Center, New York (Library hereafter ci[...] as LPA).

29 Margaret Reid, "Has the Flapper Changed?" *Motion Pict[...] Magazine,* XXXIII, (July, 1927), 28-29, 104.

30 *Black Oxen,* see also Chapter VIII.

31 *Our Dancing Daughters,* non-catalogued scrapbook, LPA.

32 Blumer, p. 184.

33 *Ibid.*

34 F. Scott Fitzgerald, "The Jelly Bean," *Six Tales of the Jazz A[...]* (New York: Charles Scribner's Sons, 1960), pp. 17-34. According to [...] biographer, Nancy Milford (*Zelda,* New York: Avon Books, 19[...] originally submitted as a Ph.D. dissertation at Columbia), Zeld[...] tragic life as "the first American flapper" illustrated the difficulty[...] creating new identities for women unrestrained by convention [...] restrained by conventional marriage. Milford quotes one of Sco[...] remarks to Malcolm Cowley about his wife, "Sometimes I don't kn[...] whether Zelda isn't a character I created myself." (p. 338.) But Ze[...] was already a rebellious Southern belle when she met Scott and such[...] original personality in her own right that he recreated her in his ficti[...] Even so, critic Jonathan Peale Bishop remarked that Scott ne[...] captured her "hard intelligence, nor her intricate emotional equ[...] ment." Significantly, Scott would not permit the publication of [...] diaries which provided material for stories such as "The Jelly Bea[...] (which they co-authored) although George Jean Nathan made Zelda [...] offer. (p. 98.) Also, stories which the Fitzgeralds co-authored w[...] published only under Scott's name. See Zelda Fitzgerald's *Save Me [...] Waltz,* an autobiographical novel (Carbondale, Ill.: Southern Illin[...] University Press, 1967).

35 *Ibid.,* p. 27.

36 *Ibid.,* p. 34.

37 *Ibid.,* p. 23.

38 O'Neill, pp. 304-306.

39 Bernice Kenyon, "Girl Graduates--Ten Years Out," *Scribne[...] LXXXIX (January, 1931), 640-43.

NOTES

Chapter VII

[1] The linking of the names of these directors is common enough ritings about American film, but it has not always been complimen-. According to Herman G. Weinberg, "Stroheim was the true ator of a 'sophisticated' cinema. ...But the art of the 'sophisticated' ma was degraded, corrupted, and commercialized by others. ilettantes appeared, with all the surface polish and superficial s which Stroheim could not or would not have. Let us be generous name no names." ("Erich Von Stroheim," *Introduction to the Art he Movies,* ed. Lewis Jacobs, New York: Noonday Press, 1960, 2.)

[2] William deMille, "Great Pictures and the Men Who Made m," William deMille papers, New York Public Library, New York.

[3] Cecil B. DeMille, *The Autobiography of Cecil B. DeMille,* ed. ald Hayne (Englewood Cliffs, New Jersey: Prentice-Hall, 1959), 12.

[4] *Ibid.,* p. 209-10.

[5] Conversation with James Card, Rochester, New York, ember, 1972.

[6] Benjamin B. Hampton, *History of the American Film Industry* w York: Dover Publications, Inc., 1970), p. 194.

[7] *Ibid.,* p. 249.

[8] Cecil B. DeMille, p. 226.

[9] A few of the amusing titles from *Why Change Your Wife?* are oduced in an illustrated pamphlet in the collection at the Library for Performing Arts, Lincoln Center, New York (Library hereafter d as LPA).

10 Ernest W. Burgess, "The Romantic Impulse and Family Di organization," *Survey,* LVII (December 1, 1926), 293.

11 *Way Down East,* see also Chapter I.

12 William L. O'Neill, *Divorce in the Progressive Era* (New Have Yale University Press, 1967).

13 *Blind Husbands,* non-catalogued scrapbook, LPA.

14 The film's original title was *The Pinnacle.* Stroheim objected *Blind Husbands,* but Carl Laemmle shrewdly put the question exhibitors and followed their decision. (Thomas Quinn Curtiss, *Vc Stroheim,* London: Angus & Robertson, 1971, pp. 101-103.)

15 At the Museum of Modern Art, I viewed a 16 mm. print whi had been acquired from Universal but was probably one of the studio mutilated properties. In contrast to a British Film Institute print whi I also viewed, the sequences are differently arranged and the film h less footage. Hughes is characterized as a wealthy American busines man rather than government official, and the ceremonial scenes of tl Hughes' arrival at Monte Carlo as well as the ambassador's subseque reception by the prince are missing. The final scene involving tl attack upon Ventucci's daughter is very much mutilated in both print Also, in neither print is there the slightest indication that Mrs. Hugh is pregnant and gives premature birth to a child, as Stroheim indicat in a plot summary he wrote. MOMA also has a 35 mm. print recent reconstructed by the American Film Institute. It has more transition footage between scenes and contains about ten additional minut viewing time. This print appears to approximate more closely the B version. I have not seen it. The Library for the Performing Arts Lincoln Center has two Universal stillbooks which contain scen missing from both the prints which I viewed, but the stills are n arranged in narrative sequence.

According to Stroheim, the MOMA print (probably the 16 mm. versio contains 7,000 of the original 21,000 feet. In contrast to *Foolish Wive* Stroheim shot only 9,000 feet while filming *Blind Husbands* and c only 1,000 feet from the final version. (Herman G. Weinberg, *Sai Cinema,* New York: Dover Publications, Inc., 1970, p. 132.)

16 Curtiss, pp. 121-22.

17 "Foolish Wives," *Photoplay,* XXI (March, 1922), in George (Pratt, *Spellbound in Darkness* (2 vols.; Rochester, New York: Unive sity of Rochester, 1966), II, 287.

18 *Foolish Wives,* non-catalogued scrapbook, LPA.

[19] Mordaunt Hall, "Persistent von Stroheim Conquered Film
ignate," *New York Times* (December 14, 1924), in Pratt, II, 286.

[20] The characterization of Mae Murray as a follies dancer in *The
erry Widow* is an exception. As Sally O'Hara, she is appealing and
tatious but also demands to be treated with propriety. And though
bivalent, she is a sensual woman who yields to her lover before the
dding and hardly comes to grief since a happy ending replaced a
re tragic one.

[21] Hampton, p. 300.

[22] *A Woman of Affairs* and *Sadie Thompson*, see also Chapter IV.

[23] Ernst Lubitsch clipping file, LPA.

[24] *Ibid.*

[25] *One Hour With You*, the 1932 sound remake by Lubitsch starred
gers Maurice Chevalier and Jeanette MacDonald. I thought it rather
ore and the Lubitsch touch heavy-handed. Richard Watts, Jr., *New
rk Herald Tribune* critic, wrote at the time the sound film was
eased: "I enjoyed it immensely, and yet, contemplating it later, I
nd that I had been grudging in my admiration, spending most of my
e recalling certain superior merits of 'The Marriage Circle.'...It
rely happened that in 'The Marriage Circle' Lubitsch hit upon a self-
staining medium, and that the addition of song and talk to something
eady complete seemed not unlike painting a handsome piece of
lpture or sticking a microphone in its mouth." (Ernst Lubitsch
ping file.) The advent of sound was not always welcomed by film-
kers and critics who appreciated the perfection of a silent medium.

[26] Herman G. Weinberg, *The Lubitsch Touch* (New York: E.P.
tton & Co., Inc., 1968), p. 57.

[27] Iris Barry, "The Cinema: Hope Fulfilled," *Spectator*, Vol. 132,
. 5003 (May 14, 1924), in Pratt, II, 275.

[28] Dorothy Dunbar Bromley, "Feminist--New Style," *Harper's*,
V (October, 1927), 555.

[29] "The Wife's Share," *One Hundred Years of the American
nale from Harper's Bazaar* (New York: Random House, 1967), 22.

[30] Sinclair Lewis, *Main Street* (New York: New American Library,
1), p. 74.

[31] *Ibid.*, p. 170.

[32] A chart titled "Marriages, Divorces and Annulments" in the
partment of Commerce *Statistical Abstract of the United States
ashington, D.C.: Government Printing Office, 1933) indicates that
number of divorces per 1,000 marriages rose from 81 in 1900 to 170

in 1930. The most interesting statistic is not necessarily the ris
divorce rate but the greater number of decrees granted to wives
opposed to husbands. The figure of 33.4 percent in 1900 increased
72.3 percent in 1930. (p. 90.)

33 Robert S. Lynd and Helen Merrell Lynd, *Middletown* (N
York: Harcourt, Brace & World, Inc., 1929), p. 127.

34 Report of the President's Research Committee on Social Tren
Recent Social Trends in the United States (New York: McGraw-Hill C
1933), p. 694.

35 Lynd and Lynd, pp. 122-23.

36 Robert L. Dickinson and Lura Beam, *The Single Woman* (N
York: Reynal & Hitchcock, Inc., 1934), p. 62. See also Chapter VI.

37 Robert L. Dickinson and Lura Beam, *A Thousand Marriages
Medical Study of Sex Adjustment* (Baltimore: Williams & Wilkins C
1931), p. 61.

38 David M. Kennedy, *Birth Control in America: The Career
Margaret Sanger* (New Haven: Yale University Press, 1970), pp. 19,
76, 106, 113, 124, 127, 160, 176, 211, 218-21, 243, 290.

39 *Recent Social Trends,* p. 683.

40 Lynd and Lynd, p. 123.

41 Katherine B. Davis, *Factors in the Sex Life of Twenty-T
Hundred Woman* (New York: Harper & Bros., 1929), p. 14. Da
conducted a study of one thousand women who responded to
questionaire about their married life. Eight hundred seventy-t
women indicated that their marriage was a happy one. (pp. 38-39.
study of one hundred married men and an equal number of marr
women living in New York City by Gilbert Van Tassel Hamilton yiel
the following results: 51 percent of the men and 45 percent of
women had "fairly" or "obviously" successful marriages. (*A Resea
in Marriage,* New York: Albert and Charles Boni, Inc., 1929, pp. 80-8
Lewis M. Terman published a study based upon 792 married coup
in California. The mean "happiness scores" were 68.40 for husba
and 69.25 for wives. (*Psychological Factors in Marital Happiness,* N
York: McGraw-Hill Book Co., 1938, p. 367.) Despite rising divo
rates, these studies indicate a relative degree of satisfaction w
marriage. It should be noted that the participants in the studies w
above average in terms of education, cultural background, and incor

42 Walter Lippmann, *A Preface to Morals* (Boston: Beacon Pre
1929), pp. 291-92.

NOTES

Chapter VIII

1 V.I. Pudovkin, *Film Acting,* trans. Ivor Montagu (London: ɔrge Newnes, Ltd., 1935), p. 151.

2 Robert Warshow, *The Immediate Experience* (Garden City, New ·k: Doubleday & Co., Inc., 1962), p. 128.

3 C. Wright Mills, *White Collar* (New York: Oxford University ·ss, 1956), p. xiii.

4 Herbert Blumer, *Movies and Conduct* (New York: The cmillan Co., 1933), p. 155.

5 Lois Wilson starred in a number of films for William deMille ▌ stresses, as does his daughter Agnes deMille, that his films were ▪ple pictures with human interest content as opposed to the spectac-·s of his more famous brother. Significantly, William deMille ·lled his name with a lower case "d" whereas his brother used the ▪ital letter. Interview with Lois Wilson, New York, November 24, ·2. Telephone conversation with Agnes deMille, New York, October 1972.

6 *Variety* (December 23, 1921), microfilm, Library for the forming Arts, Lincoln Center, New York (Library hereafter cited as ·A).

7 *New York Times* (December 25, 1921), courtesy of Lois Wilson. ·s Wilson still regards Lulu Bett as her favorite role because she felt ·ticularly suited for the part. Ironically, William deMille cast another ·ress as Lulu and actually shot footage before realizing his error and ·ssigning the role to Miss Wilson. Interview with Lois Wilson, New ·k November 24, 1972.

8 Lois Wilson agrees that as a film, *Miss Lulu Bett* has "woman's ·' aspects in the plot and characterization, but she does not regard

195

deMille's portrayal of the Deacons as an indictment against family li
in general. Interview with Lois Wilson, New York, November 24, 197:

9 Robert S. Lynd and Helen Merrell Lynd concluded in their stud
Middletown (Harcourt, Brace & World, 1929), "The minimum cost o
living for a 'standard family of five' in Middletown in 1924 wa
$1,920.87." (pp. 84-85.) A study of the American Association o
Business and Professional Women disclosed that one-fourth of th
women in clerical and publicity work and in teaching positions in 192
earned less than $1,213 annually; one-half less than $1,548; and three
fourths less than $2,004. (*Recent Social Trends,* p. 736.)

10 "Though feminists have long argued that such role reversals ar
often desirable, how many men have actually agreed to swap the dail
commuter train for domesticity? Report *Time* correspondents natior
wide: a very scant, very hardy few." Sheldon Schacter, one of th
"very scant, very hardy few," related: "At first I just lolled around th
house, doing chores, watching soap operas, and growing lonesome.
found myself waiting for Sandy to come home as the highlight of th
day. There was a dependency starting to build up in me." ("Men of th
House," *Time,* February 18, 1974, p. 76.)

11 James Monaco, *How to Read a Film,* (New York: Oxford Univei
sity Press, 1977), p. 220.

12 *The Homemaker,* clipping file, Academy for the Motion Pictur
Arts and Sciences, Los Angeles (Academy hereafter cited as AMPAS

13 *Dancing Mothers,* clipping file, AMPAS.

14 "Dancing Mothers," *New York Times Film Reviews,* 1913-196
(New York: New York Times and Arno Press, 1970), pp. 299-300.

15 *Black Oxen,* see also Chapter VI.

16 *Black Oxen,* pressbook, LPA.

17 *Variety* (January 10, 1924; January 17, 1924), microfilm, LPA

18 Gertrude Atherton, *Black Oxen* (New York: Boni & Liverright
1923), pp. 56-57.

19 Stendhal, *On Love,* trans. H.B.V. under the direction of C.K
Scott-Moncrieff (New York: Gosset & Dunlap, 1967), pp. 228-230.

Chapter IX

[1] According to Janet Dunbar in *The Early Victorian Woman: Some ›ects of Her Life,* 1837-1957 (London: George G. Harrap & Co., Ltd., 3): "No official records of maternal mortality were kept in those s, but there is a mass of evidence to show that untrained and ›mpetent midwives must have been responsible for countless deaths 1others and babies. ...Most of the medical men of that period seem ave been indifferent to strict cleanliness in childbirth cases, judging heir opposition when anyone tried to put into practice new ideas in field." (p. 23.)

[2] Steven Marcus, *The Other Victorians* (New York: Basic Books, , 1964), p. 120.

[3] *Flesh and the Devil,* see also Chapter III.

[4] See Charlotte Perkins Gilman, *Women and Economics* (New k: Harper and Row, 1966; originally published in 1898). Gilman ed that all women engage in remunerative labor and that domestic res such as cleaning and cooking, even child care, be subject to the :ient process of labor specialization as in industry. Specially trained sonnel would perform these functions for a wage and thus free 1en in the labor force from domestic drudgery. Unfortunately, 1an's concept of mass technology as a practical base for woman's 1ncipation in a socialist environment has been countered by easing privatization, as evidenced by the phenomenon of single- dwellings in suburbia. Unlike her upper class counterpart, the king wife has become saddled with double duty.

BIBLIOGRAPHY

Books

Allen, Frederick Lewis. *Only Yesterday*. New York: Bantam Boo
Inc., 1959.

Andrew, J. Dudley. *The Major Film Theories*. New York: Oxf
University Press, 1976.

Arlen, Michael. *The Green Hat*. New York: George H. Doran Co., 19

Arnheim, Rudolph. *Film*. Translated by L.M. Sieveking and Ian F
Morrow. London: Faber & Faber. Ltd., 1933.

Atherton, Gertrude. *Black Oxen*. New York: Boni & Liveright, 19

Barry, Iris. *Let's Go to the Movies*. New York: Payson & Clarke, L
1926.

Blum, Daniel. *A Pictorial History of the Silent Screen*. New Yc
Grosset & Dunlap, 1953.

Blummer, Herbert. *Movies and Conduct*. New York: The Macmil
Co., 1933.

Brown, Karl. *Adventures with D.W. Griffith*. New York: Far
Strauss & Giroux, 1973.

Brownlow, Kevin. *The Parades Gone By*. New York: Ballantine Boo
1968.

Brundidge, Harry T. *Twinkle, Twinkle Movie Star!* "Clara Bo
New York: E.P. Dutton & Co., Inc., 1930, pp. 2-12.

Calhoun, Arthur W. *A Social History of the American Family fi
Colonial Times to the Present*. Vol. III. Cleveland: Arthur
Clark Co., 1919.

Carey, Gary. *Lost Films*. New York: Museum of Modern Art, 1970.

Chaplin, Charles. *My Autobiography*. New York: Simon and Schus
1964.

nway, Michael, McGregor, Don, and Ricci, Mark. *The Films of Greta Garbo*. New York: The Citadel Press, 1968.

wley, Malcolm. *Exile's Return: A Literary Odyssey of the 1920s*. New York: The Viking Press, 1951.

awford, Morris. *One World of Fashion*. New York: Fairchild Publishing Co., 1946.

rtiss, Thomas Quinn. *Von Stroheim*. London: Angus & Robertson, 1971.

le Edgar. *The Content of Motion Pictures*. New York: The Macmillan Co., 1935.

_____. *Children's Attendance at Motion Pictures*. New York: The Macmillan Co., 1935.

vis, Katherine B. *Factors in the Sex Life of Twenty-Two Hundred Women*. New York: McGraw Hill Book Co., 1938.

Beauvoir, Simone. *The Second Sex*. Translated and edited by H.M. Parshley. New York: Bantam Books, Inc, 1964.

l, Floyd. *Love in the Machine Age*. New York: Farrar & Rinehart, 1930.

Mille, Cecil B. *The Autobiography of Cecil B. DeMille*. Edited by Donald Hayne. Englewood Cliffs, New Jersey: Prentice-Hall, 1959.

Mille, William C. *Hollywood Saga*. New York: E.P. Dutton & Co., 1939.

Rougemont, Denis. *Love in the Western World*. Translated by Montgomery Belgion. Greenwich, Conn.: Fawcett Publications, Inc., 1966.

Tocqueville, Alexis. *Democracy in America*. Vol. II. Translated by Henry Reeves. New York: A.S. Barnes & Co., 1863.

kinson, Robert Latou, and Beam, Lura. *The Single Woman: A Medical Study in Sex Education*. New York: Reynal & Hitchcock, Inc., 1934.

_____. *A Thousand Marriages: A Medical Study of Sex Adjustment*. Baltimore: The Williams & Wilkins Co., 1931.

s Passos, John. *The Big Money*. New York: New American Library, Inc., 1969.

eiser, Theodore. *Gallery of Women*. 2 vols. "Ernestine." New York: Horace Liveright, 1929, II, 527-565.

singer, Wendell S. *The Emotional Responses of Children to the Motion Picture Situation*. New York: The Macmillan Co., 1933.

erson, John, and Loos, Anita. *Breaking into the Movies*. New York: James A. McCann Co., 1921.

Ernst, Morris L., and Lorentz, Pare. *Censored: The Private Life of th Movie.* New York: Jonathan Cape & Harrison Smith, 1930.

Fiedler, Leslie A. *Love and Death in the American Novel.* New York Dell Publishing Co., Inc., 1969.

Finler, Joel W. *Stroheim.* London: Studio Vista, Ltd., 1967.

Fisher, Dorothea Frances (Dorothy Canfield). *The Homemaker.* New York: Grosset & Dunlap, 1924.

Fitzgerald, F. Scott. *Flappers and Philosophers.* New York: Charle Scribner's Sons, 1959.

_____. *The Last Tycoon.* New York: Charles Scribner's Sons 1941.

_____. *Six Tales of the Jazz Age and Other Stories.* New York Charles Scribner's Sons, 1960.

_____. *This Side of Paradise.* New York: Charles Scribner's Sons 1920.

Fitzgerald, Zelda. *Save me the Waltz.* Carbondale, Ill.: Souther Illinois University Press, 1967.

Fowles, John. *The French Lieutenant's Woman.* New York: The Ne American Library, Inc., 1969.

Franklin, Joe. *Classics of the Silent Screen.* New York: The Citad Press, 1959.

Freud, Sigmund. *The Interpretation of Dreams.* Translated and edite by James Strachey. New York: Avon Books, 1965.

_____. *On Creativity and the Unconscious: Papers on the Ps chology of Art, Literature, Love, Religion.* Translated under th supervision of Joan Riviere. Selected by Benjamin Nelson. Ne York: Harper & Bros., 1958.

Gale, Zona. *Miss Lulu Bett.* New York: D. Appleton & Co., 1920.

Giannetti, Louis D. *Understanding Movies.* Englewood Cliffs, Ne Jersey: Prentice-Hall, Inc., 1976 (second edition).

Gilman, Charlotte Perkins. *Women and Economics: A Study of th Economic Relation between Men and Women as a Factor i Social Evolution.* New York: Harper & Row, 1966 (originall published in 1898).

Gish, Lillian with Pinchot, Ann. *The Movies, Mr. Griffith and Me.* Ne York: Avon Books, 1970.

Geduld, Harry M. (ed.). *Focus on D.W. Griffith.* Englewood Cliff New Jersey: Prentice-Hall, Inc., 1971.

Glyn, Anthony. *Elinor Glyn: A Biography.* Garden City, New York Doubleday & Co., Inc., 1955.

The Golden Harvest of the Silver Screen. Los Angeles: Hunter, Dulin & Co., 1927.

Greer, Germaine. *The Female Eunuch.* New York: Bantam Books, Inc., 1971.

Griffith, Mrs. D.W. (Linda Arvidson). *When the Movies Were Young.* New York: Dover Publications, 1969.

Hall, Ben M. *The Best Remaining Seats: The Story of the Golden Age of the Movie Palace.* New York: Clarkson N. Potter, Inc., 1961.

Hall, Carrie A. *From Hoopskirts to Nudity: A Review of the Follies and Foibles of Fashion, 1866-1936.* Caldwell, Idaho: The Caxton Printers, Ltd., 1946.

Hall, Stuart, and Whannel, Paddy. *The Popular Arts.* New York: Pantheon Books, 1964.

Hamilton, Gilbert Van Tassel. *A Research in Marriage.* New York: Albert and Charles Boni, Inc., 1929.

Hampton, Benjamin B. *History of the American Film Industry from Its Beginnings to 1931.* New York: Dover Publications, Inc., 1970 (formerly titled *A History of the Movies*).

Haskell, Molly. *From Reverence to Rape.* New York: Holt, Rinehart, Inc., 1974.

Hays, Will H. *See and Hear: A Brief History of Motion Pictures and the Development of Sound.* New York, 1929.

Henderson, Robert M. *D.W. Griffith: His Life and Work.* New York: Oxford University Press, 1972.

Horney, Karen. *Feminine Psychology.* New York: W.W. Norton & Co., 1967.

Hull, Edith M. *The Sheik.* Boston: Small, Maynard & Co., 1921.

Jacobs, Lewis. *The Rise of the American Film.* New York: Columbia University, Teachers College Press, 1939.

Johnson, Diane. *The True History of the First Mrs. Meredith and Other Lesser Lives.* New York: Alfred A. Knopf, Inc., 1972.

Jordan, Jr., Thurston C. *Glossary of Motion Picture Terminology.* Menlo Park, California: Pacific Coast Publishers, 1968.

Jung, Carl, *et al. Man and His Symbols.* New York: Dell Publishing Co., Inc., 1971.

Kennedy, David M. *Birth Control in America: The Career of Margaret Sanger.* New Haven: Yale University Press, 1970.

Kirchwey, Freda. (ed.). *Our Changing Morality.* New York: Albert and Charles Boni, 1924.

Koury, Phil A. *Yes, Mr. DeMille.* New York: G.P. Putman's Sons, 1959.

Kracauer, Siegfried. *From Caligari to Hitler: A Psychological History* the German Film. Princeton: Princeton University Press, 197(

Kraditor, Aileen. *The Ideas of the Woman Suffrage Movement.* Ne York: Columbia University Press, 1965.

Lane, Tamar. *What's Wrong with the Movies?* Los Angeles: Th Waverly Co., 1923.

Lawrence, D.H. *Studies in Classic American Literature.* New York: Th Viking Press, 1966.

Lee, Raymond. *The Films of Mary Pickford.* New York: A.S. Barnes Co., 1970.

Leighton, Isabel. (ed.). *The Aspirin Age, 1919-1941.* New York: Sime and Schuster, 1949.

Lennig, Arthur. *The Silent Voice.* Albany, New York: Faculty-Stude Assn. of the State University of New York at Albany, Inc., 196

Leuchtenberg, William E. *The Perils of Prosperity, 1914-32.* Chicag University of Chicago Press, 1958.

Lewis, Sinclair. *Babbitt.* New York: New American Library, Inc., 196
_____. *Main Street.* New York: New American Library of Wor Literature, Inc., 1961.

Lippman, Walter. *A Preface to Morals.* Boston: Beacon Press, 19((first published in 1929).

Lynd, Robert S., and Lynd, Helen Merrell. *Middletown: A Study American Culture.* New York: Harcourt, Brace & World, Inc 1929.

Marcus, Steven. *The Other Victorians: A Study of Sexuality and Porn graphy in Mid-Nineteenth Century England.* New York: Bas Books, Inc., 1964.

Marion, Frances. *Off with Their Heads! A Serio-Comic Tale* Hollywood. New York: The Macmillan Co., 1972.

Marsh, Mae. *Screen Acting.* Los Angeles: Photo Star Publishing Co 1921.

May, Henry F. *The End of American Innocence: A Study of the Fir Years of Our Own Time, 1912-1917.* Chicago: Quadrang Books, 1959.

Mayer, Arthur, and Griffith, Richard. *The Movies.* New York: Bonan Books, 1957.

McLuhan, Marshall. *Understanding Media: The Extentions of Ma* New York: The New American Library, Inc., 1964.

Mellen, Joan. *Women and Their Sexuality in the New Film.* New Yor Dell Publishing Co., Inc., 1973.

Meyer, Donald. *The Positive Thinkers: A Study of the American Quest for Health, Wealth and Personal Power from Mary Baker Eddy to Norman Vincent Peale.* Garden City, New York: Doubleday & Co., Inc., 1966.

Milford, Nancy. *Zelda.* New York: Avon Books, 1970.

Millett, Kate. *Sexual Politics.* Garden City, New York: Doubleday & Co., 1970.

Mills, C. Wright. *White Collar: The American Middle Classes.* New York: Oxford University Press, 1956.

Mitchell, Alice Miller. *Children and Movies.* Chicago: University of Chicago Press, 1929.

Mitchell, Juliet. *Psychoanalysis and Feminism.* New York: Vintage Books, 1975.

Monaco, James. *How to Read a Film.* New York: Oxford University Press, 1977.

Moore, Colleen. *Silent Star.* New York: Doubleday & Co., Inc., 1968.

Morin, Edgar. *The Stars.* Translated by Richard Howard. New York: Grove Press, Inc., 1960.

Mowry, George. (ed.). *The Twenties: Fords, Flappers and Fanatics.* Englewood Cliffs, New Jersey: Prentice-Hall, Inc., 1965.

Nash, Roderick. *The New Generation: American Thought, 1917-1930.* Chicago: Rand McNally & Co., 1973.

Negri, Pola. *Memoirs of a Star.* Garden City, New York: Doubleday & Co., Inc., 1970.

Nichols, Bill. (ed.). *Movies and Methods.* Berkeley and Los Angeles: University of California Press, 1976.

Oberholtzer, Ellis Paxton. *The Morals of the Movie.* Philadelphia: The Pensylvania Publishing Co., 1922.

O'Leary, Liam. *The Silent Cinema.* New York: E.P. Dutton & Co., 1965.

O'Neill, William L. *Divorce in the Progressive Era.* New Haven: Yale University Press, 1967.

_____. *Everyone Was Brave: The Rise and Fall of Feminism in America.* Chicago: Quadrangle Books, 1969.

Ortega y Gasset, Jose. *On Love: Aspects of a Single Theme.* Translated by Toby Talbot. Cleveland: The World Publishing Co., 1957.

Paine, Albert Bigelow. *Life and Lillian Gish.* New York: The Macmillan Co., 1932.

Papashvily, Helen W. *All the Happy Endings: A Study of the Domestic Novel in America, the Women Who Wrote It, the Women Who Read, in the Nineteenth Century.* New York: Harpers & Bros., 1956.

Peters, Charles. *Motion Pictures and Standards of Morality*. New Yor
    The Macmillan Co., 1933.

Pickford, Mary. *Sunshine and Shadow*. Garden City, New Yor
    Doubleday & Co., 1955.

Powdermaker, Hortense. *Hollywood the Dream Factory: An Anthropo
    ogist Looks at the Movie-Makers*. Boston: Little Brown & Co
    1950.

Pratt, George C. *Spellbound in Darkness*. 2 vols. Rochester, New Yor
    University of Rochester, 1966.

Pudovkin, V.I. *Film Acting*. Translated by Ivor Montagu. Londo
    George Newnes, Ltd., 1935.

    _____. *Film Technique*. Translated and annotated by Iv
    Montagu. London: George Newnes, Ltd., 1933.

Quirk, Lawrence J. *The Films of Joan Crawford*. New York: The Citad
    Press, 1968.

Ramsaye, Terry. *A Million and One Nights*. 2 vols. New York: Simo
    and Schuster, 1926.

Richardson, Robert. *Literature and Film*. Bloomington, Ind.: India
    University Press, 1969.

Riesman, David, Glazer, Nathan, and Denney, Reuel. *The Lone
    Crowd: A Study of the Changing American Character*. Garde
    City, New York: Doubleday & Co., Inc., 1953.

Robinson, David. *Hollywood in the Twenties*. New York: Paperba
    Library, 1970.

Rosen, Marjorie. *Popcorn Venus*. New York: Avon Books, 1974.

Rosenberg, Bernard and White, David Manning. (eds.). *Mass Cultur
    The Popular Arts in America*. Glencoe, Ill.: The Free Pres
    1957.

Rotha, Paul. *The Film Till Now: A Survey of World Cinema*. With a
    Additional Section by Richard Griffith. New York: Funk
    Wagnalls, 1949.

Sanger, Margaret. *The New Motherhood*. London: Cape, 1922.

Sann, Paul. *The Lawless Decade: A Pictorial History of a Gre
    American Transition from the World War I Armistice an
    Prohibition to Repeal and the New Deal*. New York: Bonan
    Books, 1957.

Seabury, William Marston. *The Public and the Motion Pictu
    Industry*. New York: The Macmillan Co., 1926.

Selwyn, Edgar, and Goulding, Edmund. "Dancing Mothers," *The Be
    Plays of 1924*. Edited by Burns Mantle. New York: Dodd, Mea
    & Co., 1963, pp. 175-222.

Sheehan, Perley Poore. *Hollywood As a World Center.* Hollywood, Calif.: Hollywood Citizen Press, 1924.

Shulman, Irving. *Valentino.* New York: Trident Press, 1967.

Sklar, Robert. *Movie-Made America.* New York: Vintage Books, 1976.

Spears, Jack. *Hollywood: The Golden Era.* New York: A.S. Barnes & Co., 1971.

Stendhal. *On Love.* Translated by H.B.V. under the direction of C.K. Scott-Moncrieff. New York: Grosset & Dunlap, 1967.

Sullivan, Mark. *Our Times: The United States, 1900-1925.* Vol. V: *Over Here, 1914-1918.* Vol. VI: *The Twenties.* New York: Charles Scribner's Sons, c. 1926.

Taylor, Deems, Peterson, Marcelene, and Hale, Bryant. *A Pictorial History of the Movies.* New York: Simon and Schuster, 1943.

Terman, Lewis M. *Psychological Factors in Marital Happiness.* New York: McGraw Hill Book Co., 1938.

Thomas, Bob. *Thalberg: Life and Legend.* New York: Doubleday & Co., Inc., 1969.

Tyler, Parker. *The Hollywood Hallucination.* New York: Creative Age Press, Inc., 1944.

Vidor, King. *A Tree Is a Tree.* New York: Harcourt, Brace & Co., 1952.

Wagenknecht, Edward. *The Movies in the Age of Innocence.* New York: Ballantine Books, 1971.

Walker, Alexander. *The Celluloid Sacrifice: Aspects of Sex in the Movies.* New York: Hawthorn Books, Inc., 1966.

Warner, Jack L. *My First Hundred Years in Hollywood.* New York: Random House, 1964.

Warshow, Robert. *The Immediate Experience: Movies, Comics, Theater and Other Aspects of Popular Culture.* Garden City, New York: Doubleday & Co., Inc., 1962.

Weinberg, Herman G. *The Lubitsch Touch: A Critical Study.* New York: E.P. Dutton & Co., 1968.

_____. *Saint Cinema.* New York: Dover Publications, Inc., 1970.

West, Nathanael. *The Day of the Locust.* New York: New Directions Publishing Corp., 1950.

Wiebe, Robert H. *The Search for Order, 1877-1920.* New York: Hill and Wang, 1968.

Wilde, Oscar. *Salomé.* Paris: *Edition à petit nombre. Imprimée pour les souscripteurs,* 1907.

Williamson, Alice M. *Alice in Movieland.* New York: D. Appleton & Co., 1928.

Wolfenstein, Martha, and Leites, Nathan. *Movies: A Psychologic* *Study.* Glencoe, Ill.: The Free Press, 1950.

Women's Wear Daily. Fifty Years of Fashion. New York: Fairchi Publications, Inc., 1950.

Woolf, Virginia. *A Room of One's Own.* New York: Harcourt, Brace World, 1929.

_____. *Three Guineas.* New York: Harcourt, Brace & Worl 1938.

Zukor, Adolph with Dale Kramer. *The Public Is Never Wrong.* Ne York: G.P. Putnam's Sons, 1953.

Articles

Adams, Grace. "The Rise and Fall of Psychology, " *Atlantic Month* CLIII (January, 1934), 82-92.

Birnbaum, Lucille C. "Behaviorism in the 1920's," *American Quarter* VII (Spring, 1955), 15-30.

Bodeen, De Witt. "Pauline Frederick," *Films in Review,* X (February, 1965), 69-90.

Bolitho, William. "The New Skirt Length," *Harper's,* CLX (Februar 1930), 292-96.

Bromley, Dorothy Dunbar. "Feminist-New Style," *Harper's,* C (October, 1927), 552-60.

Brooks, Louise. "Gish and Garbo: The Executive War on Stars," *Sig and Sound,* XXVIII (Winter, 1958-59), 13-17.

Card, James. "The Films of Mary Pickford," *Image,* VIII (Decemb 1959), 172-87.

Collins, William S. "Lois Wilson," *Films in Review,* XXIV (Janua 1973), 18-36.

"Director Gish," *Photoplay Magazine,* XVII (March, 1920), 68.

Door, John H. "A Retrospective of the Griffith Era," *Los Ange Times Calendar* (June 13, 1971).

Dreiser, Theodore. "Hollywood: Its Morale and Manners," *Shado land,* V (November, 1921), 37, 61-63; V (December, 1921), 61.

_____. "Hollywood Now," *McCall's Magazine,* XLVIII (Septe ber, 1921), 8, 18, 54.

Evans, Nancy. "Good-by, Bohemia," *Scribner's,* LXXXIX (Janua 1931), 643-46.

eldman, Egal. "Prostitution, the Alien Woman and the Progressive Imagination, 1910-1915," *American Quarterly,* XIX (Summer, 1967), 192-206.

itzgerald, F. Scott, "Echoes of the Jazz Age," *Scribner's,* XV (November, 1931), 459-65.

letcher, Adele Whitely. "Mary," *Motion Picture Magazine,* XXIII (June, 1922), 22-23, 94.

reedman, Estelle B. "The New Woman: Changing Views of Women in the 1920s," *Journal of the American History,* LXI (September, 1974), 372-393.

ox, Julian. "The Country Boys," *Films and Filming,* XVIII (May, 1972), 28-36.

iordon, Henry Stephen. "The Story of David Wark Griffith," *Photoplay Magazine,* X (June, 1916), 28-37, 162-65; X (July, 1916), 122-32; X (August, 1916), 78-88; X (September, 1916), 79-86; X (October, 1916), 86-94; X (November, 1916), 27-40.

Iall, G. Stanley. "Flapper Americana Novissima," *Atlantic Monthly,* CXXIX (June, 1922), 771-80.

Ialler, Jr., John S., "From Maidenhood to Menopause: Sex Education for Women in Victorian America," *Journal of Popular Culture,* VI (Summer, 1972), 49-69.

Iardwick, Elizabeth. "Zelda," *Seduction and Betrayal.* New York: Random House, 1970, pp. 91-108.

Iarmetz, Aljean. "A Valentine for Mary Pickford, America's Sweetheart," *Los Angeles Times Calendar* (March 14, 1971).

Iarriman, Margaret Case. "Profiles," *The New Yorker,* X (April 7, 1934), 29-33.

Iofstadter, Beatrice. "Popular Culture and the Romantic Heroine," *The American Scholar,* XXX (Winter, 1960-61), 98-116.

ohnson, Julian. "Mary Pickford: Herself and Her Career, Part I," *Photoplay Magazine,* VIII (November, 1915), 53-61.

Iones, Dorothy B. "Sunrise: A Murnau Masterpiece," *Introduction to the Art of the Movies.* Edited by Lewis Jacobs. New York: Noonday Press, 1960, pp. 107-29.

Kenyon, Bernice. "Girl Graduates--Ten Years Out," *Scribner's,* LXXXIX (January, 1931), 640-43.

eSage, Julia. "The Human Subject--You, He, or Me? Or, the Case of the Missing Penis," *Screen,* (Summer, 1975), 77-82 (reprinted from *Jump Cut,* November-December, 1974).

indsay, Vachel. "Queen of My People," *The New Republic,* XI (July 7, 1917), 280-81.

"Male and Female," *Time* (September 10, 1973).

Manvell, Roger. "Revaluations-2," *Sight and Sound,* XIX (May, 1950), 130-32.

"Mary Pickford Awards," *Photoplay Magazine,* XXIX (October, 1925), 45, 109.

"Mary Pickford's Favorite Stars and Films," *Photoplay Magazine* XXV (January, 1924), 28-29, 105-107.

May, Henry F. "Shifting Perspectives on the 1920's," *Mississippi Valley Historical Review,* XLIII (December, 1956), 405-27.

McGovern, James. "The American Woman's Pre-World War Freedom in Manners and Morals," *Journal of American History,* LV (September, 1968), 315-33.

"Men of the House," *Time* (February 18, 1974), 76.

"Movie Censorship," *Movie Weekly* (March 26, 1921), 20.

Pickford, Mary. "Ambassadors," *Saturday Evening Post,* CCII (August 23, 1930), 6-7, 117-18.

_____. "Mary Is Looking for Pictures," *Photoplay Magazine* XXVIII (June, 1925), 39, 109.

_____. "When I Am Old," *Photoplay Magazine,* XXVI (February, 1925), 52.

Quarterly Review of Film Studies, guest edited by Dudley Andrew, I (August, 1977).

Reid, Margaret. "Has the Flapper Changed? F. Scott Fitzgerald Discusses the Cinema Descendants of the Type He Has Made So Well Known," *Motion Picture Magazine,* XXXIII (June, 1927), 28-29, 104.

Reppelier, Anne. "Women and War," *Atlantic Monthly,* CXV (May 1915), 577-85.

Riegel, Robert E. "Changing American Attitudes Towards Prostitution, 1800-1920," *Journal of the History of Ideas,* XXIX (1968), 437-52.

Small, Frederick James. "Mary Had a Little Tear," *Motion Picture Classic,* V (September, 1917), 35-36, 67.

Stendler, Celia. "New Ideas for Old: How Freudianism Was Received in the United States," *The Journal of Educational Psychology* XXXVIII (April, 1947), 193-206.

Stern, Seymour. "Griffith: I The Birth of a Nation," *Film Culture* No. 36 (Spring-Summer, 1965). (The entire issue is devoted to the film.)

St. Johns, Adela Rogers. "Why Does the World Love Mary?" *Photoplay Magazine,* XXI (December, 1921), 50, 110.

St. Johns, Adela Rogers. "Why Mary Pickford Bobbed *Her* Hair," *Photoplay Magazine,* XXXIV, (September, 1928), 33, 128-29.

The Survey, LVII (December 1, 1926). (The entire issue was devoted to articles about women.)

"The Vampire," *Moving Picture World,* XVIII (October 4, 1913), 51.

Villard, Osward Garrison. "Sex, Art, Truth, and Magazines," *Atlantic Monthly,* CXXXVII (March, 1926), 388-98.

Wembridge, Eleanor Rowland, "Petting and the Campus," *The Survey,* LIV (July 1, 1925), 393-95, 412.

Weinberg, Herman G. "Erich Von Stroheim," *Introduction to the Art of the Movies.* Edited by Lewis Jacobs. New York: Noonday Press, 1960, pp. 89-96.

Whitaker, Alma. "Mrs. Douglas Fairbanks Analyzes Mary Pickford," *Photoplay Magazine,* XXXIII (March, 1928), 30-31, 127.

Woolf, Virginia. "The Movies and Reality," *The New Republic,* XLVII (August 4, 1926), 308-10.

Wright, Edna. "Mary Pickford Plus Silent Money Talk," *Motion Picture Classic,* V (March, 1917), 19-21.

Yellis, Kenneth A. "Prosperity's Child: Some Thoughts on the Flapper," *American Quarterly,* XXI (Spring, 1969), 44-64.

Other Sources

American Film Institute Catalog of Motion Pictures Produced in the United States. Feature Films, 1921-1930.* Edited by Kenneth W. Munden. New York and London: R.R. Bowker Co., 1971.

Inglis, Ruth A. *Freedom of the Movies: A Report on Self-Regulation from The Commission on Freedom of the Press.* Chicago, 1947.

New York Times Film Reviews, 1913-1968. New York: New York Times and Arno Press, 1970.

Report of the President's Research Committee on Social Trends. *Recent Social Trends in the United States.* New York: McGraw-Hill Book Co., Inc., 1933.

See, Carolyn. "The Hollywood Novel: An Historical and Critical Study," Unpublished Ph.D. dissertation, University of California, Los Angeles, 1963.

U.S. Department of Commerce. *Statistical Abstract of the United States*. 1916, 1924, 1933.

Collections

Los Angeles. Academy of Motion Picture Arts and Sciences.
Barthelmess, Richard. Scrapbook, Vol. I, 1916-1920.
Bow, Clara. Clipping file.
Davies, Marion. Clipping file.
Gish, Lillian. Clipping file.
La Plante, Laura. Clipping file.
Pickford, Mary. Clipping file.
Negri, Pola. Clipping file.
Normand, Mabel. Clipping file.

Glazer, Benjamin. *Seventh Heaven*. Unpublished scripts.

Black Oxen. Clipping file.
Dancing Mothers. Clipping file.
The Homemaker. Clipping file.

Los Angeles. University of Southern California.
William deMille Papers. Scrapbook No. 3.
Claire Windsor Scrapbooks, 21 vols.

Los Angeles. Welder Daniel Private Collection.
Annie Laurie. Herald.
The Enemy. Herald.
The Four Horsemen of the Apocalypse (re-issue). Herald.
Hotel Imperial. Herald.
_____. Press Sheet.
Sadie Thompson. Herald.
The White Sister (re-issue). Herald.
The Wind. Herald.
Wings. Herald.

New York. Library for the Performing Arts at Lincoln Center.
Bara, Theda. Clipping files.
_____. Scrapbooks (non-catalogued).

_____. Scrapbook, Robinson Locke Collection (non-catalogued).

DeMille, Cecil B. Clipping files.

_____. Scrapbooks (non-catalogued).

_____. Scrapbook, Robinson Locke Collection (non-catalogued).

Dexter, Elliott. Scrapbook, Robinson Locke Collection (non-catalogued).

Garbo, Greta. Clipping file.

Gish, Lillian. Scrapbook (non-catalogued).

Lubitsch, Ernst. Clipping file.

Pickford, Mary. Clipping files.

_____. Scrapbooks. Robinson Locke Collection (non-catalogued).

Swanson, Gloria. Clipping file.

_____. Scrapbook (non-catalogued).

Valentino, Rudolph. Scrapbook (non-catalogued).

The Affairs of Anatol. Clipping file.

Black Oxen. Pressbook (microfilm).

Black Oxen. Variety (January 10, 1924). Microfilm.

Blind Husbands. Scrapbook (non-catalogued).

Blood and Sand. Clipping file.

La Boheme. Scrapbook (non-catalogued).

The Crowd. Clipping file.

_____. Scrapbook (non-catalogued).

Dancing Mothers. Press Sheet.

The Devil's Circus. Scrapbook (non-catalogued).

Don Juan. Clipping file.

The Flapper. Clipping file.

Flesh and the Devil. Clipping file.

_____. Scrapbook (non-catalogued).

Foolish Wives. Scrapbook (non-catalogued).

_____. Stillbooks.

The Four Horsemen of the Apocalypse. Clipping file.

Hotel Imperial. Clipping file.

It. Clipping file.

The Kiss. Scrapbook (non-catalogued).

Love. Scrapbook (non-catalogued).

Male and Female. Clipping file.

Man, Woman and Sin. Clipping file.

_____. Scrapbook (non-catalogued).

The Marriage Circle. Clipping file.

Miss Lulu Bett. Clipping file.

_____. *Variety* (December 23, 1921). Microfilm.

My Best Girl. Scrapbook (non-catalogued).

The Mysterious Lady. Scrapbook (non-catalogued).

Our Dancing Daughters. Scrapbook (non-catalogued).

Our Modern Maidens. Scrapbook (non-catalogued).

Romola. Clipping file.

_____. Scrapbook (non-catalogued).

_____. Stillbooks.

Sadie Thompson. Clipping file.

Sally, Irene, and Mary. Scrapbook (non-catalogued).

Salome. Clipping file.

_____. Scrapbook (non-catalogued).

The Scarlet Letter. Scrapbook (non-catalogued).

Seventh Heaven. Scrapbook (non-catalogued).

The Sheik. Clipping file.

The Single Standard. Scrapbook (non-catalogued).

Sunrise. Clipping file.

New York. Museum of Modern Art.

Marion, Frances. *The Wind.* Unpublished scripts.

New York. New York Public Library.

William deMille Papers.

Washington, D.C. Library of Congress.

Lillian Gish Papers, 16 boxes.

Interviews

deMille, Agnes. New York. Telephone conversation, October 19, 1972.

Gish, Lillian. Los Angeles. Seminar. University of California, Los Angeles (tape recording), November 26, 1968.

Gish, Lillian. New York. Telephone conversation, October 21, 1972.

La Plante, Laura. Palm Desert, California. Interview, December 2, 1971.

Mohr, Hal. Los Angeles. Interview, July 18, 1972.

ilson, Lois. New York. Interview, November 24, 1972.
indsor, Claire. Los Angeles. Interview, August 2, 1971.

FILMOGRAPHY

The following films were viewed at public screenings in Los Angele
and New York and also at the Library of Congress, Washington, D.C.
the Museum of Modern Art, New York; and at George Eastman House
Rochester, New York.

The Affairs of Anatol. Famous Players-Lasky. Dist. Paramount. Dir
    Cecil B. DeMille, 1921. (Czech titles.)

Amarilly of Clothes Line Alley. Artcraft Pictures Corp. Dir. Marshal
    Neilan, 1918.

Anna Christie. M-G-M. Dir. Clarence Brown, 1929. (silent version.

Anna Christie. Thomas H. Ince Corp. Dist. First National. Dir. John
    Griffith Wray, 1923.

Barney Oldfield's Race for Life. Mack Sennett. 1912.

Battle of the Sexes. Art Cinema Corp. Dist. United Artists. Dir. D.W
    Griffith, 1928.

Beau Brummel. Warner Bros. Dir. Harry Beaumont, 1924.

Beau Geste. Famous Players-Lasky. Dist. Paramount. Dir. Herber
    Brenon, 1926.

Beloved Rogue. United Artists. Dir. Alan Crosland, 1927.

Ben Hur. M-G-M. Dir. Fred Niblo, 1927.

The Big Parade. M-G-M. Dir. King Vidor, 1925.

The Birth of a Nation. Enoch Producing Co. Dir. D.W. Griffith, 1915

Black Oxen. Frank Lloyd Productions. Dist. First National. Dir. Frank
    Lloyd, 1924.

The Black Pirate. Elton Corp. Dist. United Artists. Dir. Albert Parker
    1926.

Blind Husbands. Universal. Dir. Erich von Stroheim, 1919.

Blood and Sand. Famous Players-Lasky. Dist. Paramount. Dir. Fred
    Niblo, 1922.

La Boheme. M-G-M. Dir. King Vidor, 1926.

Broken Blossoms. Dist. United Artists. Dir. D.W. Griffith, 1919.

The Busher. Famous Players-Lasky. Dist. Paramount. Dir. Jerome Stern, 1919.

Butterfly. Universal. Dir. Clarence Brown, 1924.

Camille. Nazimova Productions. Dist. Metro Pictures. Dir. Ray C. Smallwood, 1921.

Capital Punishment. B.P. Schulberg Productions. Dist. Preferred Pictures. Dir. James P. Hogan, 1925.

The Cat and the Canary. Universal. Dir. Paul Leni, 1927.

The Cheat. Famous Players-Lasky. Dist. Paramount. Dir. Cecil B. DeMille, 1915.

Children of Divorce. Famous Players-Lasky. Dist. Paramount. Dir. Frank Lloyd, 1927.

The Conquering Power. Metro Pictures. Dir. Rex Ingram, 1921.

The Covered Wagon. Famous Players-Lasky. Dist. Paramount. Dir. James Cruze, 1923.

The Crowd. M-G-M. Dir. King Vidor, 1928.

Daddy Long Legs. First National. Dir. Marshall Neilan, 1919.

Dancing Mothers. Famous Players-Lasky. Dist. Paramount. Dir. Herbert Brenon, 1926.

The Devil's Circus. M-G-M. Dir. Benjamin Christiansen, 1926.

Don Juan. Warner Bros. Dir. Alan Crosland, 1926.

Don't Change Your Husband. Famous Players-Lasky. Dist. Paramount. Dir. Cecil B. DeMille, 1919.

Dorothy Vernon of Haddon Hall. Mary Pickford Productions. Dist. United Artists. Dir. Marshall Neilan, 1924.

Down to the Sea in Ships. Whaling Film Corp. Dist. W.W. Hodkingson Corp. Dir. Elmer Clifton, 1923.

Dream Street. D.W. Griffith, Inc. Dist. United Artists. Dir. D.W. Griffith, 1921.

The Eagle. Art Finance Corp. Dist. United Artists. Dir. Clarence Brown, 1925.

Ella Cinders. John McCormick Productions. Dist. First National. Dir. Alfred E. Green, 1926.

The Extra Girl. Mack Sennett Productions. Dist. Associated Exhibitors. Dir. F. Richard Jones, 1923.

The Eyes of Youth. Equity. Dir. Albert Parker, 1919.

Fine Manners. Paramount. Dir. Richard Rosson, 1926.

The Flapper. Selznick Pictures. Dir. Alan Crosland, 1919.

Flesh and the Devil. M-G-M. Dir. Clarence Brown, 1927.

A Fool There was. Fox. Dir. Frank Powell, 1915.

Foolish Wives. Universal. Dir. Erich von Stroheim, 1922.

The Forbidden City. Selznick Pictures. Dir. Sidney A. Franklin, 191

The Four Horsemen of the Apocalypse. Metro Pictures. Dir. R
Ingram, 1921.

Free to Love. B.P. Schulberg Productions. Dir. Frank O'Connor, 192

A Girl in Every Port. Fox. Dir. Howard Hawks, 1928.

The Godless Girl. Cecil B. DeMille Productions. Dist. Pathe Exchang
Dir. Cecil B. DeMille, 1929.

The Goose Woman. Universal. Dir. Clarence Brown, 1925.

The Grand Duchess and the Waiter. Famous Players-Lasky. Dis
Paramount. Dir. Malcolm St. Clair, 1926.

Greed. M-G-M. Dir. Erich von Stroheim, 1925.

Heart o' the Hills. First National. Dir. Sidney A. Franklin, 1919.

Hearts of the World. Dist. State Regent. Dir. D.W. Griffith, 1918.

He Who Gets Slapped. M-G-M. Dir. Victor Seastrom, 1924.

The Homemaker. Universal. Dir. King Baggott, 1925.

Hotel Imperial. Famous Players-Lasky. Dist. Paramount. Dir. Mauri
Stiller, 1926.

Hula. Famous Players-Lasky. Dist. Paramount. Dir. Victor Fleming
1927.

The Hunchback of Notre Dame. Universal. Dir. Wallace Worsley, 192:

Intolerance. Wark Producing Co. Dir. D.W. Griffith, 1916.

Irene. First National. Dir. Alfred E. Green, 1926.

The Iron Horse. Fox. Dir. John Ford, 1924.

Isn't Life Wonderful? United Artists. Dir. D.W. Griffith, 1924.

It. Famous Players-Lasky. Dist. Paramount. Dir. Clarence Badge
1927.

Joyless Street. Dir. G.W. Pabst, 1925 (German film.)

Judith of Bethulia. Biograph. Dir. D.W. Griffith, 1913.

Kid Boots. Famous Players-Lasky. Dist. Paramount. Dir. Frank Tuttle
1926.

The King of Kings. DeMille Pictures. Dist. Producers Distributin
Corp. Dir. Cecil B. DeMille, 1927.

The King of Main Street. Famous Players-Lasky. Dist. Paramount
Dir. Monta Bell, 1925.

The Kiss. M-G-M. Dir. Jacques Feyder, 1929.

Knight of the Trail. Thomas H. Ince. 1915.

A Lady of Chance. M-G-M. Dir. Robert Leonard, 1928.

Lady of the Night. M-G-M. Dir. Monta Bell, 1925.

The Last Trail. Fox. Dir. Lewis Seiler, 1927.

a and the Geese. Biograph. Dir. D.W. Griffith, 1912.

c Time. First National. Dir. Geroge Fitzmaurice, 1928.

le Annie Rooney. Mary Pickford Co. Dist. United Artists. Dir. William Beaudine, 1925.

e Little Church Around the Corner. Warner Bros. Dir. William Seiter, 1923.

le Lord Fauntleroy. Mary Pickford Co. Dist. United Artists. Dir. Alfred E. Green and Jack Pickford, 1921.

e. M-G-M. Dir. Edmund Goulding, 1927.

e 'em and Leave 'em. Famous Players-Lasky. Dist. Paramount. Dir. Frank Tuttle, 1926.

e Light. Mary Pickford Productions. Dist. United Artists. Dir. Frances Marion, 1921.

e Mad Whirl. Universal. Dir. William A. Seiter, 1924.

dame Mystery. Pathecomedy. 1926.

de for Love. Cinema Corp. of America. Dist. Producers Distributing Corp. Dir. Paul Sloane, 1926.

le and Female. Famous Players-Lasky. Dist. Paramount. Dir. Cecil B. DeMille, 1919.

nhandled. Famous Players-Lasky. Dist. Paramount. Dir. Allan Dwan, 1924.

nhattan Madness. Triangle Film Corp. Dir. Allan Dwan, 1916.

nslaughter. Famous Players-Lasky. Dist. Paramount. Dir. Cecil B DeMille, 1922.

ntrap. Famous Players-Lasky. Dist. Paramount. Dir. Victor Fleming, 1926.

n, Woman and Sin. M-G-M. Dir. Monta Bell, 1927.

e Mark of Zorro. United Artists. Dir. Fred Niblo, 1920.

e Marriage Circle. Warner Bros. Dir. Ernst Lubitsch, 1924.

rried? Jans Productions. Dir. George Terwilliger, 1926.

rry-Go-Round. Universal. Dir. Erich von Stroheim and Rupert Julian, 1923. (Julian replaced von Stroheim about halfway through the production.)

e Merry Widow. M-G-M. Dir. Erich von Stroheim, 1925.

ss Lulu Bett. Famous Players-Lasky. Dist. Paramount. Dir. William deMille, 1921.

y Best Girl. Mary Pickford Corp. Dist. United Artists. Dir. Sam Taylor, 1927.

y Lady of Whims. Dallas M. Fitzgerald Productions. Dist. Arrow Pictures. Dir. Dallas M. Fitzgerald, 1925.

The Mysterious Lady. M-G-M. Dir. Fred Niblo, 1928.

The New York Hat. Biograph. Dir. D.W. Griffith, 1912.

Night of Love. Sam Goldwyn, Inc. Dist. United Artists. Dir. George Fitzmaurice, 1927.

Old Ironsides. Famous Lasky Corp. Dist. Paramount. Dir. James Cruze, 1926.

Old Wives for New. Famous Players-Lasky. Dist. Paramount. Dir. Cecil B. DeMille, 1918.

Orchids and Ermine. John McCormick Productions. Dist. First National. Dir. Alfred Santell, 1926.

Orphans of the Storm. D.W. Griffith, Inc. Dist. United Artists. Dir. D.W. Griffith, 1921.

Our Dancing Daughters. Cosmopolitan Pictures. Dist. M-G-M. Dir. Harry Beaumont, 1928.

Our Modern Maidens. M-G-M. Dir. Jack Conway, 1929.

Peter Pan. Paramount. Dir. Herbert Brenon, 1924.

The Phantom of the Opera. Universal. Dir. Rupert Julian, 1925.

The Plastic Age. B.P. Schulberg Productions. Dir. Wesley Ruggles, 1925.

Pollyanna. Mary Pickford Co. Dist. United Artists. Dir. Paul Powell, 1920.

A Poor Little Rich Girl. Artcraft Pictures Corp. Dir. Maurice Tourneur, 1917.

Primrose Path. Arrow Pictures. Dir. Harry O. Hoyt, 1925.

Rags. Famous Players Co. Dir. James Kirkwood, 1915.

Rebecca of Sunnybrook Farm. Artcraft Pictures Corp. Dir. Marshall Neilan, 1917.

Riders of the Purple Sage. Fox. Dir. Lynn Reynolds, 1925.

Robin Hood. Douglas Fairbanks Pictures. Dist. United Artists. Dir. Allan Dwan, 1922.

Romola. Inspiration Pictures. Dist. Metro Goldwyn. Dir. Henry King, 1924.

Sadie Thompson. Gloria Swanson Productions. Dist. United Artists. Dir. Raoul Walsh, 1928.

The Saga of Gosta Berling. Dir. Mauritz Stiller, 1924 (Swedish film.)

Sally, Irene, and Mary. M-G-M. Dir. Edmund Goulding, 1925.

Sally of the Sawdust. D.W. Griffith, Inc. Dist. United Artists. Dir. D.W. Griffith, 1925.

Salome. Nazimova Productions. Dist. Allied Producers and Distributors. Dir. Charles Bryant, 1922.

Scarlet Letter. M-G-M. Dir. Victor Seastrom, 1926.

Sea Beast. Warner Bros. Dir. Millard Webb, 1926.

enth Heaven. Fox. Dir. Frank Borzage, 1927.

Sheik. Famous Players-Lasky. Dist. Paramount. Dir. George Melford, 1921.

rting Sands. Triangle Film Corp. Dir. Albert Parker, 1918.

w People. M-G-M. Dir. King Vidor, 1928.

Single Standard. M-G-M. Dir. John S. Robertson, 1929.

ner's Dress Suit. Universal. Dir. William A. Seiter, 1926.

of the Sheik. Feature Productions. Dist. United Artists. Dir. George Fitzmaurice, 1926.

ouldering Fires. Universal. Dir. Clarence Brown, 1924.

rrows. Pickford Corp. Dist. United Artists. Dir. William Beaudine, 1926.

ge Struck. Famous Players-Lasky. Dist. Paramount. Dir. Allan Dwan, 1925.

nd and Deliver. DeMille Pictures. Dist. Pathe Exchange. Dir. Donald Crisp, 1928.

lla Dallas. Samuel Goldwyn, Inc. Dist. United Artists. Dir. Henry King, 1926.

lla Maris. Artcraft Pictures Corp. Dir. Marshall Neilan, 1917.

Student Prince in Old Heidelberg. M-G-M. Dir. Ernst Lubitsch, 1927.

ls. United Artists. Dir. John Dillon, 1920.

rise. Fox. Dir. F.W. Murnau, 1927.

e Temptress. Cosmopolitan Productions. Dist. M-G-M. Dir. Fred Niblo, 1926.

e Ten Commandments. Famous Players-Lasky. Dist. Paramount. Dir. Cecil B. DeMille, 1923.

ss of the Storm Country. Famous Players Co. Dir. Edwin S. Porter, 1914.

at Certain Thing. Columbia. Dir. Frank Capra, 1928.

e Thief of Bagdad. Douglas Fairbanks Pictures. Dist. United Artists. Dir. Raoul Walsh, 1924.

e Third Degree. Warner Bros. Dir. Michael Curtiz, 1926.

lie's Punctured Romance. Mack Sennett. 1914.

e Torrent. Cosmopolitan Pictures. Dist. M-G-M. Dir. Monta Bell, 1926.

amp, Tramp, Tramp. H.L. Corp. Dist. First National. Dir. Harry Edwards, 1926.

Tumbleweeds. William S. Hart Co. Dist. United Artists. Dir. K
   Baggott, 1925.

Underworld. Paramount. Dir. Josef von Sternberg, 1927.

The Unknown. M-G-M. Dir. Tod Browning, 1927.

Up in Mabel's Room. Christie Film Co. Dist. Producers Distribut
   Corp. Dir. E. Mason Hopper, 1926.

The Vampire. Kalem. Dir. Robert Vignola, 1913.

The Vanishing American. Famous Players-Lasky. Dist. Paramo
   Dir. George B. Seitz, 1925.

The Volga Boatman. DeMille Pictures. Dist. Producers Distribut
   Corp. Dir. Cecil B. DeMille, 1926.

Walking Back. DeMille Pictures. Dist. Pathe Exchange. Dir. Rup
   Julian, 1928.

Way Down East. United Artists. Dir. D.W. Griffith, 1920.

The Wedding March. Famous Lasky Corp. Dist. Paramount. Dir. Er
   von Stroheim, 1928.

West of Zanzibar. M-G-M. Dir. Tod Browning, 1928.

What Price Glory? Fox. Dir. Raoul Walsh, 1926.

What's Worth While. Lois Weber Productions for Famous Playe
   Lasky. Dist. Paramount. Dir. Lois Weber, 1921.

The White Sister. Inspiration Pictures. Dist. Metro. Dir. Henry Ki
   1923.

Whispering Chorus. Paramount-Artcraft. Dir. Cecil B. DeMille, 19

Why Change Your Wife? Famous Players-Lasky. Dist. Paramou
   Dir. Cecil B. DeMille, 1920.

The Wind. M-G-M. Dir. Victor Seastrom, 1928.

Wine of Youth. M-G-M. Dir. King Vidor, 1924.

Wings. Famous Players-Lasky. Dist. Paramount. Dir. Willi
   Wellman, 1929.

Woman. Dist. Hiller and Wilk. Dir. Maurice Tourneur, 1918.

A Woman of Affairs. M-G-M. Dir. Clarence Brown, 1928.

A Woman of Paris. United Artists. Dir. Charles Chaplin, 19
   (Roumanian titles.)

INDEX

225